The Cover

In 1871 merchant Henry Probasco presented this fountain, in memory of his brother-in-law Tyler Davidson, "To The People Of Cincinnati." Since then it has graced the heart of downtown, at "Fountain Square," and has become the most recognizable symbol of the Queen City. The woman at the top of the fountain is "The Genius of Water." To many people her image personifies Cincinnati. On the cover of this book she personifies the ill-starred Cincinnati citizens whose stories are recounted herein.

The Cincinnati
Crime Book

The Cincinnati Crime Book

George Stimson

SEO Library Center
40780 SR 821 * Caldwell, OH 43724

First Printing

The Peasenhall Press - Cincinnati, Ohio
1998

ISBN 0-9663494-0-7

LCCN 98-091308

Cover Art: "The Evil Genius of Water" by **Nick Bougas**

Unless otherwise credited, all photographs are by the author.

For my Father and Mother

Table of Contents

Acknowledgments

Besides the persons whose stories are recounted in these pages there are many other people and organizations who made this book possible. They include: the staffs at the Hamilton County Public Library and the Hamilton County Courthouse; the Butler County (Ohio) Sheriff's Department; the people at the Kenton County (Kentucky) Historical Society; the folks at the Harrison County (Kentucky) Public Library; the Public Library of Franklin County (Indiana); and the staff at the Franklin County Court House.

I also have to thank all of the many reporters who worked over the past ten decades at the *Cincinnati Enquirer*, the *Post*, and especially one who worked at the old *Times-Star*.

Specific people and offices who helped were Colonel Dan Wolfangel of the Hamilton County Sheriff's Department, Liz Dufour at the *Cincinnati Enquirer*, Charles King of the Kenton County (Kentucky) Public Library, and Kenneth Reis and his coworkers at the Campbell County (Kentucky) Historical and Genealogical Society.

I would also like to thank Graham P. Hunt, Jr, who remembered Pearl Bryan. (Actually, he remembered his mother remembering her.) Thanks to Cemeterian Henry Harrison; he knows where the bodies are buried. Likewise the gravedigger at the Riverside Cemetery in Falmouth, Kentucky. (The day I was there he was digging *up* a body. I didn't ask him why.)

Special thanks to David and Janet Reid.

Finally, thanks to all of my family members and friends who encouraged me to do this book.

Illustrations (after each chapter)

1. Pearl Bryan
2. Scott Jackson and Alonzo Walling
3. Much of 9th Street hasn't changed since the time of Pearl Bryan.
4. A ticket to Alonzo Walling's execution.
5. The valise, on display at the Campbell County Historical and Genealogical Society.
6. The Bryan family plot, Greencastle, Indiana. Pearl's topless headstone is on the right.
7. Pennies for Pearl.

8. George Remus
9. Imogene Remus
10. Eden Park, where George Remus killed his wife.
11. George Remus' grave in Falmouth, Kentucky.
12. The outside figures were once angels.

13. Harry Miller's New Trenton, Indiana house.
14. Captain Harry Miller
15. Harry Miller's grave in Spring Grove Cemetery.
16. The lake at General Butler State Resort Park, near Carrollton, Kentucky.
17. Heber Hicks after his arrest for the murder of Harry Miller.

18. Anna Marie Hahn
19. Anna Marie Hahn's first known victim lived in this Over-the-Rhine apartment building.
20. Jacob Wagner lived in this building on Race Street.
21. Hahn's final victim lived in this Clifton Heights home.

22. The secluded Pugh residence on Hill and Hollow Lane.
23. Robert Lyons and Foss Hopkins say the underwear don't fit.

24. The Mount Washington home shared by Edythe Klumpp and Bill Bergen.
25. Edythe Klumpp
26. Louise Bergen was murdered on this isolated road in Anderson Township.
27. Cowan Lake, in Clinton County, Ohio, where Louise Bergen's body was burned.

28. A man believed to be the Cincinnati Strangler attacked an elderly woman in the basement of this apartment building on Park Avenue. The victim survived.
29. Emogene Harrington was slain in the basement of the Clermont Apartments.
30. Lois and Frank Dant lived in this Price Hill apartment building.
31. The trail in Burnett Woods where Jeanette Messer was strangled to death.
32. Barbara Bowman
33. The site of the Lark Café, 1989.
34. Barbara Bowman was murdered at this intersection in Price Hill.
35. Alice Hochhausler was murdered in this Clifton garage.
36. The first-floor hallway of the Brittany Apartments.
37. Posteal Laskey
38. The Soul Lounge, 1997.

39. Jerry and Linda Bricca
40. Debbie Bricca
41. An officer from the SPCA leads Thumper from the Bricca house after the discovery of the bodies there.
42. The house on Greenway Avenue in 1997.

43. Charity Ruppert's home in south Hamilton.
44. James Ruppert
45. - 50. The Ruppert family graves.

51. Dale Henderson
52. Dale Henderson kidnaped his Cincinnati victim from this shopping mall parking lot.

53. Alton Coleman
54. Debra Brown
55. Alton Coleman and Debra Brown killed a woman in this Norwood residence.
56. 15-year-old Tonnie Storey was found dead in this building in Walnut Hills.

57. Donald Harvey killed over twenty people when he worked at Drake Hospital on Galbraith Road.
58. Donald Harvey

59. Della Dante Sutorius
60. The Symmes Township house where Dante Sutorius killed her husband.

Preface

Cincinnati is a unique place. Since its founding over two centuries ago on the banks of the Ohio River in what is now southwestern Ohio, it has evolved into a city that stands quite apart from any other in the United States.

Initially founded as Losantiville in 1788, the settlement was renamed three years later by the first governor of the Northwest Territory, Arthur St. Clair. St. Clair, a veteran of the Revolutionary War, named the place Cincinnati after the Society of the Cincinnati, a group of fellow ex-officers from the Continental Army which took its name from the Roman hero Cincinnatus. Cincinnatus, like many of the soldiers in this country's war of independence, left his fields in order to serve his country on the battlefield.

Any claims native Americans may have had on the territory were effectively quashed by the Battle of Fallen Timbers in 1794. A year later, 500 settlers lived in the village.

Since the Ohio River was one of the main routes to the vast western frontier, Cincinnati soon became a major stopping point for immigrants who were headed west. Many of these persons decided to stay and settle down in the growing city.

By 1812 steam-powered boats began appearing on the nation's rivers. Soon they were a major means of transport for people and goods moving to and from the frontier. Because of its prime location on the Ohio River, Cincinnati became a major center for commerce. Its population grew swiftly. The early log cabins were replaced by permanent structures of brick and stone. Social and religious institutions began to flourish. The city developed a reputation as a fast-growing settlement with many opportunities for work and wealth. German immigrants began arriving in the 1830s. The Irish came a decade later.

Cincinnati soon became one of the busiest commerce centers in the country. Riverboats crowded the waterfront area known as the public landing. The riverfront became the economic heart of the city. Its busy commerce fueled the fixed businesses and a population which continued to grow and

13

spread out from the river basin, over the surrounding hills, and into the new suburbs beyond.

In 1842 Charles Dickens visited Cincinnati and called it a "beautiful city; cheerful, thriving, and animated." By then the population was over 50,000 and growing fast. Seventeen years later the figure had risen to 160,000. Soon the city was the sixth largest in the United States.

When Henry Wadsworth Longfellow visited the city he was so impressed with its beauty and vitality that he praised it as "The Queen of the West, in her garlands dressed, on the banks of the beautiful river." Cincinnati has been known as the Queen City ever since.

But ironically, the river-centered philosophy that caused Cincinnati's spectacular growth was also responsible for its decline when, shortly after the Civil War railroads began replacing rivers as the main method for transporting goods. As riverboat commerce declined, so did the rising fortunes of the Queen City. Population growth slowed, and the city settled down into a stable period of slow progress that lasted well into the Twentieth Century. Some observers have said that this era of calm and minimal development left the city with an indelibly conservative, or even provincial, character.

But the character of Cincinnati was determined by more than just geography and economics. It was also determined by the sort of people who made the city their home. The German and Irish immigrants have already been mentioned. There were also individual persons who helped make Cincinnati the city it is.

Daniel Drake arrived here at the age of 15 in 1800. After meeting a frontier doctor, he developed an interest in medicine and became a physician. He then dedicated the rest of his life to elevating the field of medicine. In 1817 he founded the Medical College of Ohio, the first medical school west of the Alleghenies. Drake's tireless work for the advancement of science, education, and culture made him early Cincinnati's best-known citizen. His work is remembered to this day: The Drake Center, a long-term health care facility on Galbraith Road in the Cincinnati neighborhood of Hartwell, is named after him.

Another well-known Cincinnatian was Nicholas Longworth. Longworth came to the city in the early 1800s and began a career as a lawyer. He soon branched out into real estate. He also had a great interest in horticulture and was a leading proponent of grape growing in the area. A grape industry did indeed flourish in the Cincinnati area until a "black rot" wiped out most of the vineyards in the 1850's. By then Longworth was worth $10 million – perhaps the second richest man in the United States. Longworth paid back the city where he had achieved such success by leaving much of his property to the city of Cincinnati upon his death. One of his vineyards eventually became one of Cincinnati's finest gems – Eden Park.

Another big name in Cincinnati is Taft. Alonzo Taft arrived here in 1839, also eager to purse a career in law. Many of his descendants followed his example and achieved amazing success. William Howard Taft, born in Mount Auburn in 1857, was the only man ever to become both President of the United States and Chief Justice of the United States Supreme Court. His son, Charles Phelps Taft, II, was active for years in Cincinnati politics and also served in the Hamilton County Prosecutor's Office.

Daniel Drake. Nicholas Longworth. William Howard Taft. All of these names resonate the history of Cincinnati.

But the history of Cincinnati is more than just the stories of the entrepreneurs, politicians, and other notable individuals who have made the city their home. For like anything else, Cincinnati is the sum of its parts. And, like anything else, Cincinnati has its good parts and its bad parts.

This book is about some of the bad parts.

George Remus. Anna Marie Hahn. Donald Harvey. All of these people were, in their time, as well-known in Cincinnati as anyone named Drake, Longworth, or Taft. But you won't find their names in any tour guide or on a bronze plaque. That's because these people were well-known for the wrong reason: all of them were killers, Cincinnati murderers involved in sensational crimes. All of their stories were prominent in the news and public consciousness for months, years, and, in some cases, decades. And all of them are, for better or worse, a part of the history and character of this Queen City.

George Remus. Anna Marie Hahn. Donald Harvey. These names resonate the criminal history of Cincinnati.

That criminal history is what this book is about.

How did I select which crimes to include in this book? The only criterion I had was that they had to involve murder.

To me, murder is the most interesting crime for several reasons. First, I'm interested to know at what point a person is willing to commit the high taboo of taking another person's life. What circumstances make someone decide to do it? I also like to see how the authorities catch these individuals. What mistakes do the murderers make that lead to their captures? And, if the authorities *don't* catch the killer, why don't they? Is the story a good mystery?

Murder can be *very* interesting.

The thirteen cases in this book all meet that minimum murder standard, but they also all have some element that makes them stand out from most of the other homicides that have unfortunately occurred in the Queen City during the last century. All of the crimes in this book went beyond the interest of the local Tri-State area to become national or even international news stories. These killings transcended the "common" murders. Many of the crimes or criminals acquired the colorful and descriptive nicknames so often assigned by enthusiastic members of the news media: The Head and Hands Murder. The Cincinnati Strangler. The Angel of Death.

Several of the crimes I chose came to mind immediately from my own memory. I still vividly remember the fear that the Cincinnati Strangler case generated. (My grandmother lived a block away from one of the victims.) So, I started with the cases I remembered. Then I asked my parents what famous crimes they remembered, and what crimes their parents remembered. That got me back as far as Pearl Bryan and I figured that a century ago was a pretty good place to start. (Actually, before Pearl Bryan there *were* no high-profile murders in the Queen City. True, there were plenty of killings, but none if them achieved anything near the notoriety associated with the cases described in this book.)

Most of these cases ended with arrests and convictions. Quite a few of the convicted individuals got the death penalty. But some were acquitted. And some were never caught....

Not every decade in the last hundred years is represented here, and some decades are represented more than once. Still, these stories comfortably span the period.

They also span the city, for these crimes occurred (or had other relevant locales) in virtually all sections of Cincinnati and the surrounding Tri-State area. In the Afterward I have given the present status of most of the locations that figured in the stories in this book, an armchair tour of the shadow side of the Queen City.

Many of the cases recounted in this book provoked considerable controversy when they were current news, and it is still easy to get an argument going on some of the more recent examples, like the Cincinnati Strangler. With that in mind, I would stress that this book is not intended to be the complete or final word on any of the events described herein. It is, rather, a general guide to the criminal careers of some of the more well-known (if sometimes unknown) persons who have made their dark marks on Cincinnati and the surrounding area during the last one hundred years.

Cincinnati, March, 1998   G.S.

The Murder Of Pearl Bryan

The murder of Pearl Bryan was Cincinnati's first major, well-publicized homicide, the one people called the "Crime of the Century." All the elements of the case lent it both to intense public interest and sensational news reporting. There was the image of a poor country girl meeting her tragic end in the big city. There was the scandalous subject of out of wedlock pregnancy. There was a question of innocence or guilt. And there was a missing head.

On Saturday February 1, 1896 a young man named Johnny Hewling made his way to his job at the John Lock farm, which was located off Alexandria Pike in Fort Thomas, Kentucky. The Lock farm was on a road that would later be Grandview Drive, just west of the Fort Thomas business district. In 1896 Fort Thomas was not much more than a wide spot in the road, with only a few businesses, a couple of saloons, and a tollgate. Johnny Hewling worked for the Locks as a farm hand.

The property line of the Lock farm was secured by a wooden fence. Just inside the fence at the main entrance to the property was a grouping of privet bushes. As Johnny Hewling passed the privets he noticed something that sent him rushing to the Lock residence. What he saw was the headless body of a young woman.

After the Locks confirmed Hewling's gruesome discovery, John Lock ran to the nearby Army post (where the only telephone in Fort Thomas was located) and called Campbell County Sheriff Jule Plummer.

When Sheriff Plummer arrived on the scene he observed the body lying on its back with its arms flung up over the shoulders. A huge pool of blood covered the ground, spreading out from where the head had been severed from the neck. The dead woman was wearing only a cotton dressing gown. There was no sign of her head.

News of the grisly find spread quickly and many morbid sightseers converged on the apparent crime scene. They soon overwhelmed the area, trampling bushes and obliterating footprints that may have been important clues. There were so many spectators that the Locks set up a concession stand and sold refreshments to the crowd.

Sheriff Plummer knew at once that the situation was beyond his experience and that he would need outside help. "I'm the sheriff of this county and I think I'm a good sheriff, but I know I'm not a detective," he later explained. Plummer made a call to the Detective Division of the Cincinnati Police Department.

The Chief of the Detective Division in 1896 was Larry Hazen. In response to Sheriff Plummer's call, Hazen sent two of his most able investigators, John J. "Jack" McDermott and Cal Crim, to the crime scene.

By the time McDermott and Crim arrived at the Lock farm the body of the unfortunate woman and some apparent personal effects had already been removed to an undertaker's parlor in nearby Newport. An examination of the scene revealed evidence of a great struggle. The vegetation in the area was splattered with blood, even on branches six feet above the ground. There was a large pool of coagulated blood on the ground. But there was no blood trail, which led investigators to conclude that the woman had been killed and decapitated at the scene. Officers found women's clothing, including a new shoe, on a nearby roadway. Also on the roadway were fresh carriage tracks.

An examination of the body and personal effects at the funeral parlor provided no immediate information as to the identity of the deceased. The hands of the dead woman were soft, indicating that she had not been a manual laborer. Several rings had obviously been removed from her fingers. Authorities assumed that the rings had been taken as a means of preventing identification of the dead girl. Among the personal effects were a blood-stained union suit, a checkered kimono, a corset, and the woman's shoe.

Many people viewed the body at the mortuary, but no one was able to identify the remains.

McDermott and Crim decided to trace the personal effects found near the body as a means of identifying the victim. To do this they took the shoe to a Cincinnati shoe factory where they learned that it had been manufactured by a company in Portsmouth, Ohio. Crim contacted an employee of the Portsmouth factory and was told that the shoe had been sold to the Lewis and Hayes clothing outlet in Greencastle, Indiana.

On Monday February 3 McDermott, Crim, and Sheriff Plummer traveled to Greencastle to follow the lead of the shoe. At Lewis and Hayes an employee checked records and discovered that shoes of the style and size of the one recovered in Fort Thomas had been sold to only three customers. Two of the customers were checked and it was easily determined that the shoe did not belong to them. The third pair of shoes had been sold as part of a graduation outfit to one Pearl Bryan.

Pearl Bryan was the 20-year-old daughter of Mr. and Mrs. Alexander Bryan. The Bryans lived on a farm near Greencastle. Pearl was a recent graduate of DePauw University, which was located in the Indiana town.

The Cincinnati Crime Book

When McDermott and Crim went to the Bryan residence Mr. and Mrs. Bryan told them that their daughter was not there. The parents, too, were wondering about Pearl. She was supposed to be visiting friends in Indianapolis. But the friends had not heard from her. And the news from Cincinnati about the headless body found across the Ohio River was making everyone apprehensive as to her welfare.

Mr. and Mrs. Bryan had another daughter who owned a women's hat store in Greencastle. When the detectives visited her their search for the identity of the dead woman was ended. The daughter readily identified the kimono found near the body as one she had loaned to her sister Pearl.

With the identity of the corpse virtually certain, officials questioned family and friends of the victim to learn what they could. They were particularly interested in why Pearl ended up in Fort Thomas after telling her relatives that she was going to Indianapolis.

The relatives said that the reason for the trip to Cincinnati may have been because of a relationship Pearl had developed with one Scott Jackson.

Scott Jackson was 28 years old. An attractive man, he had light brown hair and often wore a mustache or beard. Pearl had met him the previous year at DePauw University. Jackson was related to a faculty member at the university and had resided there until he moved to Cincinnati to become a student at the Cincinnati Dental College, located downtown at Court Street and Central Avenue.

As the Cincinnati detectives continued to question Pearl's relatives they found one of them, Will Wood, a cousin of Pearl, especially helpful. Wood told McDermott and Crim that the relationship between his cousin and Scott Jackson was the most intimate kind. Wood also said that the relationship was in trouble.

Based on this information, Crim wired authorities in Cincinnati and told them to detain Scott Jackson for questioning. He was picked up at his lodgings in a rooming house at 220-222 9th Street, downtown.

Jackson admitted that he knew Pearl Bryan, but said he had only seen her in Greencastle. He claimed that he was not very well acquainted with the missing girl. He was certainly not her sweetheart.

Despite these denials, Jackson was kept in custody.

Scott Jackson had a roommate in his quarters on 9th Street, and authorities also questioned him thoroughly. He was Alonzo Walling.

At 21, Alonzo Walling was seven years younger than Jackson. He was also a student at the Cincinnati Dental College. At first, Walling denied knowing Pearl Jackson. Then he admitted that he had heard his roommate mention her vaguely. Police took Walling into custody too.

In the meantime, new revelations in Cincinnati added more sensational aspects to the already shocking crime. An autopsy revealed that Pearl Bryan had ingested a large quantity of cocaine shortly before her death. And she had been four to five months pregnant.

19

Police surmised that if Pearl Bryan was carrying Scott Jackson's unwanted child, that may have been enough motive for the dental student to want to do away with his paramour.

Police now had a murder victim, a possible motive, and two suspects behind bars. But it looked like they soon wouldn't have the latter, because even though Jackson and Walling's accounts of the familiarity between Jackson and Pearl were at odds with the reports from Greencastle, that discrepancy itself was not enough to charge them with any crime. If police didn't come up with some strong evidence, the two men would have to be turned loose.

Then police got the break they needed.

This case had received much publicity, and there were few people in the area who were not familiar with the murder mystery. Among the people who were following the case were several employees of the John Church Company, then located downtown at 4th and Elm Streets. These workers remembered that on the afternoon of January 31 there had been a loud argument on the street outside the building. The workers were on their lunch break, so they were able to pay close attention to the dispute. It was between a woman and two men. Apparently the three persons were headed to the Central Train Depot at 3rd Street and Central Avenue, because the woman said she was taking a train home to tell her brother of her problems and that he would take care of them. The employees identified the arguing trio as Scott Jackson, Alonzo Walling, and Pearl Bryan.

Further information came from two employees of a saloon which was owned by Dave Wallingford and located at the corner of Plum and George Streets, just around the corner from the rooming house where Jackson and Walling lived. After reading of the identity of the dead girl and the holding of the two dental students the saloon employees contacted the police.

The saloon workers said that on the evening of January 31 they had seen Pearl Bryan in the company of Scott Jackson and Alonzo Walling in the private sitting room of the saloon. One of the employees said that he had seen Scott Jackson slip something into Pearl's drink. This, police thought, must have been when Pearl ingested the cocaine found in her system.

Confronted with these witness statements, Scott Jackson simply denied everything. But police suspected that Alonzo Walling was the weaker of the pair, and they interrogated him relentlessly in an effort to get him to confess.

Their assessment was correct. After many hours of questioning he finally gave up and exclaimed, "Jackson killed her! He gave her dope and killed her! How he got her across the river I don't know, but I tell you I had nothing to do with it!"

Jackson, confronted with his roommate's confession, suggested otherwise. He sent authorities to check out Walling's locker at the Cincinnati Dental College. When they did they discovered a pair of muddy, blood-stained trousers.

The Cincinnati Crime Book

Informed of this discovery Walling cried, "He can't do this! He's the real murderer – not me! I can find you evidence!"

Walling then directed police to a sewer at John and Richmond Streets, a few blocks from the 9th Street rooming house. There they recovered another pair of bloodstained pants and a bloodstained shirt. Both belonged to Scott Jackson. In the pocket of the pants were two handkerchiefs with the monogram "P.B."

Scott Jackson and Alonzo Walling were charged with murder. But many loose ends still remained. Where had the murder actually occurred? (This was important from the jurisdictional standpoint in determining who would eventually prosecute the case.) How had the trio gotten from David Wallingford's saloon in Cincinnati to the Lock farm in Fort Thomas? And lastly, but most intriguingly, where was Pearl Bryan's head?

The first of these questions was apparently answered by evidence at the scene where the body was discovered. Police concluded from the trampling and breaking of the bushes and the fact that blood had spurted high enough to splatter branches over six feet off the ground that Pearl had been decapitated while still alive at the entrance to the Lock farm.

The second question was answered when an informant came forward and identified Jackson and Walling as the two men he had seen soliciting a carriage driver on the corner of George and Elm Streets late on the night of January 31. The informant said that the two men and a woman had gotten into the carriage and then headed in the general direction of Kentucky. The carriage driver was described as an elderly black man. An appeal was made for this coach driver to come forward.

Several days later a Cincinnati policeman was casually chatting with a carriage driver in Mount Auburn. Soon the conversation turned to the widely-publicized Pearl Bryan case. The carriage driver, an elderly black gentleman, said, "I understand that the police want to locate that fellow who drove them across the river."

"They certainly do," the officer said.

"Well, if they find him, will he be hanged?" the man asked. The officer assured him that the driver would not be hanged and would more probably be regarded as a good citizen. "All right," the man said. "I trust you. I'm the man that drove that carriage!"

The coachman told the police that on the night of January 31 he had gone downtown to watch the drill for the Caldwell Colored Guards. After the drill, as he was on his way home, a carriage pulled up beside him on Elm Street. The driver of the carriage asked him if he would like to earn $5.00. The driver said he was a doctor and that he had a sick girl in the back of the coach. He said that he was taking the girl to her home in Kentucky and needed someone else to drive them there. The black coachman agreed to drive and climbed up on the seat next to the "doctor." Then they headed toward Kentucky. The girl could be heard moaning loudly inside the coach.

But as they rode along it began to occur to the driver that something was wrong, that the girl in the coach was probably being taken somewhere against her will. He suddenly wanted no part of this late night ride. When he suggested to the man next to him that he wanted out of the deal the man produced a revolver and said, "You will stay with us. What's more, you better not tell about anything you see or hear. If you do, we will find you and kill you. And if anything happens to us so we can't reach you, we've got pals who will take care of you."

After what seemed like an eternity, the "doctor" finally told the driver to pull over by an overgrown grove of trees off Alexandria Pike in fort Thomas. "The girl's house is down that way," he said. "You will wait here."

The "doctor" and another man in the carriage dragged the girl out of the back. She could barely stand up. The two men supported her on their shoulders and disappeared into the dark grove of trees. Soon the driver heard sounds of a struggle, then a loud scream. He didn't wait around to find out what was happening. "Now I was afraid they would kill me when they got back," he told the policeman. "So I jumped off the seat and ran. I ran until I all but dropped dead. I got home at four o'clock and went straight to bed, and didn't say a thing to a living soul."

The coach driver's story was supported by his mention that at the Fort Thomas scene he had tied the horse to a railway iron that was lying on the ground. The bloody clothes found in the sewer had been weighted with just such a railway iron. Also, a cab company in Walnut Hills reported that two men resembling Jackson and Walling had rented a cab on the night of January 31. The cab had not been returned, but was found on February 1 abandoned on a Cincinnati side street. Finally, a toll collector on the Ohio River bridge recalled a carriage being driven by an elderly black man late on the night of January 31.

The coach driver identified Alonzo Walling as the man who had been next to him in the driver's seat.

Now police knew how Pearl Bryan got to Fort Thomas. The only mystery that remained was: Where was her head?

One theory held that Pearl's head had been dropped into the Ohio River. But a better theory was that Jackson and Walling disposed of the head somewhere in downtown Cincinnati on the night after the crime.

One of the items seized as evidence after Jackson and Walling became suspects was a leather valise. The valise, formerly the property of Pearl Bryan's sister, would have easily accommodated a human head. The interior of the valise contained privet leaves, bloodstains, and particles of earth which were later determined to be the same as that at the crime scene at the entrance to the Lock farm in Fort Thomas. The bartender at Jack Legner's saloon, another downtown watering hole, located at 9th and Plum Streets, said that on the evening after Pearl's death Jackson and Walling had given him the valise to hold for safekeeping. The bartender did not look inside the case, but he noticed that it was weighted as if it contained a bowling ball. The next night Jackson retrieved the case.

If the head was in the valise, Jackson may have secreted it somewhere in his rooming house or even buried it in the basement there. Others pointed out that it was only a few blocks from Legner's saloon to the Cincinnati Dental College. In the basement of the college was a large furnace which heated the building and was also used as a trash incinerator. Pearl's head may have ended up there.

After the arrests of Jackson and Walling, Pearl Bryan's family traveled to Kentucky and met with Jackson. They pleaded with him to reveal the whereabouts of the head. Pearl's sister literally begged on her knees for him to reveal the head's location. Jackson coldly replied that since he had not killed Pearl he knew nothing of the whereabouts of her head. "I can't tell you anything about it," he said.

Scott Jackson and Alonzo Walling were scheduled for separate trials, with Jackson's being first. It was decided that since the bloodstains at the Lock farm and the testimony of the carriage driver indicated Pearl had been killed in Fort Thomas the defendants would be tried at the county seat for Campbell County in Alexandria, Kentucky.

Jackson's trial began on April 21, 1896. The main witnesses for prosecution were Sheriff Plummer and Cincinnati detectives McDermott and Crim. Crim was on the stand for three and a half days.

While Jackson was ably defended, there was little his attorney could do to refute the state's evidence. On May 14 the jury returned with a guilty verdict and fixed the penalty at death.

Walling's trial was shorter, lasting from June 2 to June 18. Most of that time was spent trying to select a jury that was not prejudiced against the defendant. Scott Jackson took the stand and put all the blame for the murder on his hapless former roommate. His testimony, and the other evidence, had its effect, and Walling was also found guilty and sentenced to death.

Both men appealed their cases to the Kentucky Court of Appeals, but those appeals were denied. Kentucky Governor William O. Bradley set March 20, 1897 as the execution date. Jackson and Walling were housed in the Newport Jail while they awaited their deaths.

On March 20 Scott Jackson and Alonzo Walling climbed the steps to the scaffold in the yard of the Newport Jail. There had not been a hanging in the Cincinnati area for over a dozen years, and a huge crowd gathered to witness the event. Walling appeared more shaken in anticipation of his fate. Jackson shocked the crowd by singing hymns, including "The Sweet Bye And Bye." But, as the noose was fastened around his neck, he, too, showed signs of nervousness.

Black hoods were placed over the condemned men's heads and at 11:40 a.m. Sheriff Plummer pulled the trapdoor lever and sent them dropping to their deaths. For a few minutes the suspended bodies were motionless. Then the men began to twitch and struggle as the ropes slowly strangled them to death. Walling was pronounced dead at 11:55, Jackson six minutes later.

But the case was not really concluded with the executions of the convicted men. For years debate raged over whether the punishment for Alonzo Walling had been too severe. Many observers, including Cal Crim, believed that Walling, while not completely innocent, had nevertheless been somewhat under the evil influence of the older and more worldly Scott Jackson. Crim later characterized Walling's execution as a "miscarriage of justice."

And of course, the execution of the two men did not solve the mystery of whatever happened to Pearl Bryan's head.

In 1953 the old 9th Street neighborhood where Jackson and Walling once roomed had changed quite a bit. Then on the corner of 9th and Elm Streets was a medical clinic whose owner wished to add a parking lot to the west of the clinic. To make room for the lot all the buildings on the north side of 9th Street, including Jackson and Walling's former rooming house, were demolished. Workers on the wrecking crew were advised to keep an eye out for Pearl's head. It took 45 days for the five man crew to demolish the buildings, and although they did find a false floor, they found no sign of the missing head. Still, the workmen conceded that if Jackson had buried the head in the dirt floor of the basement of his rooming house it would have been covered up, probably forever, by the debris of the demolition.

So, the mystery of the missing head endures to this day. It may rest under the pavement of the parking lot which now sits on the north side of 9th Street between Elm and Plum Streets. It may have been incinerated in the furnace in the basement of the old Cincinnati Dental College. It may have been tossed into the Ohio River.

But one place the head definitely is not is with Pearl Bryan's body in the Forest Hill Cemetery in Greencastle, Indiana. The large Bryan family plot is high on a hill there, near the Veterans Memorial. Pearl's grave is marked by a headstone at the end of a long row of deceased kin. Like the body in the grave, the headstone has no top. Years ago some unknown person removed the part of the stone with the inscription. All that remains is the marker's stone base.

After over 100 years people still visit the burial site of the innocent country girl who went away to her unfortunate end in the big city of Cincinnati so long ago. And, as a sort of tribute, the visitors leave pennies on what's left of Pearl Bryan's tombstone – heads sides up, of course.

The Cincinnati Crime Book

The Ballad of Pearl Bryan

Young ladies if you'll listen, a story I'll relate,
Which happened near St. Thomas in the old Kentucky state.
It was January the 31st, that awful deed was done,
By Jackson and Walling. How cold Pearl's blood did run!

But little did Pearl think when she left her happy home,
That the grip she carried in her hand would hide her head away.
She thought it was a lover's hand she could trust both night and day,
But alas! It was a lover's hand that took her life away.

But little did Pearl's parents think when she left her happy home,
That their darling child in youth would nevermore return.
Her aged parents, you know well, a fortune they would give,
If Pearl could but return to them, a natural life to live.

Now all young girls take warning, for all men are unjust.
It may be your truest liver; you know not whom to trust.
Pearl Bryan died away from home on a dark and lonely spot.
My God, believe me girls, don't let this be your lot.

(author unknown)

Pearl Bryan.
(Courtesy Campbell County Historical and Genealogical Society)

Scott Jackson and Alonzo Walling.
(Courtesy Campbell County Historical and Genealogical Society)

Much of 9ᵗʰ Street hasn't changed since the time of Pearl Bryan.

COMMONWEALTH OF KENTUCKY
vs.
ALONZO WALLING

March 20th, 189

Admit Mr. *C. A. Yelton*

TO THE PLACE OF EXECUTION.

Jule Plummer

SHERIFF CAMPBELL CO., K

Not good without Seal. Not transferabl

A ticket to Alonzo Walling's execution. (Author's collection)

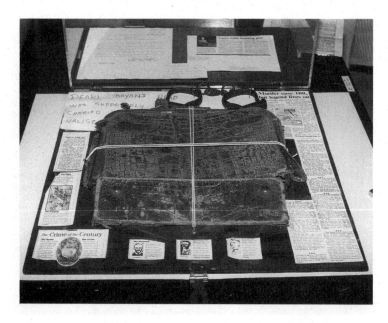

The valise, on display at the Campbell County Historical and Genealogical Society.

The Bryan family plot, Greencastle, Indiana.
Pearl's topless headstone is on the right.

Pennies for Pearl.

The King Of The Bootleggers

On January 16, 1919 the United States Constitution was amended to prohibit the manufacture, sales, transportation, import or export of intoxicating liquors within the United States. One year later this 18th Amendment went into effect and the grand experiment called Prohibition began.

With much of the liquor world now against the law, the drinking public went underground and America entered a decade of general lawlessness that would become known as "The Roaring Twenties." The 1920s were the decade of the hip flask, the speakeasy, and the bootlegger. An illegal subculture emerged, presided over by enterprising (if criminal) men who, in addition to getting rich and powerful by breaking the nation's new laws, became some of the most well known personalities of the time – men like Dutch Schultz, Bugs Moran, and Al Capone.

One of the most notable of these enterprising and well known men operated out of Cincinnati, Ohio. His name was George Remus. At the height of his career he ran a bootlegging operation that supplied most of the Midwest with illegal liquor. But George Remus did not become well known just because of his bootlegging activities. He was also the principle character in one of the city's (if not country's) most unusual murder cases.

George Remus was born on November 13, 1878 near Berlin, Germany. His parents brought him to the United States when he was only three or four years old. After their arrival in this country, the family settled in Chicago, Illinois, where there was a large German immigrant population, including Remus relatives. Remus's father Frank easily found steady work as a day laborer. Soon George had four siblings – three sisters and a brother.

Young George Remus loved to read and was always a good student in school. But in 1890 Frank Remus was forced to stop working because of ill health. George, the elder son, had to quit school and find work to help support his family.

His first job was in a drug store owned by an uncle. He also took classes in pharmacology. While he never completed the classes, by 1895 he had obtained a license to practice the science. That same year he bought his own drug store. In order to get the deed to the property Remus lied about his age, saying he was 21 when in fact he was two years younger.

George Remus was a good businessman. By the time he was really 21 he had purchased another drug store, the house he was living in, and a farm in Wisconsin. He still loved to read and developed a fondness for good food. But he neither smoked nor drank.

It didn't take long for the life of a druggist to lose its challenge, so Remus entered law school, taking night classes. It only took him two years to complete the three year load of courses, and he was admitted to the Illinois Bar at age 24.

As an attorney, Remus handled mostly criminal cases, including murder. He often resorted to unconventional tactics in defending his clients. In one instance, he defended a man accused of poisoning his wife. The man's conviction seemed to be a done deal until Remus' closing statement. As he spoke to the jury, Remus picked up an exhibit in the case – the bottle which held the rest of the poison that the defendant had allegedly given his wife. "There has been a lot of talk about poison in this case," he said, "but it is a lot of piffle. Look." He then drank the rest of the poison and continued his statement. The shocked jury expected him to collapse and die, but he didn't. So, they concluded that there was no poison involved in the case and acquitted the defendant. What the jurors didn't know was that Remus, as a pharmacologist, was familiar with poisons and had taken the antidote for the poison in the bottle just before addressing them.

In another case Remus defended a man charged with killing his wife. The man pleaded innocent by reason of insanity. Remus said that when the defendant killed his spouse he had been under the influence of a "transitory insanity" which Remus defined as "a condition in which a man may commit an act and then fall asleep, and when he wakes up he will have no knowledge of what he has done, but will be perfectly sane." Remus' strategy resulted in the man being sentenced to fifteen years instead of getting the death penalty.

But not all of his clients were so lucky. Remus did lose some cases and he did have some clients executed. As a result, he joined the Anti-Capital Punishment Society. As a member of this group, he met and occasionally worked with a man who would become one of the premier criminal defense attorneys of all time, Clarence Darrow.

In late 1895 Remus married a woman he met in one of his drug stores, Lillian Hansen. Nine years later the union produced its only child, a daughter named Romola. This marriage was not destined to last, however, and in early 1919 Lillian sued for divorce, saying he "hasn't supported me to speak of for five years." In the divorce settlement Remus was ordered to pay his wife $50,000 plus $25 a week alimony.

The divorce was well-timed, for by then Remus had taken up with another woman, Mrs. Imogene Holmes. In fact, he had already been seeing Mrs.

The Cincinnati Crime Book

Holmes, a divorcee, for several years. Imogene eagerly became the new woman in George Remus' life.

Remus was a successful lawyer, and he enjoyed the profession. By 1919 he was earning $50,000 a year. His flamboyant courtroom style had earned him the sobriquet "The Napoleon of the Chicago Bar." But in 1920 something happened that would forever change the course of George Remus' life. The 18th Amendment to the United State Constitution, which prohibited "the manufacture, sale, or transportation of intoxicating liquor" went into effect in January of that year. The passage of this law created a new class of criminal, the bootlegger. Since Remus was a criminal attorney, it wasn't long before he had several bootleggers as clients. Always alert, he quickly noticed a curious fact: many of these men made much more money at bootlegging than he made as a lawyer. As he later frankly recalled, "I was impressed with the rapidity with which those men, without any brains at all, piled up fortunes in the liquor business. I saw a chance to make a clean-up."

But Remus didn't move hastily into his new enterprise. He carefully studied the Volstead Act, the legal implementation of the Prohibition Amendment, and discovered that it had many exceptions and loopholes. The new law did not make it illegal for citizens to buy liquor and possess it in their homes. But it was against the law to manufacture, sell, barter, transport, import or export, or deliver alcoholic beverages. And there were exceptions even to these restrictions. For example, alcohol used for religious or medicinal purposes was still permitted. It was the sale of so-called "medicinal whiskey," through government bonded outlets, that was especially interesting to George Remus. He learned that not only was such liquor legal, but that 80% of the bonded whiskey in the country was located within 300 miles of Cincinnati, Ohio. Further investigation showed that many of the owners of the distilleries which produced medicinal liquor were not aware of the true marketing possibilities for their products, and thus they could be induced to sell their manufacturing operations at a good price.

Remus arrived in Cincinnati in late 1919. With him came Imogene Holmes and her daughter from her previous marriage, Ruth. Soon after their arrival, Remus and Mrs. Holmes were married in Newport, Kentucky.

After settling into the Queen City, he bought his first distillery for $10,000. Within a year he owned over a dozen more liquor manufacturing plants and distribution centers – all of it legal.

Remus enjoyed his new profession. "I went into it mostly for the thrill and excitement," he said. He had no problem justifying his new profession. "Prohibition is wrong," he said. "It is not accepted by the great majority of people and, therefore, bootlegging is not criminal."

The money started coming in fast, and Remus knew how to spend it. In addition to his other interests, he had always yearned to achieve a high position socially. One way to do this, he reasoned, was to have an impressive home. So, he purchased a ten-acre property with a 20-room mansion located at the intersection of 8th Street and Hermosa Avenue (825 Hermosa) in Price Hill. He quickly invested much of his profits from his businesses into the estate, and spent many thousands of dollars to furnish the house and landscape the grounds.

After settling into the house, the Remuses began giving extravagant parties, all in an attempt to crash high society. The most famous of these parties occurred on New Year's Eve, 1921. Over 200 people were invited to the affair. One of the highlights of the evening was the dedication of a new $100,000 indoor swimming pool that Remus had built. After making a short speech about the pool to his assembled guests, Remus jumped into it fully clothed. After that spectacle, he presented the male guests with expensive jewelry. The female guests each received a brand new car.

But Remus was denied his wish to become a major member of Cincinnati society. Despite the extraordinary opulence of the New Year's Eve affair (and despite the fact that he had invited the society editors of the local newspapers, who, however, chose not to attend) no mention of the party was made in the society pages of the papers. George Remus never realized his dream of becoming the social equal of people like the Seasongoods and the Tafts.

Despite the social setbacks, however, Remus's bootlegging business thrived. By legally owning both production and distribution outlets, he had the legal basis for his empire, i.e. legitimate ownership of a large stockpile of liquor. Then all he had to do was get the product to the public. This could be done by several methods. One was to steal the liquor out of its storage barrels and replace it with water and alcohol to fool government inspectors. Or Remus would have his men hijack his own delivery trucks and then redistribute the booze through illegal retail outlets. Still another way was to create phony drug companies and have "medicinal whiskey" shipped to these businesses, from which it would eventually make it to the drinking public.

To facilitate the logistical aspects of his business, Remus purchased a farm near Westwood and converted it into a storage and distribution center. This farm became known as the "Death Valley Ranch." Located just outside the Cincinnati city limits, Death Valley was perfect for Remus' purposes. Barreled liquor, either legally transferred or from hijacked trucks, would arrive and be bottled for distribution to retail outlets and individual consumers. People could buy liquor right at the ranch or phone in an order and have it delivered. Independent bootleggers from throughout the Midwest also got their wholesale booze there.

Business boomed. Remus bought more distilleries until he owned almost a dozen. Eventually his entire operation would employ over 3,000 men. Helping Remus oversee this constantly expanding empire was George Conners, a former agent for the Internal Revenue Service who had become Remus's best friend and second in command.

But bootlegging was not without its risks. The Death Valley Ranch was a heavily guarded operation. Remus' liquor trucks always carried armed men and were escorted by vehicles containing more armed men. Occasionally there were shootouts on the rural roads around Cincinnati as Remus' men fought to protect his liquor from would-be hijackers.

Another risk was that the sheer size of the operation attracted too much unwanted attention from the authorities. Although Remus was ostensibly a lawyer and the Death Valley Ranch did have some livestock on it to give it the appearance of a typical farm, it was well-known by just about everybody that the whole setup was a bootlegging operation. In fact, by the end of 1921 George Remus was already known as the "King of the Bootleggers."

The only way Remus could continue to run his operation was if law enforcement authorities didn't look at it, and the only way their attention could be deflected from an operation the size of Remus' was to be bribed to look the other way. Remus avoided investigation by Cincinnati officials because any investigation would reveal that his liquor was ending up in the stockpiles of some of the city's most prominent and upstanding citizens. One time an investigator for the U.S. Treasury Department presented his accumulated evidence on Remus to local law enforcement officials and was told "Go back to New York and forget it."

Remus had guardian angels outside of Cincinnati as well. The main one of these was Washington DC-based Jess Smith. Smith had no official position with the U.S. government, but he was the best friend and right-hand man of United States Attorney General Harry Daugherty. Smith and Daugherty were so close that they even lived together in the same apartment. In 1921 Remus was introduced to Smith in New York City. The two men reached an agreement wherein Remus would make large cash payments to Smith in return for the promise that neither Remus nor any of his men would ever be prosecuted for bootlegging. Remus always made these payments, which would eventually total almost half a million dollars, to Smith personally. Remus also paid Smith for government whiskey certificates, papers which greatly facilitated the transfer of liquor. Smith may have made another half million on this side deal.

With distilleries, a distribution center, and bribed officials from Cincinnati to Washington, Remus' operation took off. "I now felt that no matter what happened I was safe," he said years later. "I believed that I had the Justice Department fixed and regardless of any attempts that might be made to prosecute me, I would never go to prison. When you have Washington fixed you don't need to worry about fixing anybody else. I had my man in the Department of Justice, right next door to the Attorney General's private office. That was enough for me. I had plenty of permits, and I began operating more openly than ever."

But if all of these factors were running in Remus's favor there were other realities operating against it. One was the pressure put on the government by certain citizens to do something about the obvious non-enforcement of the country's prohibition laws. Another was the realization that Remus could not buy everybody off. There was, as Remus later recalled, "not enough money in the world to buy up all the public officials who demanded a share." Worse, there were actually some public officials who couldn't be bought at all.

Then, in October of 1921, a man arrested for illegal whiskey transportation told authorities that he had obtained the liquor from the Death Valley Ranch and that the ranch was a major liquor distribution center for most of the Midwest. Armed with this information, federal prohibition agents descended on the farm, arrested ten men, seized $40,000 worth of illegal booze, and confiscated an impressive array of firearms. Inside one of the buildings agents found mounds of paperwork implicating numerous local citizens from all strata of society in the area's liquor trade. Remus, in Cincinnati at the time of the raid, was not arrested.

That situation didn't last long, however. Authorities put pressure on the men arrested during the raid and eventually got some of them to name Remus as the leader of the bootlegging operation. On October 31, 1921 Remus appeared in court to face charges of conspiracy to violate the Volstead Act. He pleaded not guilty. His bond was set at $50,000 – the highest ever set by the Federal Court in that district. Remus paid it and was set free pending his trial.

Understandably, Remus was furious with Jess Smith. He had paid the friend of the United States Attorney General close to $1 million for protection and now he was facing substantial charges. Remus met with Smith at least four times between his arrest and the following April. On each of these occasions Smith assured Remus that he had nothing to worry about. On each of these occasions Remus gave Smith about $10,000.

In April 1922 the Grand Jury returned four indictments against George Remus and over a dozen of his associates. The trial began on May 8. The government presented a mountain of evidence against the defendants. Scores of individuals testified that they had either participated in the operation, had bought illegal liquor at Death Valley, or had been offered bribes by Remus. The evidence was overwhelming. After only two hours of deliberating the jury found all fourteen defendants guilty. Remus received the maximum allowable penalty: two years in the federal penitentiary at Atlanta, Georgia, and a $10,000 fine. At a second trial on related charges Remus was also found guilty and sentenced to one year in the Montgomery County jail and fined $1,000. Remus immediately appealed both verdicts and remained free on bond.

While awaiting the outcomes of his appeals, Remus traveled to Washington, DC to have a few words with his supposed guardian angel, Jess Smith. Extremely angry, Remus yelled, "The conviction is there. What assistance will you give now?"

"There is no likelihood," Smith assured him, "of you ever going (to jail) at anytime."

The Cincinnati Crime Book

Remus met several times with Smith during this period. He gave Smith another $30,000 with the understanding that the verdict from the Court of Appeals would be favorable. That court was scheduled to rule in early June, 1923.

On May 30 Jess Smith was found dead in the Washington apartment he shared with the Attorney General of the United States. The official verdict in the death was that Smith had committed suicide by shooting himself in the head. Some people later contended that he had been murdered.

Six days later the Court of Appeals upheld Remus's convictions. He continued appealing his case up to the United States Supreme Court but was denied all the way. Finally, his time as a free man ran out.

Remus arrived at the federal penitentiary in Atlanta in late January, 1924. He promptly paid off prison officials in return for a private cell, good food, and an easy job in the prison library.

His main objective now was to get out of prison. Toward that end, he began providing information to an agent of the (then just) Bureau of Investigation, Franklin L. Dodge, Jr. Remus gave Dodge information on the corrupt public officials whose cooperation had aided him in his bootlegging endeavors. Remus wrote to his wife Imogene and asked her to try and get Dodge into his corner.

Imogene Remus had moved to Atlanta to be close to her husband while he did his jail time. She often visited him at the prison. In accordance with Remus's wishes, she contacted Franklin Dodge. Dodge was tall and handsome. He was also single and known to enjoy the company of beautiful women. When Imogene Remus contacted the agent on her husband's behalf, Dodge refused even to consider the notion of intervening. Still, despite these refusals, Imogene Remus continued to be seen with the good-looking government man.

George Remus heard that his wife was seeing Dodge, but he thought she was only doing what he had asked her to do – trying to influence the government man on his behalf. Therefore, he was shocked when his wife sent him a letter announcing her intention to divorce him. On August 30, 1925 Imogene officially served him with the divorce papers, charging him with, among other things, cruelty. This letter arrived just days before Remus' scheduled release from prison.

Remus responded, "My wife must have been misled and ill-advised. I have showered luxuries upon her and she has stood by me through my imprisonment here. We have been devoted to each other." He was shocked by the allegations in his wife's petition for divorce. And he believed he knew the real reason his wife wanted to leave him: she was in love with Franklin L. Dodge.

George Remus was released from federal prison on September 2, 1925. All the other sentences he had received were thrown out on double jeopardy grounds, but he wasn't out of trouble. He still had to face trial in a case involving the theft of over 30,000 gallons of Jack Daniel's whiskey from their St. Louis distillery in 1923. In fact, he was immediately taken into custody on these charges upon his release from Atlanta.

The Jack Daniel's affair began in May 1923 and basically involved Remus and some associates planting a worker in the distillery who would look the other way while whiskey was pumped out of the warehouse through a hose to another building where it would be re-barreled and sent on its way. The barrels back at Jack Daniel's would then be topped off with water and pure alcohol. This would satisfy any cursory examiner.

This plan worked fine until September, when the inside man was replaced. One night the replacement got thirsty for whiskey and tapped one of the barrels that had been topped off. When the man tasted the supposed whiskey, he discovered it was just water and alcohol. When he checked the other barrels, he discovered the same thing. He then alerted Prohibition officers of the theft.

The Feds closed the operation down but did not immediately arrest any of the men who had set up the elaborate scheme. Instead, they steadily gathered information and evidence until they were able to obtain indictments. By December 1925 they were ready to go to trial. And the government had a star witness: George Remus.

Remus decided to testify for the government because in his eyes he had been cheated in the Jack Daniel's deal. At a point early in the siphoning operation a local criminal gang known as Egan's Rats had become aware of the scam and demanded a cut of the action. That cut had come out of Remus's share of the profits, and he felt that he had been robbed.

Remus testified on December 16 for over two hours. Because of threats against his life, he was allowed to carry a firearm for his own protection, even though he was still officially a federal prisoner.

Remus's testimony was vague but effective. On December 18 the jury convicted all but two of the defendants. Calling the Jack Daniel's affair "The biggest conspiracy I ever heard of," the judge imposed fines on the convicted men and sentenced them to various lengths of time in custody.

Remus went back to Cincinnati. Several months later, all charges against him in connection with the Jack Daniel's affair were dropped because of his cooperation. But by then, George Remus was already becoming consumed with an obsession which would culminate in his most serious criminal act and would lead to one of the most unusual murders trials in the history of the United States.

By 1926 George Remus was convinced that his wife and Franklin Dodge were lovers and were involved in a longstanding conspiracy to destroy him. He discovered that Dodge had been a major player in the 1921 raid on the Death Valley Ranch. Remus now felt that Imogene had assisted Dodge in that action and that their affair had begun long before that date.

The Cincinnati Crime Book

Imogene Remus had power of attorney over her husband's financial empire while he was doing his time in Atlanta. Upon his release, Remus discovered that his bootlegging operation was not just a shambles, but that it was gone altogether. Imogene had sold many of his distilleries at prices far below their true value. Remus believed she had used some of the profits to buy expensive gifts for Franklin Dodge. Remus later said that his wife also sold all of the expensive contents of the mansion in Price Hill. When he arrived there after serving his prison sentence all he found was a cot, a table, and a chair.

Franklin Dodge would always deny allegations that he was romantically involved with George Remus's wife. "The charges are absolutely false," he said on one occasion. "I deny them without qualification. They have no foundation in fact and the attack upon me is wholly unwarranted and manifestly unfair." Dodge said he had first met Imogene Remus in January 1925.

In addition to his marital and monetary setbacks, George Remus had another new problem. His legal presence in the country was becoming an issue. His arrival in this country, as a young boy in the early 1880s, was not well-documented. There was no record of his father ever becoming a naturalized U.S. citizen. If it could be determined that George Remus was an illegal alien, he could be deported to Germany. Remus was convinced that his wife and Franklin Dodge were behind this action as well.

George and Imogene Remus appeared in court on numerous occasions relating to their upcoming divorce throughout early 1927. They also spent much of the year gathering evidence to use against each other. In September Remus's attorneys bowed out of the case, so Remus decided he would represent himself. The divorce trial was scheduled to begin in Hamilton County's Domestic Relations Court on October 6, 1927.

The divorce trial would never take place. But a spectacular murder trial would.

October 6, 1927 was a Thursday. About an hour before the divorce proceedings were to begin, Imogene Remus and her daughter from her first marriage, Ruth, left Imogene's residence at the Hotel Alms on Victory Parkway and got into a taxicab to go meet her attorney before their appearance in court. As they proceeded south towards Eden Park, Imogene noticed that they were being followed by George Remus, who was being driven in another car behind them. Frightened, she exclaimed, "My God, there's Remus in that car!" She told the cab driver to speed up. He did, but Remus' driver kept pace.

The two vehicles proceeded along victory Parkway and into Eden Park. As the cars reached the straight section of road just past the gazebo, Remus' driver overtook the taxicab and forced it off onto the sidewalk on the right side of the road. Remus then left his car and ran towards the cab. As Imogene Remus tried to get out of the cab and run away, Remus grabbed her.

The Cincinnati Crime Book

"Now, you decomposed mass of clay, I've got you!" he yelled at his wife. He then pulled a small, pearl handled revolver from his pocket and pressed it to Imogene's stomach.

"Oh Daddy, you know I love you. Daddy don't do it!" she screamed.

George Remus pulled the trigger once.

As blood began flowing from her stomach, Imogene broke away from her husband and staggered into the morning rush-hour traffic. "For God's sake won't somebody help me?" she pleaded. Soon a motorist stopped and took her and her daughter to Bethesda Hospital. By then, Imogene had lost consciousness. She would die two hours later without regaining it.

Remus' driver had panicked and driven off, so Remus walked away from the scene to Gilbert Avenue. There he got a ride with a motorist who took him to the Pennsylvania Railway Station. An hour later he presented himself at the Central Police Station, downtown. "I want to give myself up," he told the cops. "I've shot my wife." He was immediately taken into custody.

Remus never acted like a guilty man. Shortly after his arrest, he told police, "I am now at peace after two years of hell. I'm satisfied I've done right." Later that day he told reporters, "I am entirely responsible for the act I committed.... I shall make no defense of insanity. I feel I was justified doing what I did. I owed this to society.... If you have a clear conscience, you have nothing to fear, and consequently why should I run away? A man who feels that he has performed a duty to society and that he has committed no moral wrong does not run away from the consequences of his act, but would do just as I have done, give himself up."

In Chicago, Remus's first wife defended her ex-spouse. "(Imogene) made his life so miserable that he was driven to (kill her). She made him a pauper. Again and again she threatened his life. Why, George Remus wouldn't hurt a fly."

Remus' daughter from his first marriage, Romola, arrived in Cincinnati late in the evening of the day of the shooting. She announced her wholehearted support for her father.

The day after his arrest George Remus appeared in Cincinnati Municipal Court where he pleaded not guilty. He added that he wanted a speedy trial and that he intended to represent himself at that trial. "Remus will defend himself," he asserted. "After all, it is I who will be tried for murder. Death is staring me in the face, and I say to you frankly that I will defend myself. Remus will play a lone hand." (Remus often referred to himself in the third person.) He was then returned to his cell to await an indictment from the Grand Jury.

Although Remus did intend to defend himself, he knew that since he was to be jailed during the proceedings he would need the help of an outside attorney. For this assistance, he hired Charles Elston, a young criminal lawyer who had at one time been a prosecutor.

The Cincinnati Crime Book

On October 14 the Grand Jury indicted George Remus for the murder of his wife. He pleaded not guilty. The trial was scheduled to begin a month later in the Common Pleas Courtroom of Judge Chester R. Shook. The state's case would be presented by Hamilton County Prosecutor Charles P. Taft. Taft was the son of William Howard Taft, the former President of the United States and then current Chief Justice of the U.S. Supreme Court. Charles Taft and George Remus developed an immediate and everlasting dislike for each other.

Remus spent the month before the trial accumulating evidence of his wife's supposed treachery against him. Under Remus' direction, Charles Elston obtained court orders to open several safe deposit boxes in Chicago and in Lansing, Michigan, in an attempt to locate Remus' missing fortune. They found nothing, although an official at the Lansing Bank identified Franklin Dodge as one of the people who had used the box. Dodge, a Lansing resident, denied the accusation. "If (Imogene) had a safety box here or visited Lansing, I know nothing about it," he claimed.

Remus announced that he planned to plead justifiable homicide. "Anyone who thinks I'm insane needs a mental examination himself," he said.

Charles Elston confirmed the strategy. "We expect to prove conclusively that Mrs. Remus and Franklin Dodge, Jr. carried on a love affair and that they conspired to deprive Remus of his property while he was in jail. (This is) clearly a case of the unwritten law."

As if to indicate that the upcoming trial would not be typical, Remus added, "Remus the lawyer is fighting for Remus the defendant, and he will make the fight of his life for his life." Remus' flamboyant courtroom style in Chicago was well-known, and courtroom observers expected nothing less at this trial. They would not be disappointed.

The trial began with jury selection on November 14, 1927. Hamilton County Courtroom Number Two was packed with spectators minutes after the doors were opened. It would remain full throughout the duration of the trial. Judge Shook banned cameras, typewriters and telegraph equipment from the room, declaring, "This case must be tried without confusion and in the usual dignified, calm manner. The atmosphere pervading the Courtroom must be consistent with the best traditions of American judicial procedure."

The first day of jury selection went well except for a shouting match that erupted between Remus and Assistant Hamilton County Prosecutor Carl Basler when the latter referred to George Conners as "Remus' lieutenant."

Nothing further happened until the third day. Remus, since he was defending himself, was allowed to question the perspective jurors and to address the court. At one point a dispute arose when Prosecutor Taft mentioned that Remus had been disbarred by the Chicago Bar Association for allegedly questionable activities. Remus jumped to his feet. "A nice statement to be made by the son of the Chief Justice of the Court! He knows that the defendant is charged with murder and he makes these statements for no other purpose than to cause prejudice as a result of these newspapermen that are here.... It has been the pleasure of this defendant to appear before that High Chief Justice (prosecutor Taft's father, William Howard Taft), but the specimen as given by the offshoot of that great, renowned character is pitiful." Remus was shaking with rage. "Five hundred judges and members of the Chicago Bar have volunteered to come down here as character witnesses and, just because the son of the Chief Justice in this wonderful United States makes that kind of assertion...." His voice trailed off. He then approached the prosecution table, shook his fist in the startled Taft's face and said, "Man, if I had you in the corridor, I would wreck you physically!"

Basler jumped up. "Get back on your side or I'll punch you!" he threatened.

Judge Shook hammered his gavel and regained control of the courtroom. Taft asked the judge to prevent Remus from making any future such outbursts, but since Remus was acting as his own attorney there was nothing Shook could do but assign Sheriff's deputies to physically restrain the defendant if he lost control of himself.

Commenting on the judge's threat of physical restraint, Remus said, "They may bind Remus, they may truss him, they may entangle him in chains. But they will never halt his mind, and they will never silence these lips."

By the end of that third day a jury of ten men and two women was selected. Charles Taft made a motion to have the panel sequestered and Judge Shook granted it. The first duty of the jury was to visit the scene of the crime in Eden Park and Remus' mansion in Price Hill. Then court was dismissed for the weekend. Opening statements would be given on the following Monday, November 21.

The State of Ohio's opening statement was delivered by Assistant Hamilton County Prosecutor Walter K. Sibbald. "The State's evidence will show that George Conners, George Klug (the driver of Remus's car on the day of the shooting), and Blanche Watson of Covington, Kentucky (Remus' secretary) were with Remus in his room at the Sinton (Hotel on October 5, 1927). We will show that they plotted to kill Mrs. Remus." In Eden Park, Sibbald continued, Remus "approached his wife, who had left the taxicab, (and) his actions were so deliberate that as he walked to the taxicab he slowly drew his revolver from his pocket and as he fired he said something abusive to the woman he was killing. After the shooting (he) put the revolver in his pocket and calmly walked away from the scene."

Remus had a sore throat, so spectators were disappointed that they would not get to see the defendant make his own opening statement.

Remus had since learned that there was no common law in Ohio that justified killing one's spouse, so the defense had, after all, changed to an insanity plea. Therefore, in addition to the usual cast of characters in a murder trial (defendant, prosecutor, judge, etc.), three state-appointed psychiatrists (then called "alienists") were present in the courtroom, seated on a platform behind and above the judge. These doctors would determine whether Remus had been insane at the time of the shooting, or whether he was presently insane. These doctors could also halt the proceedings at any time if they determined that the defendant was acting irrationally.

Charles Elston spoke for the accused man, saying, "We will introduce evidence to show that for two years prior to the killing George Remus was insane and that on the morning of the killing the insanity was brought out by a series of circumstances and facts which had turned this otherwise normal man into an insane man.... At the time of the slaying George Remus was not a free agent, he was not a sane man, he was not a normal man, he was not able to entertain deliberate preparation and malice such as the law contemplates in a first-degree murder." Elston contended that the insanity was caused by Remus' knowledge of the affair between his wife and Franklin Dodge. "He learned the truth about (the affair) after he got out of prison in 1925, and we claim that since that day he has been insane. We expect to show that his mind snapped because these things bore down so heavily on him. Because, after all, he is just human."

After opening statements, the state called its first witnesses, people who had witnessed the shooting in Eden Park. The driver of Imogene Remus' taxicab testified how Remus' car had forced him to the side of the road. Once the vehicles were stopped, Remus advanced on the taxi. The cab driver said he didn't witness the actual shooting, but he heard the gunshot just after Remus told his wife, "I'll get you!" After the shooting, the driver said, he had driven off in search of assistance. By the time he returned to the scene with a policeman, everybody else was gone.

A motorist testified to taking the mortally injured Imogene Remus and her daughter to Bethesda Hospital. He added that they had stopped on the way to pick up a police lieutenant.

Doctors from Bethesda testified about Imogene Remus dying in the emergency room there.

Then the prosecution introduced witnesses who were supposed to prove that Remus had conspired with the others (none of whom, however, had been indicted) to kill his wife. An employee from the Sinton Hotel said that she had often seen Blanche Watson at the hotel, where Remus had a suite of offices. Cross-examining this witness, Remus suggested that there was nothing unusual about Watson being at the suite because she was his secretary.

Imogene Remus' divorce lawyer was called and testified that George Remus had filed no paperwork in regard to the anticipated divorce trial. The state said that this proved Remus knew there would be no divorce trial because he planned to murder his wife before the case reached that point. Remus countered that he had indeed obtained some depositions for the case, but that they had simply not been filed yet.

The state called George Klug, the driver of Remus' car on the morning of the shooting. Klug surprised the prosecution by contradicting many earlier statements he had made to them while they were preparing their case. On the stand, Klug apparently didn't even remember most of the earlier statements. He did recall picking up Remus at his Price Hill mansion and driving him to the Hotel Alms at about 7:00 a.m. on October 6. (George Klug didn't seem to know much about anything else. Although he described Blanche Watson as Remus' secretary, he was unable to explain exactly what kind of business Remus was in.)

After Klug's testimony, court recessed until Friday since the next day, Thursday, was Thanksgiving Day. In keeping with the holiday, Remus told the press that he was "Thankful! Yes, a million times thankful for the peace of mind, soul, and being that no verdict can rob me of, and which now, on this day of thanks, is my solace."

When court resumed on Friday another witness to the shooting , Imogene Remus's daughter Ruth, took the stand. Dressed in black, the young woman recalled the events leading up to the pursuit into Eden Park and the cars coming to a halt there. "Mother opened the taxicab door and started to get out," she said. "And Mr. Remus approached her and grabbed her by the wrist and pulled her out of the cab. It took me some time to recover myself, but I followed. (Outside the cab) I asked (Remus) what he was going to do, but he had already shot her. Then he hit her in the head. He held the muzzle of the pistol close to her body. I heard her scream, 'Oh Daddy dear, you know I love you!' He swore at her. Terrible language. Then she said, 'Don't do it Daddy, don't do it!' I saw the pistol in his right hand. After the shot, I grabbed him by his coat lapel and said, 'You don't know what you are doing.' He answered, 'She can't get away with that!'" After Remus left the scene, Ruth said, she had flagged down another car to take her mother to the hospital. On the way, in the car, "Mother was lying on the floor. I was trying to help her, but she was suffering terribly although conscious and able to talk. She said, 'I know I'm dying.' I said, 'No, you're not.' I couldn't believe it. Then she said, 'Isn't it terrible of George to do this?'"

On cross-examination Charles Elston did not attempt to disprove Ruth's version of the events in Eden Park. The young woman had been a sympathetic witness for the prosecution and it wouldn't have been wise to attack her in front of the jury. But he did get the young woman to admit that she and her mother had visited Lansing Michigan, home of Franklin L. Dodge.

The next day the three court appointed alienists delivered their opinions of the mental condition of the defendant. Their report, which was not read to the jury, concluded that "Basing our conclusions upon conversations with and examinations of the said George Remus, including our observations of him in the Courtroom during the progress of this trial so far, we are of the opinion that the said George Remus is now sane and was on October 6, 1927, sane."

The only testimony the jury heard that day was from the man who had driven Remus downtown to Pennsylvania Station after the shooting. After that, the state rested its case.

The defense's first move was to have the alienists removed from their impressive seats high up behind the judge to a less exalted location behind the jury. Then Elston got to the heart of the defense's case – the mental condition of George Remus.

In order to demonstrate that Remus often "lost it" when he was angered, the defense called a series of witnesses who testified as to the defendant's behavior under stress.

Over prosecution objections, the court had ruled that the defense could present evidence of any relationship between Imogene Remus and Franklin Dodge in order to explain the defendant's diseased state of mind when he shot his wife.

The first witness in this vein was the former caretaker of Remus' Price Hill mansion. William Mueller testified that he had seen Dodge at the residence on three occasions. He also described how Imogene had been removing property from the house and telling him it was all right because "Mr. Remus will never come back here. We are going to have him deported. Everything is fixed up. He will go back (to Germany) the way he came – without any money."

An attorney who had represented Remus on other matters testified that when the subject of Imogene Remus and Franklin Dodge came up "Remus would become much worked up, strike his body, raise he hands above his head and to my mind appeared like a maniac. (Then) he would quiet down, apologize, and then go back and do the same thing over. It happened twice during one conference. His face would become distorted."

A former Common Pleas Court judge testified that he had witnessed Remus walking through his empty house after his release from Atlanta, "wringing his hands, uttering cries of amazement that he had been treated in that manner." The judge recalled Remus' obsession with Imogene and Dodge. "We would be talking about matters entirely foreign to (their supposed affair) and Mr. Remus would give way to an outburst. Uncanny laughter would resound through my office.... (Remus) raved and raved and raved. His eyes became glassy. He told me he was being watched by detectives and gunmen, and left my office without making one coherent statement."

The next witness, a former United States District Attorney, testified similarly. "(Remus said), 'That man Dodge has taken my wife's affections. Franklin L. Dodge has taken my wife after I trusted her, and ruined my life forever.' (Remus') muscles were contorted, his face was drawn, and his eyes were glassy. He left my office without making a coherent statement with reference to (what he originally came to discuss)."

Another witness, a Pulitzer Prize winning reporter for the *St. Louis Post Dispatch* testified that Remus had been convinced that his wife and Dodge were plotting to murder him during the Jack Daniels trial in Indianapolis. "He was in an agitated state of mind and behaved like a wild man," the journalist said. On another occasion, when Remus was informed that Imogene and

Dodge were together, "(He) at once flew into a rage.... His struggles were so violent that I was knocked to the floor."

A childhood friend of Remus, who had become reacquainted with the defendant in 1925, told how he had made a divorce settlement offer to Imogene on George's behalf. When she turned the offer down, the friend recalled, "Remus was absolutely insane.... He tore his clothes off. He took off his collar and his coat and vest. Why, he actually tore them right off! Then he took off his shoes and threw them out the window. This fit lasted for hours and hours.... He was insane."

Another acquaintance told the court how Remus could "be as solemn and sonorous as an Archbishop, but when his wife and lover were mentioned he would jump up like a man with a hornet in his pants and rave like a maniac.... He was crazy as a bedbug.... His neck swelled up like a cobra's."

Then George Conners, Remus' best friend and right-hand man, took the stand. He gave lengthy testimony about the deterioration of the relationship between George and Imogene Remus. He recalled the numerous alleged death plots against Remus that were instigated by his wife. Imogene had even threatened his own life, Conners said. He remembered Remus' rage over his wife's spending. On one occasion Remus had told him, "If I get a hold of her I'll take her by the back of the neck into every store in Cincinnati and make her pay her own bills."

On December 7, a Harry Truesdale was testifying that Imogene Remus had actually offered him $10,000 to kill George Remus. Truesdale said that Imogene had given him a $250 down payment on the murder and told him where Remus could be found. Upon hearing this testimony, Remus suddenly began to weep uncontrollably. Judge Shook immediately had the jury escorted out of the courtroom. Remus became hysterical. "Your Honor, can we have an adjournment?" he cried. The judge agreed and everyone went into his chambers. Remus' wailing could still be heard in the courtroom. After about fifteen minutes it became clear that the defendant wasn't calming down ("My God, I can't stand it!" he screamed.), so he was taken back to his cell to regain his composure.

The prosecutors alleged that Remus had staged the dramatic breakdown for the benefit of the jury. They pointed out that Truesdale's planned testimony was already known by Remus. Supporters of Remus countered that if he had planned the performance for the jury he would not have asked for an adjournment and had the jury removed from the courtroom before he performed most of the "act" in the judge's chambers.

Whatever the true cause of the outburst, its effect on the jury was obvious and real. Some of the jurors had been observed crying as they were led from the courtroom.

By late afternoon the alienists had examined Remus and determined that he was recovered enough for the trial to continue. But court was already adjourned for the day.

The Cincinnati Crime Book

The next day the courtroom was filled early. Hundreds of people tried to get in, both to see the follow-up to the previous day's outburst and to see one of the most famous men in the country: Clarence Darrow. The renowned attorney had agreed to testify as a character witness for his old friend George Remus.

When everyone was assembled in the courtroom, Remus stood and said, "Your Honor, I want to apologize to you and the jury for my unmanly conduct of yesterday." Judge Shook said nothing, and the trial resumed.

After Harry Truesdale completed his testimony about being hired to kill Remus, Clarence Darrow was called to the stand. Darrow told the jury that he had known the defendant for over thirty years. He characterized Remus as a good citizen and a good attorney. "(Remus') reputation as a lawyer, I believe it to be good," Darrow said. "It was good. I say it from the fact that I never heard it questioned.... (But) I know that he was a very emotional man, and somewhat unstable."

After Darrow, several more witnesses testified as to Remus' good character. Then the defense called its last witness, a former Municipal Court judge from Chicago who testified that when Remus visited him after his release from Atlanta "He wasn't the same man I had known. He looked wild and would jump up and walk around. He was standing there leaning against the wall scratching his head and crying out, 'Oh my God! Mrs. Remus is driving me crazy! She won't talk to me! She is driving me crazy!'"

With that testimony, the defense rested its case.

Charles Taft began the prosecution's rebuttal case, trying mainly to counter the scenario of marital treachery that had been presented by the defense. The state also called witnesses who testified as to the apparent sanity of the defendant.

Cincinnati Police Sergeant George Dooley was the first officer to talk to Remus after he turned himself in on October 6. "He said he shot his wife," Dooley recalled. He also remembered Remus referring to his wife as a "decomposed mass of clay" and Franklin Dodge as a "parasite." Remus "talked plainly" and was "calm and collected," Dooley said. "From his behavior I concluded he was sane."

Another officer who was present during the initial interrogation of Remus said that he was "courteous, intelligent, coherent, and without any regret for what he had done."

Ruth Remus, still dressed in mourning black, testified that her mother and Remus' marriage had begun to sour long before his incarceration in Atlanta. She recalled a card game in which Imogene had chided her husband for making a bad play. "He picked up a five pound box of candy and threw it at her." On another occasion, she had entered her mother's room after Imogene had an argument with Remus and "found mother standing there, very scared, her nose bleeding and her dress stained with blood." Things didn't improve when Remus went to jail, Ruth said. "Mother tried to do things for Mr. Remus when he was in prison, but the things she did did not please him. He would get angry at her and she would leave the prison in tears." Ruth admitted that Imogene had hired Harry Truesdale, but only to follow Remus and catch him with another woman.

Both the prosecution and defense rested their rebuttal cases on December 15. (The defense called no rebuttal witnesses.) Charles Taft then pointed out that the alienists had not testified, so Judge Shook reopened the case so the jury could hear their conclusions. The alienists stated unanimously that in their opinions Remus was not insane at the time of the shooting or at the present time, and that the insane episodes testified to during the defense's presentation of its case were merely "expressions of violent hate expressed with the appropriate degree of anger."

The prosecution and defense rested their cases again on December 17. All that was left was for each side to make its closing argument.

Charles Taft argued for the state. He called the shooting of Imogene Remus "the most atrocious murder in the history of Cincinnati." He reiterated an earlier state claim that Remus had killed his wife because he feared she would disclose too many of his illegal activities during the divorce trial. He called Remus a coward for not testifying. "(He) will throw a fit in front of you, go down on his knees, maybe throw himself into a faint. He certainly will weep, but he wouldn't let the state cross-examine him, for he knew it would hang him.... There never was a case where the defendant was so clearly guilty of cold-blooded, calculated, ruthless murder than this. You can only find him guilty of first degree murder and you can show him no mercy.... There will be just one time when the people of the State of Ohio will be safe from George Remus and that is when he is dead."

Charles Elston closed for the defense. He mocked the state's contention that Remus had plotted to kill his wife with George Conners, George Klug, and Blanche Watson. "Blanche Watson, who had no stain on her name, has been branded a murderess.... Where is one solitary scintilla of evidence in the case to brand (the alleged conspirators) as murderers? I don't think there was ever made in this courtroom or in any other court any accusation that was less justified than that one." Elston contradicted the prosecution's image of Imogene Remus as an innocent wife. "When Remus came to Cincinnati to engage in the bootlegging business, his wife came with him. He made money and she knew how he made it. She enjoyed it luxuriously. She never said, 'George Remus, I don't want that money – you made it bootlegging.'" Elston lambasted Franklin Dodge. "They try to make Franklin L. Dodge Jr. look like an eminent gentleman, but I tell you if it had not been for Franklin Dodge, George Remus would not be charged with murder and you would not be here."

Closing arguments were interrupted while court recessed for the weekend. Remus commented to reporters that he planned to finish the closing arguments for his case himself. Hinting at what that argument might be, he said, "Fancy yourself in prison, locked behind the bars and for months and months knowing that the woman to whom you had given everything in life, your very soul, was in the arms of another man. Wouldn't it drive you to madness? Wouldn't it?"

Again the courtroom was jammed when the proceedings resumed on Monday December 19. Elston resumed the defense's closing argument with an attack on the character of Franklin Dodge ("the dirty rotten skunk.... that filthy louse") and said that the alienists' report that Remus was insane at the time of the shooting should be ignored. "Turn (Remus) loose for Christmas," Elston said. "That time when there's peace on earth and good will to men. Bring a peace of mind to a man who has suffered the tortures of hell for more than two years. Let George Remus be judged in the spirit of peace on earth and good will to men. I know then you will have righted the greatest wrong that has ever been done to any man."

Then, George Remus stood up.

"Here before you stands Remus, the lawyer," he began. "In that chair there" – he indicated his now empty seat – "sits Remus, the defendant, charged with murder. The eyes of the whole civilized world have been turned on this case and on George Remus, the murderer of his wife." Remus defended his career as a bootlegger, calling the Volstead Act "one of the greatest criminal and legal abortions of all time.... This prohibition law is making hypocrites out of our judges, our prosecutors, and our citizens as well." He contrasted himself with the prosecutor. "This defendant started in life at $5 a month.... I would gladly lay down my life today for one drop of the blood which flows in the veins of your prosecutor, son of that noble statesman, the Chief Justice of the United States, and a former President, but ladies and gentlemen we could not all be born with a golden spoon in out mouths like Charles P. Taft the second." He attacked Franklin Dodge, "that social leper, that contemptible mass of human nothingness that was kicked out of the Department of Justice, who used his badge as an agent of the United States government to enter my home and debauch my wife." He ridiculed the prosecution's unproven claim that he had conspired with George Conners ("so noble and beautiful a character") and Blanche Watson to kill his wife, and said that only an insane person would kill someone in broad daylight in front of witnesses.

"I have suffered tortures of living hell for two years," Remus concluded. "I am not asking for mercy, but justice. The defendant does not desire any sympathy or compassion in any shape or form whatsoever. If you, who have a higher power than the President of the United States in this case, feel that the defendant should go to the electric chair, do not flinch. The defendant will not flinch. The defendant stands before you in defense of his honor and the sanctity of his home. The defendant is on trial for that. If that is a crime, punish him. As you ponder on your duty bear in mind that which is most sacred is your home and your family. I thank you. Merry Christmas to you."

The final words for the prosecution were split between Assistant Prosecutors Carl Basler and Walter Sibbald.

"What's this all about?" Basler asked the jury. "Why, it's about a cold-blooded murder: the murder of Mrs. Remus and how he lay in wait for her. The issue in this case is murder, and don't forget it. He grabbed that warm, pulsating human being and shot her down in cold blood.... If you want to do right by your fellow citizens and churchgoers, you will come back after you have deliberated and say, 'He is guilty. He must die.'"

Walter Sibbald concluded with a summary of the prosecution case and rebuttal of defense contentions. Then the state rested. Judge Shook gave the case to the jury at 1:00 p.m. on December 20. He gave them five possible verdicts, none of which was outright acquittal. After fifteen minutes the jury indicated that it had not reached a verdict, so the judge adjourned the court for an hour and a half for lunch.

At 2:15 the jury resumed deliberating. At 2:55 they announced that they had reached a verdict. Excluding the lunch break, they had deliberated for just over half an hour.

Everyone was reassembled in the courtroom and the jury came in. The foreman handed a note with the verdict to the court clerk, who then read the decision to the anxious crowd: "We the jury, on the issue joined, find the defendant not guilty of murder, as he stands charged in the indictment, on the sole ground of insanity."

After a few seconds of silence, the courtroom erupted in cheers. "Thank you, thank you!" Remus exclaimed to the jurors. "I wanted American justice and I thank you for it."

Spectators who filled the courthouse corridors began chanting "Not guilty - hurray! Not guilty - hurray!"

The jurors later said that it had only taken ten minutes to reach the verdict, but that they had wanted to eat. "I wanted to go back then (when we reached the verdict)," the foreman said, "but we finally decided to wait until after lunch." He added, "If we could have acquitted him clean we surely would have done so. We decided that the man had been persecuted long enough."

Remus told reporters, "Thank God for a verdict that lifts the greatest burden man must ever stand. God alone knows the thing that is in my heart at this moment. The rest of my life I will dedicate to stifle the insult that is upon our statutes known as the national prohibition act."

The prosecution was in a much different mood. In a statement to the press Charles Taft said, "To characterize the verdict as a gross miscarriage of justice is to us a trite expression and is utterly inadequate to express half the truth of so nauseating a situation."

If a large portion of the public thought the verdict just, there were also many who were dismayed by the jury's decision. In an editorial, the *Cincinnati Enquirer* asked how a jury of lay persons could be expected to make decisions on the sanity of a defendant. Calling the death of Imogene Remus an "adroitly planned killing" the editorial hoped that "Possibly the time will come in the United States when juries will be required to take into account the character, intelligence, and impartial interest of (expert) witnesses in murder trials more than they now take into account the maudlin sympathies and testimonies of lay witnesses."

An out of town reporter was more blunt. Calling the case "the damndest thing I ever saw," he asked, "Is that the way they always do things down here?"

On December 28 George Remus appeared in Hamilton County Probate Court for a hearing on his sanity. Two days later the judge in that court declared Remus "insane and a dangerous person to be at large" and ordered him sent to the Lima State Hospital for the Criminally Insane.

Remus entered Lima on January 6, 1928, exactly three months after he gunned down Imogene Remus in Eden Park.

After the verdict, Remus quickly filed a habeas corpus writ with the Court of Appeals in Allen County, claiming that he was no longer insane and therefore should be released from custody. The hearing on the writ lasted several weeks before the judges concluded that Remus was now sane and entitled to his freedom. The State of Ohio immediately appealed the court's ruling to the Ohio Supreme Court. While this appeal was in progress, Remus was still held at Lima.

George Remus remained at Lima until June 29, 1928. He was released that day after a 4 to 3 favorable vote by the Ohio Supreme Court on his writ of habeas corpus. Remus was told of the court's decision as he worked on the hospital's farm. He rushed to his quarters and began packing. "It's wonder, wonderful," he exclaimed. "I am going back to Cincinnati. I am so satisfied with the decision of the court that I am unable to say just what my plans will be. But anyway, I'm going back to Cincinnati with the least delay and I intend to stay there."

Remus was gone from the hospital within a half hour of the court's decision.

Ohio Attorney General Edward Turner said the state would not attempt to have the Justices' decision reversed. "No, we will not appeal," he said. "We are through."

Remus's attorney, Charles Elston, said, "I am certainly glad that it's all over," and added, "There can be no further appeal as there is no constitutional question involved on which the state might take the case to the United States Supreme Court."

George Remus did return to Cincinnati, but his life was never quite the same. The trial for the shooting of his wife had seriously depleted what little was left of his fortunes. Most of his associates from his bootlegging endeavors had deserted him. He kept a relatively low profile. He opened offices in the Keith Building on Walnut Street downtown where he ostensibly operated a real estate business. He was sued for back taxes, but fought the suit and was discharged of all tax liens against him in 1929. The deportation

The Cincinnati Crime Book

proceedings against him never went anywhere. There were rumors that he was involved in bootlegging, but no proof of this was ever produced. He never achieved the levels of wealth or flamboyance that he had established before his arrest in 1921.

Prohibition ended on December 5, 1933 after the 26th state ratified the 21st Amendment which repealed the 18th. But by then George Remus' days as the "King of the Bootleggers" were already long over.

Remus married his secretary, Blanche Watson, and the couple set up house in Covington, Kentucky. He formed the Washington Construction Company, the main purpose of which was to tear down his former mansion in Price Hill and subdivide the ten-acre lot into smaller residential units. The extravagant swimming pool, however, was spared the wrecker's wrath and remained opened for many years for use by the public.

During the remaining years of his life Remus' name occasionally made it into the newspapers, usually connected with old charges and lawsuits left over from his bootlegging days or with new business ventures.

George Remus died at his home at 1810 Greenup Street in Covington, Kentucky on January 20, 1952. He had been in ill health for the last few years of his life due to a stroke. The man who at one time reportedly had a $20 million fortune left no will. Whatever possessions he had went to his widow and daughter.

Remus' passing caused almost as much notice as if he had been a former mayor of Cincinnati. The *Cincinnati Enquirer* called him "fabulous" in its obituary headline. An editorial in the *Times-Star* compared Remus to the Great Gatsby. A well-known local newspaper columnist who knew Remus remembered him as "thoughtful.... charitable.... a gentleman."

About fifty people attended the memorial service for George Remus at the Allison and Rose Funeral Home in Covington. Among the mourners were Remus' wife Blanche and his ever-loyal daughter, Romola. The expensive casket was surrounded by over 25 floral arrangements. The Reverend Morris Coers, of Covington's Immanuel Baptist Church, presided over the service. His theme was "He that is without sin among you, let him cast a stone...."

George Remus was buried in the family plot of his third wife, Blanche Watson, in the Riverside Cemetery at Falmouth, Kentucky. The monument marking the plot had three human figures on top. Originally, the outside figures were angels. But sometime after Remus was interred someone removed the angels' wings.

Perhaps that someone believed that George Remus didn't deserve to rest with angels.

George Remus. (*The Cincinnati Enquirer*/Michael Snyder)

Imogene Remus. (*The Cincinnati Enquirer*/Michael Snyder)

Eden Park, where George Remus killed his wife.

George Remus' grave in Falmouth, Kentucky.

The outside figures were once angels.

The Head And Hands Murder

The Head and Hands Murder did not occur in the City of Cincinnati, but most of the people involved with the case were from there and the story was dominant in the local press for many months. And even today, after over 60 years, the ghastly decapitation murder of Cincinnati Fire Captain Harry Miller still stands as one of the most brutal and bizarre crimes in the area's history.

It all started on June 12, 1936 with a disturbing find along the bank of the Mill Creek about seven miles southeast of Carrollton, Kentucky. Early that Friday morning a farmer walking on the bank came upon a macabre collection of debris, things that had not been there when he passed by the same spot the previous evening. After looking closely at the objects in front of him, the farmer hurriedly left and summoned authorities.

When authorities arrived they quickly confirmed that the farmer's concern was justified. A thorough examination of the scene was made. The plants and grasses in the area were splattered and smeared with blood. Scattered about were several bloodstained articles of a man's clothing and three bloodstained handkerchiefs. There was a thirty-inch length of clothesline, also bloodied. Three fishing poles, tied together with string, had been carelessly discarded. Also discarded was an axe, smeared with blood but otherwise brand new. Most ominous were two very large pools of blood. It appeared as if someone had attempted to hide the pools by pouring dry cement over them.

The police were convinced that some violent and probably criminal act had occurred on the creek bank, but they didn't know what. There was not yet enough evidence to point a criminal investigation in any specific direction. They made routine inquiries in the area but were unable to come up with any further information about or explanation for the bloody scene. All they could do was wait and hope that some other evidence would present itself. A week later, it did.

On June 19 a passerby poking around in a culvert along Kentucky State Route 55 between Eminence and Shelbyville made a horrific discovery. Stuffed inside the drain was the headless body of a man. The dead man's ankles had been bound with wire and his arms were tied together at the wrists with clothesline. The man's hands had also been cut off. Neither the head nor the hands were found with the corpse. A closer search of the area turned up a packet of matches from a restaurant in Harrison, Indiana, and an iron rod about three feet long and three quarters of an inch thick.

The culvert where the body was found was located about twenty miles south of the place where the blood pools and other items were found along the Mill Creek. Authorities quickly made a connection between the headless corpse and the bloody debris found at the creek.

There were several factors pointing toward such a connection. For one thing, the clothesline used to bind the corpse's wrists looked identical to the length of line found on the creek bank. Bloody clothing had been found at Mill Creek; the dead man was unclothed except for underwear. Finally, the body had powdered cement on it. Powdered cement had been scattered over the pools of blood at Mill Creek.

Now police had more to go on. But they still did not know who the victim was, much less who was responsible for his demise.

The gruesome series of discoveries in Kentucky finally reached its end on Sunday, June 27. On that day three boys were escaping the early summer heat by taking a swim in the lake at the General Butler Resort Park. General Butler Park was located on U.S. Highway 42, only a few miles from Carrollton. As the boys swam in a shallow area of the lake, they were attracted by a school of fish that was swarming around a cardboard box lying just under the water's surface. As the inquisitive boys pulled the box to the surface they were able to see inside of it, and what they saw made them drop the box and go running for the local sheriff.

Inside the box was a human hand.

When Carroll County Sheriff Walton Banks arrived at the scene the box was hauled out of the lake and given a closer inspection. The box, measuring about 7 by 14 by 28 inches, had been filled with cement and then tied shut with a length of clothesline. But the cement in the box did not completely cover the contents, and it quickly became evident that the boys had not been mistaken when they thought they saw a human hand. In fact, the box contained not one hand, but two. And that was not the worst of it. The box also contained a severed human head.

Authorities immediately connected this dreadful package to the headless corpse found in the culvert by Route 55 and to the bloody debris found along the Mill Creek. The most obvious connection was the fact that the head and hands found in the lake accounted for the parts missing from the body from the culvert. Additionally, the lengths of clothesline found on the creek bank, around the wrists of the mutilated corpse, and around the box in the lake all seemed to be the same type of line. The head and hands had been severed very neatly. That pointed to the brand new ax found at Mill Creek as possibly being the cutting instrument. Finally, cement was a factor at all three scenes.

The Cincinnati Crime Book

It had been scattered over the blood pools at Mill Creek, was present on the body found in the culvert, and had been used to fill the box found in the lake.

Now the police had a complete body and some evidentiary clues. The next step in their investigation was to determine the identity of the decedent.

All investigators knew for sure was that the victim was a white male who appeared to be in his late sixties or early seventies. They began canvassing all communities in the area, looking for any instance of an older white male who had been reported missing.

Since the evidence found so far had been scattered over a fairly wide area, the search for a reported missing person was equally wide and extended beyond Kentucky into communities in southeastern Indiana. In one of these cómmunities, New Trenton, Indiana, police learned of a missing person who fit the description of the corpse. The missing man, Harry Miller, was a retired Captain from the Cincinnati Fire Department. He had not been seen since June 11, the day before the farmer discovered the bloody scene along Mill Creek.

Harry Richard Miller was born on November 8, 1873, in Cincinnati, Ohio. His father, John Miller, had been a Marshall in the Cincinnati Fire Department, so when the time came for Harry to choose a career he chose fire fighting. He joined the department on December 17, 1896. During his career he served in numerous firehouses, including Engine Company No. 9 (4th and Mill Streets), Ladder Company No. 12 (Paddock and Reading Roads), and Engine Company No. 32 (Rockdale Avenue). By 1908 he had risen to the rank of captain.

Captain Miller worked enthusiastically for the Fire Department until he retired in May of 1930. Several years before that he purchased a cottage near New Trenton. The small orange-colored cottage, which he used as a summer residence, was located on 24 acres of land along the shores of the Whitewater River, about half a mile from where U.S. Route 52 cut through the center of the small town.

During his summers Miller settled easily into country life. He was well liked by the locals, who regarded him as something of a "gentleman farmer." They called him "Cap" Miller.

Harry Miller was well-known for his fondness for food. This fondness caused him to be a regular guest at a local tavern where he talked openly with the locals. He had no qualms about discussing his life with New Trenton's townsfolk. He always told his neighbors when he would be leaving town, and he always told stories about his trips when he returned.

The only time Captain Miller didn't tell anyone about taking a trip was when he left for the last time.

On June 11, the day before Miller's final trip, he was in the local eatery, and he was talkative as usual. Waving a letter, he complained about a person who was always asking for money. He said that the person had just sent him the letter and was demanding a $1500 "loan." He added, however, that he would not give the person the money. Miller then dropped the subject of the letter and, after commenting about possibly attending a firemen's benefit in Cincinnati, left the tavern. That was the last time he was seen alive.

Authorities suspected that the dismembered body was that of the missing fire captain. Their suspicions were given weight when three New Trenton men whose interests had been aroused by a newspaper article about the headless corpse traveled to Carrollton to see if the body was indeed that of the missing Harry Miller. Noting a scar under one eye and some gold dental work, the trio concluded that the corpse was that of their absent neighbor.

Further confirmation of the identity of the body came from Covington, Kentucky police detective Albert Selter. After viewing the head, Selter also said the dead man was Miller. Selter had been acquainted with Miller for several years.

Harry Miller had a sister, Miss Flora Miller, who lived on Crown Street in Cincinnati. A few years younger than her brother, Flora Miller had once been an opera singer, touring the United States, Canada, and Europe under the stage name Florence D'Ephia. She was also a talented artist and an art collector. When Harry Miller wasn't summering in New Trenton, he stayed at Flora's house in the city.

Sheriff Banks contacted Flora Miller by telephone to see if she could shed any light on the awful fate that had apparently befallen her brother. When the head of the dead man was described to her, Flora became hysterical. She was sure that the dead man was Harry. She told Banks that she had received a postcard on June 19 from her missing brother, postmarked June 17 in Cleveland – a week after he had disappeared. On the card Miller explained that he was on a trip and asked his sister to look after his property in New Trenton while he was away.

At Sheriff Banks' urging Flora Miller agreed to go to Carrollton to provide whatever help she could in the investigation.

With identification fairly certain, police questioned friends of Captain Miller to try and determine a reason for the brutal slaying. Everybody they talked to pointed to the same possible motive: money. Harry Miller had lots of it.

Firemen who had worked with Miller told authorities that he had been lucky in the stock market and that he didn't hesitate to brag to anyone who would listen about his good fortunes. In fact, Miller told people that he had made more money in the stock market since he retired from the Cincinnati Fire Department than he had in his entire career as a firefighter. Miller also made money in real estate dealings. Friends of Miller from New Trenton told police that the fire captain never had less than $150 on his person, and that he flashed the money frequently.

On June 30 Flora Miller viewed the head in Carrollton. She was unable to make a positive identification. Captain Miller's dentist was then located, and said he would look at the head on July 3. Because of recent unusual dental work done on the missing man, the dentist said he would have no difficulty in making an identification. He said that a general description he had of the dental work done on the head already tallied with the work he had done on Miller.

Authorities continued to delve into the world of Captain Harry Richard Miller.

An close examination of Miller's New Trenton home revealed that he had apparently left the residence in a hurry. Scraps of food from a recent meal were found on a plate on a table. Miller was notoriously neat, and he never would have left food out if he had gone on a planned trip. Further, no clothing such as he would have taken on a trip was missing. A neat stack of *Cincinnati Enquirers* lay on a table. The date on the last issue was June 11, the last day Miller was known to be alive. A neighbor inspected the property to see if he noticed anything out of place. The only thing he saw was that an iron rod from the gate of the property was missing. The rod had been used to prop the gate open and had been there the entire twelve years Captain Miller had lived on the property. The description of the missing rod tallied with that of the iron rod that was found near the decapitated corpse in Eminence. Another thing missing from the New Trenton property was Captain Miller's car. It had not been seen since a neighbor observed it on the day Miller was last seen alive.

To some investigators robbery appeared to be the motive for the slaying. Miller had no known enemies, so there seemed to be no other motive. But others didn't think that such an elaborate and apparently well-executed crime would have been committed for the hundred or so dollars that Miller was known to carry on him.

Since the evidence of the crime was scattered over such a wide area, in two states, jurisdiction was a problem for investigating officers. Some believed that the absence of the iron bar from the Miller property, coupled with the evidence of severe blows to the dead man's head, indicated that the crime had been committed in New Trenton. But Carroll County officials were convinced that the murder had occurred there. They had a witness, a woman who lived near the Mill Creek, who said she had heard three gunshots on the night of June 11. Miller, before being beheaded, had been shot twice in the head and once in the body.

Sheriff Banks was confident that there would be an early solution to the crime. "It won't be long before we make an arrest," he said on July 1.

On July 3 the dentist positively identified the severed head as that of the missing Captain Miller.

A few days later Miller's missing car was traced to a garage in the Cincinnati neighborhood of Walnut Hills. It had been stored there the day after Miller disappeared. A former employee of the garage was arrested and questioned. He said that he had released Miller's car to a man he did not know on June 13. The car was still missing.

The Cincinnati Crime Book

The practice of arresting people for questioning is a law enforcement tool from a bygone age. While the tactic may seem outrageous to today's observer, it was commonly used in the 1930s. Thus police also arrested, in lieu of further developments, Captain Miller's sister, Flora, and her chauffeur/secretary Heber L. Hicks. Miss Miller and Hicks were arrested at Captain Miller's New Trenton house and then held incommunicado in a jail in Indiana. Authorities said that the pair would be held until the investigation into the crime was over.

That investigation continued, delving into the business dealings of the deceased. Harry Miller's financial endeavors with stocks and bonds were well known, so police were looking for anyone who may have tried to sell any stock certificates which might have been stolen during the murder. Thus they learned that an individual had approached a Cincinnati broker with $100,000 worth of securities that he wanted to liquidate. The individual told the broker that the owner of the securities "would never be heard from again.... he burned up in an automobile." The broker was suspicious of the man and his story, and refused to handle the transaction. But he told his associates about the suspicious offer and word of it got to the cops. Thinking that the securities might be part of Captain Miller's missing wealth, authorities were very interested in finding the man who offered to sell them. Unfortunately, the broker was out of town on vacation, so investigators would have to wait awhile before they could talk with him and get a description of the man who had tried to sell the securities.

While police waited to talk with the broker, they followed up on another interesting lead: they discovered that Harry Miller had been engaged to be married. When they talked to Miller's fiancee, they learned a lot more about the personal life and relationships of the dead man.

For one thing, the fiancee told police, Harry Miller's sister was always hitting him up for money. About a year earlier, the fiancee said, Miller had begrudgingly given $300 to Flora after complaining, "What, again?" Also, Miller was concerned about the relationship between his sister and her chauffeur/secretary, Heber Hicks. Hicks, according to the fiancee, had been the victim in the hijacking of a liquor shipment a few months earlier. After this incident, in which both the liquor and Hicks' own car were stolen, Flora Miller had purchased a new car for him. Captain Miller "hated Hicks," the fiancee said. She added that Miller planned to change or add to his will after they were married on September 20, 1936.

These revelations were very interesting to authorities. And especially interesting was the emerging picture of Heber L. Hicks. It turned out that Hicks had a history of run-ins with the law, having been arrested as recently as June 20, for reckless driving. When arrested, Hicks had blood on his hands and face. He said that the blood was the result of "a fight at a river camp." Hicks appeared before a judge and was sentenced to five days in jail and ordered to pay a $10 fine. Both the jail sentence and fine were suspended.

61

The Cincinnati Crime Book

But reckless driving was the least of Heber Hicks' character flaws. Further investigation revealed that he had served 11 years in a penitentiary in Kentucky – for murder. In 1918, when he was 20 years old, Hicks strangled and shot a young widow in Clay, Kentucky. Robbery was the motive for the crime. He had even cut off one of the woman's fingers in order to get her rings. Hicks was sentenced to life imprisonment for the crime, but he was released after serving 11 years.

Because of this information, authorities began looking very, very closely at the life and activities of Heber L. Hicks. They found out a lot. For one thing, they discovered that Hicks was a good friend of the garage employee who had dealt with Captain Miller's car on June 12 -13. The employee soon identified Hicks as the individual who left the car at the garage early on June 12. After the garage employee quit his job (the day he released Miller's car) he had even gone on a trip to Louisville with Hicks. It was also noted that Heber Hicks fit the preliminary description police had of the man who had tried to pass the questionable securities in Cincinnati in late June.

On Saturday, July 4, 1936, police concluded that they had enough information to make an arrest and issued warrants which read: "Flora Miller (and Heber L. Hicks) did on the 11th day of June in the County aforesaid, unlawfully, willfully, feloniously, and with malice aforethought shoot and wound one Harry Miller with a pistol loaded with powder, a leaden ball, and other hard substance; and did thereafter unlawfully dismember the body of said Harry Miller by cutting off the two hands and head and from which shooting and wounding and dismembering of the body of said Harry Miller did there and then die in Carroll County (Kentucky)."

In addition to the warrants for Miss Miller and Hicks, authorities also issued four "John Doe" warrants in the belief that others as yet unknown were also involved with the crime.

While these warrants had been issued in Carroll County, Kentucky, the police were actually still not sure where the murder had occurred. Kentucky authorities backed their claim for jurisdiction with the evidence of the woman who said she heard three gunshots about two miles from the Mill Creek on the night of Miller's disappearance. Indiana police countered that Miller was killed in front of his New Trenton home, where he was bashed over the head with the iron bar. Then, they believed, the body was transported to Kentucky for disposal. While officials sorted out the jurisdictional discrepancy, Flora Miller and Heber Hicks were held in jail in Indiana.

By now, 66-year-old Flora Miller was already being described in the press as "eccentric." An interview she gave the *Cincinnati Enquirer* shortly after her brother's body was discovered hinted at her feisty and perhaps fantastic nature. Interviewed in her Crown Street home, Miss Miller declared, "If the police don't clear this case up in a few days, I'll bust this thing wide open myself. You know, I'm a 'dick' (detective) myself. I did a lot of work for (the Cincinnati police chief), and I've worked all over the Northwest for William

J. Burns (detective agency)." Commenting on her brother's well-known ability to defend himself she remarked, "If that's Captain Miller who was murdered down there, the time came when his 'dukes' weren't enough."

As noted earlier, police interrogation methods in the 1930s were somewhat less sophisticated and concerned with the rights of suspects than they might be today. Heber Hicks was subjected to continuous and intense questioning after his murder warrant was issued. There can be little doubt that officers used all of the "third degree" techniques that were standard practice in that day. And after three days of questioning, their persistence finally paid off. Heber Hicks broke down and admitted that he had been involved in the murder of Captain Harry Miller. By late in the night of July 7 he had signed a complete confession. Finally, the story of what had happened on the night of June 11, 1936 came to light.

Hicks said that the murder had been committed to gain possession of some $120,000 worth of stock certificates which had been hidden in a strongbox in Flora Miller's Crown Street home without her knowledge. He said that he had hired three men to carry out the crime. He himself, he claimed, had been at a motion picture show with Flora Miller when the crime actually occurred.

As Hicks initially described the murder, he said that Captain Miller had been killed in his New Trenton home. There was a terrific struggle before the victim was finally felled by a blow from the iron bar. "(The men I hired) told me that the lick was first struck in the kitchen with the metal pipe," Hicks' confession stated. "And after several licks the man went down on his front porch, and in the scuffle someone went into the screen. There was blood on the porch. They mopped that up with water." The men placed Miller into an automobile and headed south on Indiana State Highway 56. At a place along the Ohio River, opposite Warsaw, Kentucky but still on the Indiana side, Miller was shot three times. Still, Hicks said he did not think Captain Miller was actually dead until the car reached Madison Indiana, some 75 miles from New Trenton. The men then crossed the river into Kentucky. The body was dismembered along the Mill Creek and disposed of in the locations where it was eventually found. The original plan called for the body to be disposed of at least 400 miles away from New Trenton, in Tennessee.

The three men were each paid with $400 cash and 100 shares of stock of Bethlehem Steel. The stocks were taken from the strongbox in Flora Miller's house.

Hicks said that he had planned the crime for several months before it was committed.

As for the motive for the murder, Hicks said, "I figured that if (Captain Miller) was out of the way then Miss Flora Miller would receive the estate and that I indirectly would benefit from it, because of the fact that I was employed by Miss Miller."

Hicks' confession completely exonerated Flora Miller. She was released from jail the same night Hicks signed his confession.

The Cincinnati Crime Book

Heber Hicks was charged with first degree murder and held at the jail in Brookville, the county seat of Indiana's Franklin County. His trial was scheduled to begin on December 3, 1936. Authorities issued arrest warrants for the other three men he had named as his accomplices in the crime. They were John Joseph Poholsky, William Kuhlman, and Frank Gore Williams. All three men had previous criminal records.

While Hicks waited for his trial and police sought the other suspects, a bizarre event occurred that contributed yet another macabre chapter to the already unusual case. When Captain Miller's body was first found it had been interred in a cemetery in Shelbyville, Kentucky. But his head and hands had been buried in the Odd Fellows Cemetery in Carrollton. On Saturday, November 7, 1936 the various portions of the corpse were returned to Cincinnati for burial in a single grave. The re-internment was arranged by Flora Miller. Captain Miller – all of him – was buried in the Miller family plot at Spring Grove Cemetery. His association with his beloved Cincinnati Fire Department followed him into death; his headstone identified him for eternity as "Captain Harry R. Miller."

The next big break in the case came on November 18, 1936, when Indiana State Police arrested John Joseph Poholsky. This arrest was the result of a tip from a person wishing to cash in on a $3000 reward that had been offered in the case by Flora Miller. Poholsky was arrested as he entered his rooming house in Warren, Ohio. He offered no resistance to the arresting officers and readily admitted that he had participated in the robbery of Captain Miller. But he denied being directly involved in his murder.

John Poholsky was 35 years old. He lived in Cincinnati and was employed as a day watchman at the Laurel Homes housing project. He earned $2.50 a day at that job.

Poholsky made a confession shortly after his arrest that differed in several major respects from the confession given by Heber Hicks. One of the major differences was that Poholsky claimed that Hicks had not only been present when the crime was committed but that he had been an active participant in the murder.

Poholsky told police that Hicks had initially approached him in April, 1936, with an offer to pay him $2000 "to bury a dead man." Poholsky had a steady job and said no thanks. A week later Hicks made the offer again, but upped the payment to $3000. Poholsky still wasn't interested. When Hicks raised the payment to $5000, though, he finally agreed to go in on the plan.

The murder was originally scheduled for June 4, but the plan was foiled because Captain Miller was away at the dog races in Harrison, Indiana. On June 11, the plotters made their second attempt.

According to Poholsky, he, Hicks, Kuhlman, and Williams arrived at Captain Miller's home at about 9:30 p.m. on June 11. Hicks planned to introduce Kuhlman and Williams to Captain Miller as two whiskey salesmen who wanted to sell a hijacked load of liquor. Because Poholsky was a laborer and his appearance was not high-class enough to fit in with Hicks' "whiskey salesmen" scenario, he would wait in the car while the trio subdued Miller. Poholsky said that when the four men arrived at Miller's house all the lights were on and the radio was playing loudly.

While Poholsky waited in the car, the other three men went into the house and began socializing with the unsuspecting Captain Miller. When Miller walked into his kitchen to get a glass of water for a whiskey chaser, William Kuhlman struck him over the head with the iron bar. Miller began to struggle. Hicks called out for Poholsky to assist them, but by the time he got to the house Miller was already on the front porch, bleeding and unconscious.

Hicks told his accomplices to load the body into the car and to dispose of it in the manner they had previously discussed. He would remain at the New Trenton house and clean up any evidence that was left from the struggle that had occurred there.

With the body loaded into their car the trio drove to Madison, Indiana, and then crossed the Ohio River into Kentucky. At a spot near Carrollton, Miller's head and hands were cut off. Poholsky admitted that he did the dismembering. The men had intended to bury the body near Carrollton, but the ground was too hard to dig in, so instead they took the body to the location near Eminence where it was stuffed into the culvert. After disposing of the body, the men backtracked to Carrollton and dumped the head and hands into the lake at General Butler Resort Park.

Once the body, head, and hands were disposed of, Poholsky, Kuhlman, and Williams returned to Cincinnati. Poholsky went to work at his job at Laurel Homes that afternoon. He continued to report for work normally until the day he heard that Heber Hicks had been arrested. Then he left town.

Poholsky said that his total payment from Hicks for his participation in the murder/dismemberment of Harry Miller was $55.

Poholsky waived extradition and was taken to the jail at Brookville, where Heber Hicks already waited. It was the first time the small jail had ever held two murder suspects at the same time.

In Indianapolis, Captain Matt Leach, head of the Indiana State Police, told reporters that his department would intensify the search for William Kuhlman and Frank Williams. He described both men as "desperate," and said that he expected to have to "shoot it out" with the two ex-cons.

On December 7, 1936 jury selection began in the murder trial of Heber L. Hicks in Brookville, Indiana. A panel was seated after one day and testimony began the next day.

The first witness for the prosecution was John Poholsky. Poholsky described the crime in a cool and conversational manner that shocked the spectators in the courtroom. Hicks was tense as Poholsky testified.

He told about how Hicks had approached him in early April and "asked me if I wanted to make some easy money." Poholsky told Hicks he wasn't interested. But Hicks kept asking him, eventually providing more details about the job. "Hicks said he wanted me to cut a man's head and hands off. He didn't say who he was. He offered me $2000; then, at a second meeting he offered $5000 and said he would have it one or two weeks after the job was pulled."

On the night of the murder, Poholsky said, the four men purchased three bottles of whiskey in Harrison and then headed for Miller's house in New Trenton.

"I sat in the auto while the other three men went into the home. I heard someone cry out soon afterwards and other muffled cries. Then someone called to me. I found Captain Miller lying on the front porch.

"One of Captain Miller's hands was holding one of Kuhlman's wrists. With his other hand Captain Miller held a lead pipe we had taken there in the auto. Kuhlman, with his free hand, was beating Captain Miller with a blackjack.

"Miller collapsed then and I saw Hicks standing in the door. He gave me a towel to wrap around Captain Miller's head." The bloody towel had been recovered by police and was offered into evidence.

Poholsky said that while Hicks stayed at Miller's house to clean up and destroy evidence, he and the others loaded the injured man into the car and sped away.

But the intended victim was not subdued yet. "We drove away, and when Captain Miller groaned more and made a fuss near Madison, Indiana, Kuhlman held Miller down with his left hand while he fired three shots into his body."

After crossing the river into Kentucky, the men attempted to bury Captain Miller, but the spot they selected for the grave was too rocky to dig in. They then cut off Miller's head and hands and placed them in the cardboard box. Frank Williams poured concrete into the box. The body was then stuffed into the culvert before the men drove back to the lake in General Butler Resort Park and threw the head and hands filled box into it.

Testimony continued the next day, December 11, as the farmer who found the site of the disturbance by the Mill Creek described what he saw there.

But the real event of that day occurred over two thousand miles away from the courtroom. Early that morning police in Portland, Oregon arrested William Kuhlman.

Kuhlman, the alleged triggerman in the Miller slaying, had been arrested without incident after committing a $1000 robbery at the Broadway Theater in downtown Portland. He readily admitted his identity and said he knew that he was wanted in Indiana. After about 24 hours in custody he began talking about his role in the Miller crime.

Most of what he said tallied with the confession of John Poholsky, but with one major difference. While Kuhlman admitted that he had shot Captain Miller, he said that Poholsky had also fired shots into the injured man. Kuhlman said that Heber Hicks had been present at the crime scene. After the crime, Kuhlman said, Hicks gave the three accomplices stocks certificate as payment for their participation. Kuhlman sold his through a broker in Cleveland and netted $2500.

Authorities were anxious to get William Kuhlman to Brookville to testify in the ongoing trial of Heber Hicks. Franklin County Sheriff George Pulskamp and John Barton of the Indiana State Police flew to Portland and retrieved the prisoner.

Other testimony in the Hicks case included that of the Henry Green, who testified that he was aware of several meetings the alleged murderers had held at Poholsky's residence at 30 W. Court Street in the days prior to the crime. He also said that he had rented the garage space in Walnut Hills for Captain Miller's car and later drove the automobile to Cleveland. In Cleveland, he said, he lived in a tourist camp with Poholsky, Kuhlman, and Williams. He had seen the men pass $1000 bills.

On December 16 William Kuhlman took the stand and testified that Frank Gore Williams had held the flashlight while John Poholsky dismembered Harry Miller's body.

Then the state rested its case. That same day Frank Gore Williams was arrested in San Francisco. It is probable that Williams' arrest came as a result of information provided by William Kuhlman.

Williams was arrested at his workplace, the men's furnishings section of a downtown department store. He admitted his part in the kidnaping of Captain Miller, but denied participating in the murder. In fact, he denied even knowing that Captain Miller had been killed until he later heard the news on the radio.

Williams was returned to Indiana.

On Friday December 18 Heber Hicks took the witness stand and testified in his own defense. Hicks' strategy was to place the blame for the crime on the sister of the dead man, Miss Flora Miller.

Hicks said that Flora Miller had a much greater motive for the murder of her brother than he did. He testified that she had been accessing Captain Miller's safe in her Crown Street home for some time and that she had forged her brother's name to secure the mortgage on the Crown Street home, to the tune of $12,000. Hicks said that he had originally confessed to the crime and exonerated Miss Miller because she offered him $25,000 to do so and promised to get a good Cincinnati defense lawyer to handle his case.

Hicks said that he had informed Captain Miller that Flora had forged the mortgage certificates.

Flora Miller needed almost $400 a month to cover her debts, Hicks testified. So, in January 1936, she began plotting to get into the safe Captain Miller had at her house. The key to the safe was kept in a locked wardrobe. Hicks obtained the services of a locksmith from Covington to open the wardrobe so Flora could get the key. Once she had the key, Hicks said, she began plundering the safe.

Hicks also claimed that Flora Miller and John Poholsky had been acquainted for years in connection with the liquor business and that the two "carried on."

In its cross-examination of the defendant the prosecution sought to discredit Hicks' new version of the crime. But Hicks stuck to it, at one point tossing a copy of his first confession into the lap of the seated prosecutor and saying, "That story was made up in my own mind to save someone else."

Hicks left the witness stand on December 19, and the defense quickly concluded its case. The jury got the case on Monday, December 21. After four hours of deliberating, they announced their verdict: guilty. The jury also set the punishment for the crime at death.

The judge asked the convicted man if he had any statement to make. "I have violated no law of Indiana," Heber Hicks replied.

The judge then told the convicted man, "You will remain at the Brookville jail for two weeks and one day. Then you will be taken by the sheriff of Franklin County to the Indiana State Prison at Michigan City where he will deliver you into the custody of the warden."

The judge paused. The courtroom was quiet.

"You, Heber L. Hicks, will on April 10, 1937, before sunrise, be put to death by electric current in accordance with the verdict of this jury and the laws of the state of Indiana."

As he was led from the courtroom, Hicks repeated, "I have violated no law of Indiana."

When news of the guilty verdict and death sentence reached the Franklin County Jail, there were chants of "good, good, good" from John Poholsky and William Kuhlman. "We're not afraid to die," they said, "but we want to see Hicks die first."

But Heber Hicks did not die first. Several legal appeals postponed his death sentence. In the meantime, John Poholsky, William Kuhlman, and Frank Gore Williams were all found guilty of the Miller murder, sentenced to death, and executed.

By the spring of 1938 time was running out for Heber Hicks. As his imminent execution neared, Flora Miller spoke to the press about her former chauffeur. Still referring to him by his nickname, she said, "I feel sorry for his mother, (but) for Jimmie I have no sorrow. But still I can't say anything detrimental about the man. When he worked for me he was always a perfect gentleman. I never heard him even use a swear word." Miss Miller said she had no hard feelings about her former employee. She added that she hoped the condemned man would reveal the whereabouts of Captain Miller's still-missing securities before he died. (Hicks had been asked about this prior to one of his earlier postponed execution dates. His response was, "Ask her, she knows.") "I don't think he believes in God," Flora continued. "I have nothing to say about (Hicks' fate). I think God guides everything, and what is to be is to be...."

The Cincinnati Crime Book

Heber L. Hicks was finally executed on May 6, 1938.

There was a bizarre epilogue to the Head and Hands Murder case almost twenty years later when, on March 4, 1954, a Cincinnati Probate Court judge issued a mental health warrant for Miss Flora Miller. The warrant was the result of an incident the previous Sunday night when the now 83-year-old woman had become violent in her rooms at the Hotel Alms.

Police were called to the scene. Flora barricaded herself inside the apartment and threatened to shoot through the door if anyone tried to gain entry. Undeterred, police broke down the door and took the elderly woman into custody. She was taken to Cincinnati General Hospital where it was reported that she was suffering from hallucinations.

Staff at the Hotel Alms said that Miss Miller, who now called herself "Florence" Miller, had only left her rooms twice since she moved there shortly after her brother's death nearly two decades earlier.

On March 19, 1954, at a hearing in Probate Court, Flora Miller was declared "mentally ill." She was placed in a sanitarium.

The court then ordered an auction of a fabulous collection of possessions that Flora had accumulated over the years. Most of these were kept in a house at 993 Lenox Place, in Avondale. Although Miss Miller purchased the house ten years earlier she never lived in it and rarely even visited it. Instead, she used it as a storage place for the antiques, bric-a-brac and other personal property that she had collected throughout her life. The house, and the carriage house behind it, were filled with the collection of antiques.

Included in the auction were a 150-year-old cherry desk from France, a set of gold etched Louis XIV chairs, imported rugs and china, countless pieces of furniture, theatrical costumes, artworks, pianos, and even a surrey with a fringe on top.

Perhaps the most notable item up for bid was a 1934 Pontiac automobile. The car had only 4000 miles on it. It was the car that had formerly been chauffeured by Heber L. Hicks. It had not been driven since 1936.

The sale did not include Harry Miller's New Trenton home, which had passed to his sister after his untimely death.

There was a driving rain and wind as about 200 people showed up for the auction. The items went quickly, including the Pontiac sedan. It was sold for $140.

Flora Miller died at the Emerson A. North Hospital on April 29, 1962. She was 91 years old. She was interred in the Miller family plot in Spring Grove Cemetery, but her grave was not marked.

Her true role, if any, in her brother's murder was never determined.

Harry Miller's New Trenton, Indiana house.

Captain Harry Miller. (AP/Wide World Photos)

Harry Miller's grave in Spring Grove Cemetery.

The lake at General Butler State Resort Park,
near Carrollton, Kentucky.

Heber Hicks (left) after his arrest for the murder of Harry Miller.
(AP/Wide World Photo)

Anna Marie Hahn

Mention the name Anna Marie Hahn to anyone who lived in Cincinnati in the late 1930s and you'll get instant recognition – and with good reason. Anna Hahn was a Cincinnati archetype, a German immigrant with ties to the city's Over-the-Rhine neighborhood (the area of downtown stretching north above Central Avenue – formerly the Erie Canal, the "Rhine" – to the base of the Clifton hill). But Anna Marie Hahn is remembered for more than just the fact that she was a member of one of the major immigrant groups to shape the character of Cincinnati. She was also a serial killer fifty years before that term was even coined. And she was a female one, to boot. Finally, Anna Marie Hahn is remembered because she was the first woman to be put to death in Ohio's electric chair.

The story of Anna Marie Hahn began to unfold not in Cincinnati, but over 1200 miles away in Colorado Springs, Colorado. On July 30, 1937 three persons got off a train in that city and registered at the Park Hotel there. One of the persons registered was George Obendorfer, an elderly cobbler who made his home at 2150 Clifton Avenue in Cincinnati. The other two guests were Mrs. Anna Marie Hahn and her young son, Oskar. Mrs. Hahn signed the registry book for all three of them.

Soon after his arrival in Colorado Springs, George Obendorfer fell ill and was taken to a hospital. By August 1, he was dead. Doctors were initially unable to determine a cause of death.

But Colorado authorities were suspicious because the death of the cobbler was so sudden and unexplainable, and they began to make inquiries into the circumstances surrounding it. They discovered that Obendofer had been registered at the Park Hotel, apparently with Anna Marie Hahn and her son. They also discovered that the hotel was investigating the theft of $300 worth of diamonds which had been stolen from its proprietress.

In an attempt to locate the missing gems, police went to local pawnshops for a lead on anyone who might have recently attempted to sell any diamonds. At one shop the owner said that a woman with a boy had indeed tried to pawn such jewels. This made police even more anxious to locate the woman who had registered into the hotel with George Obendorfer.

While making more inquiries police discovered that on July 24 a woman claiming to be Mrs. George Obendorfer had presented his passbook from a Cincinnati bank at a Denver bank in an attempt to withdraw $1000 from the account. Bank officials had refused. Police were certain that this woman was Anna Marie Hahn.

By this time Anna Marie Hahn had returned to Cincinnati. But Colorado Springs police had already determined that she was from the Queen City and, since they felt they had enough evidence to hold her on suspicion of grand larceny in the theft of the hotel jewelry, they contacted Cincinnati authorities and asked them to pick her up. Cincinnati police did just that.

When asked by Colorado authorities about the death of George Obendorfer Anna Hahn responded, "Why do you call me? This man is a perfect stranger to me. I met him on the train from Denver. He was Swiss. I felt sorry for him and only was trying to help him." Police were somewhat puzzled by Anna's defensive response. They were further puzzled because they also knew that George Obendorfer was also from Cincinnati and that he was not just a "perfect stranger" to Anna Marie Hahn.

George Obendorfer was 67 years old. He had lived in Cincinnati for the last 46 years of his life. He immigrated there from Russia. He was a cobbler, working at the trade until a few years before his death. He had married and had three children and eight grandchildren.

Relatives of George Obendorfer were immediately suspicious about his sudden demise. Until his death he had been in excellent health. The relatives were also suspicious of his recently developed relationship with Anna Marie Hahn.

Police learned more about Anna Marie Hahn too. Most of the initial information came from Anna herself. She said that she had come to Cincinnati from Germany in 1929. In Germany she had been a school teacher in Munich. At that time she was married to a doctor from Vienna, Austria. The couple had one son, Oskar. The family arrived in the United States together, but the doctor died shortly after they got here.

Anna decided to stay in the country. She had relatives in Cincinnati's large German community, so she moved there. At a German dance at the Hotel Alms she met Philip Hahn, who worked as a telegraph operator. Soon they were married. Philip then quit his job with the telegraph company and opened two delicatessens, which he operated with his new wife.

Anna Hahn came to Cincinnati to visit relatives, an aunt and uncle, but they both died shortly after her arrival. She continued to live in their house, at 2970 Colerain Avenue, with her husband and her son from her first marriage.

In 1937 Anna Marie Hahn was 31 years old. She was somewhat plump but not unattractive looking. She had a thick German accent and blonde hair. That blonde hair would become the main description used in reference to her in news accounts in the months, years, and decades ahead. Often she would be referred to simply as "the blond."

Police learned more about Mrs. Hahn from relatives and friends of the late George Obendorfer. They said that although he was retired and no longer worked regularly he would still occasionally make shoe repairs for relatives or friends. This is how he met Anna Hahn. She had a shoe that needed repairing and a mutual friend directed her to the retired cobbler. Obendorfer made the repair and struck up a friendship with her.

Confronted with these details, Anna then admitted that she did know Obendorfer. She confirmed meeting him in his shoe shop on Clifton Avenue and added that in the course of subsequent conversations she mentioned going on a trip to the Rocky Mountains. Later she had been surprised, she said, that while en route to the mountains she met Obendorfer at the Union Station in Chicago and learned that he, too, was going to Colorado. She admitted that in Colorado Springs she had registered with Obendorfer at the Park Hotel but said that after he took ill and went to the hospital she had no further contact with him.

The story of an elderly German gentleman suddenly dying after a newly established association with a woman sounded familiar to investigators in Cincinnati because since June they had been investigating the sudden death of Jacob Wagner, a 78-year-old retired gardener who lived at 1805 Race Street in Over-the-Rhine. Although it was initially believed that Wagner died of heart disease, an old friend was suspicious of his sudden death and had his body exhumed for a thorough autopsy. That autopsy was still in progress when the developments in Colorado Springs came to light.

Police learned from neighbors of Wagner that several weeks before his death he had been approached by a woman claiming to be a relative. That woman, police determined, was Anna Marie Hahn. When Wagner said that he had no living relatives the woman then said that she had an interest in helping the elderly and inserted herself in his household. The neighbors said that they had often heard Wagner and his new friend discussing money. After Wagner's death the woman went into his home and searched his belongings.

But there was more. There appeared to be a series of individuals who had come into contact with the same mysterious woman. And all of those persons had been strangely and adversely affected by that contact.

An elderly woman, Olive Luella Koehler, who lived in the same Over-the-Rhine apartment house as Jacob Wagner, was also befriended by the female visitor, who again claimed to have an interest in helping elderly people. A woman who ran a confectionary in the same block told police that she had twice sold ice cream to this interested visitor, who then gave it to Olive Koehler. The second time Mrs. Koehler ate the ice cream she became so ill that she had to be placed in Longview Hospital. Neighbors suspected that the visitor had then absconded with a valise containing cash and securities belonging to Mrs. Koehler.

After this, the woman had approached Mrs. Koehler's sister, Mary Arnold, who lived nearby on Race Street. Mrs. Arnold was 95 years old. It was not difficult for the visitor to convince the old woman that she was an old friend. Mrs. Arnold later said that her "old friend" talked her into cashing a check so she could buy her some new clothes. The visitor also offered Mrs. Arnold some beer. She declined.

When Mary Arnold refused the beer she made a good choice. George Heis did not. Police learned that Heis, who lived at 2922 Colerain Avenue, had accepted a beer from the friendly female suspect a year earlier. Whereas Heis had previously enjoyed good health, after drinking the beer he was immediately stricken ill and had not left his bed since.

Based on the apparent theft of the jewelry from the Park Hotel in Colorado Springs, authorities there issued a warrant charging Anna Marie Hahn with grand theft. Because of this warrant she continued to be detained in Cincinnati and was eventually taken to the Hamilton County prosecutor's office, where she was questioned by Prosecutor Dudley M. Outcalt and Assistant Prosecutor Frank Gusweiler. As the saga of the mystery woman and the series of illnesses and sudden deaths around her began to unravel, one investigator told the press, "This story has just started. There will be a lot more to this."

By the time Colorado Springs authorities asked for Anna Marie Hahn to be detained, police in Cincinnati were already investigating still another strange death which had occurred in her orbit. On July 6, George Gsellman, 67, had died in his room at 1717 Elm Street, just around the corner from the block where Jacob Wagner, Olive Koehler, and Mary Arnold lived. George Gsellman had died of some sudden and violent illness shortly after a visit by Anna Marie Hahn. On August 2, Gsellman's body was exhumed from the Baltimore Hill Cemetery. A preliminary examination revealed the presence of a metallic poison, probably arsenic, in the body.

By now authorities were also getting more information on the case of Jacob Wagner. His autopsy had revealed no trace of metallic poisoning in the body, but police did find a bottle in his room that contained arsenic. Police theorized that Anna Hahn may not have wanted to use arsenic on Jacob Wagner since her association with him had been so well-observed by his neighbors and acquaintances.

Arsenic is an easily detected poison should authorities decide to look into the cause of a person's sudden death after a violent illness. But croton oil is not. Croton oil is a drug which was used rather commonly as a household remedy before the turn of the century. Although not particularly dangerous in small doses, a large amount taken internally has a usually fatal effect on the heart, especially if administered to someone who is sick or old. Croton oil breaks down quickly in the body and will not be readily detected during a perfunctory autopsy.

The Cincinnati Crime Book

During her questioning Anna Marie Hahn was confronted with a bottle of croton oil which had been given to authorities by her husband Philip. Philip Hahn said he had taken the bottle, a half ounce size marked "Croton Oil Poison X," away from his wife after he had recognized in himself some of the symptoms of croton poisoning. He hid the poison in his locker at work. "I kept it intending to turn it over to police in case anything happened," he said. He added that since he worked at night he was not entirely familiar with his wife's comings and goings.

Anna Hahn admitted that she had purchased the croton oil, on July 20, 1936, but she denied giving it to Jacob Wagner. A pharmacist who operated a drug store in North College Hill confirmed the purchase, telling police that he sold the oil to Anna Marie Hahn, whom he knew as a good customer with good integrity. The druggist told police, "(Mrs. Hahn said) her former husband was a German druggist who used croton oil in his practice frequently and that she was thoroughly familiar with its use."

The more police investigated the background of Anna Marie Hahn the more it became apparent that the investigator's prediction "There will be a lot more to this," was accurate. It seemed as though everywhere the woman went there were suspicious deaths and shady monetary deals.

In addition to cases of George Obendorfer, George Heis, George Gsellman, and Jacob Wagner and his neighbors, there was Albert Palmer, a 72-year-old resident of 2416 Central Parkway. Palmer died on March 27, 1936, apparently of a heart attack after having been ill for three weeks. Palmer's relatives told police that he had frequently gone to horse race betting establishments in Elmwood Place with Anna Marie Hahn. They added that after these excursions the elderly man appeared as if he was doped. After Mr. Palmer's demise his relative were unable to locate a $4000 estate they believed he had. Anna admitted borrowing $2000 from Palmer, and a promissary note in that amount was found in a search of her house.

Then there were Mr. and Mrs. Johannes Oswald, an uncle and aunt of Anna Marie Hahn. According to Anna, both Oswalds had died shortly after her arrival in Cincinnati in 1929. By one account she had inherited the Colerain Avenue house as a result of their deaths. But Anna claimed instead that she got the house when still another elderly relative died.

In addition to these deaths there were three suspicious fires, one of which occurred at a restaurant operated by Anna Marie Hahn and her husband at 3007 Colerain Avenue. She collected $300 for that fire. The other two fires occurred at the Hahn residence, one on June 2, 1935 and the other on May 20, 1936. In the first fire another tenant of the building narrowly escaped being burned to death. Anna collected a little over $2000 for these two fires.

When authorities spoke to Anna's son, Oskar, they got more details on the train trip to Colorado Springs. Oskar said that, contrary to his mother's claim that they had met George Obendorfer by chance in Chicago, she had purchased the old man's ticket to Colorado at Cincinnati's Union Terminal.

Oskar added that on the train he had given Obendorfer over a dozen glasses of water to drink. He said that Obendorfer appeared to get ill after the train left Denver.

With the investigation still in its preliminary stages authorities could only say that because of the mysterious set of circumstances surrounding Anna Marie Hahn she was either the most cold-blooded and calculating murderess in the history of Cincinnati crime or she was merely an unfortunate figure caught up in a remarkable series of coincidences.

But while Anna admitted knowing most of the deceased she denied having anything to do with their deaths, insisting that she had only been trying to help them. "Look at me," she told a reporter. "Do I look like a woman who would do things like that? Tell me. Yes, this is what I get for being kind. That was my only interest in them – just to be kind. I who am the mother of such a fine boy! I should raise a hand against anybody? Do I look like somebody who would hurt people?"

Police know that a murderer's appearance is seldom relevant, and on August 10, 1937 they arrested Anna Marie Hahn and charged her with the murder of Jacob Wagner.

Her trial began two months later, on October 11. By then the case had become a sensational story, and the courtroom was packed with curious spectators. It would be standing-room-only throughout the trial. The case was heard by Common Pleas Court Judge Charles S. Bell. The state's case was presented by Hamilton County Prosecutors Dudley Outcalt, Loyal Martin, and Simon Leis. Anna Marie Hahn was defended by Joseph H. Hoodin and Hiram Bosinger, Sr.

That first day Anna appeared in court wearing a two-piece black crepe dress with a fitted blouse. She wore little make-up. Around her neck was a gold crucifix that she would wear for the duration of the trial.

A jury was selected consisting of eleven women and one man, an unusual gender representation for that time. (The one male member would, however, eventually be elected jury foreman.)

The state's case was very strong. The motive for the murder, they said, was money. Anna needed it because of bad investments and horse-racing debts.

Prosecutors presented witnesses who recalled the defendant's association with the dead man. The agonizing death of Jacob Wagner was recalled in great detail by the hospital employees who had attended him as he died. Anna was linked to poison by the recounting of the discovery of arsenic in a bottle in a purse at her home. The manager of a branch of the Fifth/Third Bank testified that Anna had tried to make several unauthorized withdrawals from Wagner's bank account. A city chemist testified that Wagner's body had enough arsenic in it to kill four men. A handwriting expert testified that Jacob Wagner's will, which left everything to the defendant, was a forgery penned by Anna Marie Hahn.

Anna sat expressionless as all of this damaging testimony was presented.

The Cincinnati Crime Book

A major victory for the prosecution came when Judge Bell allowed information regarding the other poisoning cases to be introduced into evidence in order to show a homicidal pattern of behavior by the defendant. A secret exhumation and autopsy of Albert Palmer's body revealed a lethal dose of arsenic in his system. His internal organs, as well as those of Jacob Wagner, were actual exhibits at the trial. Anna Hahn reacted with noticeable horror when a physician displayed the viscera to the jury. George Heis, the only person known to have survived Anna's ministrations, testified that he had been in excellent health until he had eaten food prepared by the defendant.

Although defense counsel cross-examined most of the state's witnesses, they were unable to shake any of the damaging testimony. The prosecution rested its case on Friday October 29.

The defense began its presentation the following Monday, with Anna herself testifying on her own behalf. Her strategy was simple: deny everything. The prosecution's case, she said, was "lies, all lies." Prosecutor Outcalt cross- examined Anna for over an hour, but she stuck to her story and never lost her composure.

The defense rested its case on November 4.

In his closing argument to the jury Prosecutor Outcalt painted a grim picture of Anna Hahn as a woman who was willing to do anything, even commit murder, for monetary gain. "She is sly, because she developed her relationships with old men who had no relatives and lived alone. She is avaricious, because no act was so low but that she was ready to commit it for slight gain. She is cold-blooded, like no other woman in the world, because no one could sit here for four weeks and hear this damaging parade of evidence and display no emotion. She is heartless, because nobody with a heart could deal out the death she dealt to those old men. We've seen here the coldest, most heartless cruel person that ever has come within the scope of our lives."

Outcalt concluded his argument by saying, "In the four corners of this courtroom stand four dead men. Gsellman, Palmer, Wagner, Obendorfer! From the four corners bony fingers point at her and they say: 'That woman poisoned me! That woman made my last moments an agony! That woman tortured me with the tortures of the damned!' And then, turning to you they say, 'Let my death be not entirely in vain. My life cannot be brought back, but through my death and the punishment to be inflicted upon her, you can prevent such a death from coming to another old man.' From the four corners of this room, those old men say to you 'Do your duty!' I ask of you, for the state of Ohio, that you withhold any recommendation of mercy."

Defense Attorney Hoodin did his best in his closing argument, but there was not much he could say to refute the mountain of state's evidence. He suggested that some of the Over-the-Rhine witnesses had been mistaken in their perceptions of Anna Hahn's relationships with the dead men. "I will not say that a single witness lied," Hoodin said, "but this case has had such

79

widespread publicity that it would have been impossible for these witnesses not to have had preconceived ideas before they ever came into this courtroom, and particularly this is true of the witnesses from Wagner's neighborhood, where the case has been the chief topic of conversation for months." Indicating his client, Hoodin concluded, "Although she is no angel, she is not guilty of the murder of Jacob Wagner."

The case was submitted to the jury on Friday, November 5. Almost 100 witnesses had been called and 137 exhibits presented during the four week trial. The trial transcript consisted of 450,000 words, and printed out to over 1500 typed pages. It was one of the longest trials on record in Hamilton County up to that time.

The next day the jury announced that it had reached a verdict after deliberating for a little over two hours. All of the case principals were brought to the courtroom, which was packed with spectators anxious to hear the verdict. Judge Bell warned against any outbursts. "The court has been informed that the jury has arrived at a verdict," he said. "There must be no demonstration. Anyone doing so will be punished for contempt of court." Bell glanced around and noticed a man peering through the transom from the hallway. "Get that man out!" he shouted to a bailiff.

With everyone present and order established the jury foreman read the decision: guilty with no recommendation for mercy.

Anna Marie Hahn was still, and then bowed her head. Under the defense table her hands twisted a handkerchief.

The jury was polled and asked if their verdict was unanimous. It was. The guilty determination had been reached on their first ballot, the foreman said. It had taken two more ballots to decide that the defendant deserved no mercy.

Court was adjourned and Anna was taken back to the jail. On the way her stoic composure finally left her and she practically ran the last few yards to her cell. Once inside she slammed the door shut and hung a dress over the window in the door so no one could see her. Then she wept.

The verdict was a historic one for the Ohio judicial system. The lack of a recommendation for mercy meant that Anna Marie Hahn would automatically be sentenced to death. No woman had ever before been executed in Ohio's electric chair.

The jury foreman told the press that at no time had there been any question as to Anna's guilt. He said that the defendant's stoicism during the trial had worked against her. "She sat there unmoved... she showed no emotion," he said. "If I had been in her shoes, I would have showed plenty of emotion, believe me."

On November 10 Anna Hahn's attorneys announced that they were prepared to appeal the verdict all the way to the United States Supreme Court. Lead defense counsel Hoodin said, "It will be a long time before the sentence imposed on Mrs. Hahn is carried out."

The defense filed a motion for a new trial. Judge Bell denied the motion. Before pronouncing the sentence he asked the defendant if she had anything to say.

"I have," Anna replied. "I'm innocent, Your Honor."

Judge Bell then formally sentenced Anna Marie Hahn to die in the electric chair. "It is ordered, adjudged, and desired by the court that the defendant, Anna Marie Hahn, be taken hence to the jail in Hamilton County, Ohio, and that within thirty days hereof the Sheriff of Hamilton County shall convey the said defendant to the Ohio Penitentiary and deliver her to the warden thereof, and that on the 10th day of March, 1938 the said warden shall cause a current of electricity sufficient to cause death to pass through the body of the said defendant, the application of such current to be continued until the said defendant is dead." Turning to Anna he concluded, "And may God, in His infinite wisdom, have mercy on your soul."

Anna was moved to the Ohio State Penitentiary on December 1, 1937. But she would not be executed on March 10. Various appeals filed by her attorneys postponed her appointment with the chair. Her case went to the Ohio Supreme Court, and then up to the United States Supreme Court. In the meantime she waited in her cell on death row.

There, in late May 1938, Anna gave an interview to a large contingent of local and national media. The "prisoner press conference" was a first in the history of the Ohio State Penitentiary. For an hour the condemned woman answered questions about her life, the trial, and her probable fate.

When asked whether she thought she had received a fair trial she said, "No, it was not fair in any respect. They said things about me in the trial which I didn't even know about myself. They blackened my character without reason." She was angry at the mostly female jury that had convicted her. "I didn't know that women could do such a thing to another woman, particularly when so many of them were mothers." Asked about the bottle of arsenic found in her purse she responded, "In all my life I have never even known what arsenic is. I don't believe there was any arsenic in that purse, and if there was I certainly didn't put it there." She said she was finished with betting on horses. "I don't even know who is running in the Kentucky Derby," she said. On her chances of a commutation of her sentence by the governor she said, "I have always felt that Governor (Martin) Davey was a fine man and I have always admired him. I have a feeling that he will spare my life for the sake of my son, if not for myself."

Months passed while the legal maneuvering went on. Anna stayed in her death row cell. She seemed to adjust well to her confinement and spent her time reading, sewing, listening to the radio, and writing to relatives and her attorneys.

But although Anna Hahn put on a surface facade of confidence in being vindicated, she was, by some accounts, a worried woman. Frequently after awakening in the morning she would ask, "Did I dream? Did I talk in my sleep?"

Anna had good reason to be worried. Both the Ohio and United States Supreme Courts refused to block her execution. And on December 6, 1938 Ohio Governor Davey completely sealed her fate by refusing to interfere with the decisions of the courts. "I have decided not to intervene in the case of Mrs. Hahn," the Governor said in a formal statement. "Frankly, something inside of me has sort of rebelled against the idea of allowing a woman to go to the chair.... And yet, the crimes committed by Mrs. Hahn were so cold-blooded, so deliberately planned and executed, that they horrified the people who followed her trial. Her crimes were committed in remorseless deliberation for money. She was willing, in her almost inhuman way, to let these old men die in agony, without showing a quiver of emotion or any remorse, or any repentance. The guilt of Mrs. Hahn seems clearly proven.... I am genuinely sorry. I wish sincerely that this tragedy of an imperfect world had not come to me for a decision. But the responsibility is mine under the law, and it could not honorably be evaded. So the decision is made, and I hope that somehow or other, society will be benefitted."

When the warden of the Ohio State Penitentiary told Anna of the governor's decision she cried, "Oh my God! I didn't think he would do that to me!"

Anna's execution was scheduled for 8 o'clock the next evening. Her lawyers immediately filed a request for writ of habeas corpus in the United States District Court. Judge Mel Underwood denied the request.

The next night, Wednesday December 7, 1938, Anna Marie Hahn kept her historic appointment with Ohio's electric chair. By all accounts, she did not go well to her death.

When they came to get her from her cell she protested, "Oh heavenly father! Oh God! Oh God! I can't go! I won't go!" She could barely walk to the death chamber and collapsed when she reached it. After being revived with spirits of ammonia she was strapped into the chair. "Don't do that to me," she begged, "Oh, no, no, no. Warden Woodard, don't let them do that to me."

Warden Woodard answered, "I am sorry, but we can't help it." He was crying.

Anna began to wail, "Please don't. Oh, my boy. Think of my boy. Won't someone, won't anyone, come and do something for me? Isn't there anybody to help me.... anyone, anyone. Is nobody going to help me?"

Anna called for the prison chaplain. "Father, come close," she said. Father John Sullivan conferred with her and together they began to recite the Lord's Prayer. Midway through the prayer the electric current was applied, and Anna's body arched violently as the electricity flowed through it. At 8:13 p.m. she was officially pronounced dead.

The next day, December 8, Anna Marie Hahn's body was buried in unconsecrated ground at the Holy Cross Catholic Cemetery in Columbus

Ohio. The service was presided over by prison chaplain Sullivan. In attendance were Anna's lawyers, Warden Woodard's wife, the matron who attended Anna at the prison, and several members of the press. There was only one floral arrangement, a basket of flowers marked "From Cincinnati Friends."

A few days later Anna Marie Hahn's picture was hung in Ohio's death chamber, joining the pictures of 213 men who had already been electrocuted by the state.

But the story of Anna Marie Hahn did not end with her execution and burial. It was noted that just before being led to her execution Anna had handed four letters to her attorney. Now rumors began to spread that the letters were Anna's confessions to the murders of which she had been accused. One rumor said that a newspaper syndicate in New York had been offered exclusive rights to the contents of the letters for $75,000.

Any rumors of the Hahn letters ended when her attorney Joseph Hoodin revealed on December 17 that the letters had been sold to a Cincinnati newspaper and that the money derived from the sale would be used to pay for the future education of her son, Oskar Hahn.

On December 18 the *Cincinnati Enquirer* boldly announced that the letters would be published exclusively in that newspaper on the following two days.

The letters were bombshells. In them, Anna Marie Hahn admitted that she had indeed been guilty of all the crimes of which she had been accused. They were remarkable documents of admission and reflection.

"I don't know how I could have done the things I did in my life," Anna wrote. "Only God knows what came over me when I gave Albert Palmer that first one, that poison that caused his death.... When I stood by Mr. Wagner as he was laid out at the funeral home I don't know how it was that I didn't scream out at the top of my voice. I couldn't in my mind believe that it was me.... I can't believe it even today.

"I couldn't believe it when in court those people came to the room and told the jury how they said these men died. I was sitting there hearing a story like out of a book all about another person. As things come to my mind now and as I put them on this paper I can't believe I am writing about things I did myself. But they must be about me because they are in my mind and I know them. God above will tell me what made me do these terrible things. I couldn't have been in my right mind when I did them. I loved all people so much. Now I am so close to death; death is all around me. I have been here (on death row) for what seems another lifetime already. Several other people in this place have been called out."

After telling the story of her life in Germany and coming to the United States, Anna recounted the set of circumstances that she claimed ultimately led to her murderous activity.

"I went into business again, always thinking about my boy that I would have money to raise him properly.... But business was bad again and this time before I lost everything I sold it to pay all my debts. In a little while though, this money went. My husband and I had been out of work and I started worrying about my boy's future. I became crazy with fear that my boy and I would starve. I signed some notes for my husband; because I had signed these notes they threatened to take my Colerain Avenue house away from me to sell the house over my head and throw me and my boy out into the street. Then it was that I started gambling and playing the race horses. I went to a place out in Elmwood where you could play the races just like at a race track. I wanted to make some money for my boy."

At the betting parlor she met Albert Palmer. Although their relationship began friendly enough, Anna was soon borrowing money from the old man.

"I paid much of it back. Then when I didn't pay it back fast enough to suit him, then it was that he wanted me to be his girl.... He threatened me that if I didn't do what he asked he would get his attorney to get the rest of the money that I borrowed from him. I told him to please wait and give me a chance.

"But he wouldn't leave me alone. He came to my house and threatened me again. He had brought some oysters and wanted me to go home with him. God knows that I did not want to kill him, and I don't know what put such a thought in my head. I don't remember now how it was I only remember that suddenly I remembered that down in the cellar was some rat poison.... Something in my mind kept saying to me, 'Give him a little of this and he won't trouble you any more.'

"It was then that he again insisted I be his girlfriend or he would have to have his money at once.... and I don't know what made me do it, but I slipped some of the poison in the oysters. I told him to go on home and he left at the same time, threatening what he was going to do to me."

After Palmer left Anna didn't hear from him for several weeks. Finally Palmer's sister called and told Anna that Palmer had taken ill and was in a hospital.

"I visited him just as soon as I could and he was very nice to me. He told me that he was sorry the way that he had treated me. I prayed that he would get well. Nobody knows the things that went through my mind. I told the nurses and doctors to do everything they could to make him well, but on Holy Thursday, Mr. Palmer died. Only I knew why, but I couldn't understand what made me do such a thing.... for weeks after he was buried I felt I would lose my mind because way down in my heart I really did not want this awful thing to happen to him.

"It must have been fear for my family's future to just make me do it. Only God knows why I should have done and why I did this thing and some day He will explain what was in my mind and what made me sin so."

Anna went on to the next elderly gentleman.

"I had met George Heis while I was still in business, just before Mr. Palmer died. I had borrowed some money from him to pay Mr. Palmer. Mr. Heis held some of my notes for the money that I had borrowed. But I didn't poison him. Mr. Heis is alive and well today and that is proof that I didn't poison him. God knows that I didn't.

"I was getting along nicely and that terrible experience with Mr. Palmer was going out of my mind like a dream...."

Jacob Wagner was next. Anna had met him years before, and the two were distantly related. At first they had a friendly relationship, visiting each other frequently. But eventually the friendship soured when Jacob Wagner accused Anna of stealing some of his bank books. Wagner claimed that Anna had altered the books in an attempt to get money from the accounts. He and Anna went to his bank, a Fifth/Third, and showed the books to a bank official.

"(The official) told Mr. Wagner right away they were not good and that the amounts of money in them was forged. He told Mr. Wagner to bring the book back June 1 (1937), because the Monday was a holiday and that he would turn the books over to the police and maybe prosecute me. Mr. Wagner told me all about this and I invited him to come to my house on Sunday and I could give him a good dinner.

"Mr. Wagner did not come to my house that Sunday and I started to get crazy with fear. All the thoughts about Mr. Palmer's case, what I had done when not in my normal mind, came back to me. I got scared that if the police would start questioning me maybe all this about Mr. Palmer would come out."

Anna decided to see Wagner and try to convince him not to prosecute her. Before she left her house, she said, "I don't know what put the things in my mind but all of a sudden I found some poison in my hands. I put it in my pocketbook."

Anna visited Wagner on the afternoon of May 31. He told her he was taking the books to the bank the next day.

"Then something cried out in me to stop him, so that all my troubles wouldn't start again. I don't know what guided my hand but I fixed him some orange juice and placed a half of a teaspoon of the powder poison, which I took from my purse in the glass. Mr. Wagner drank it down. I stayed with Mr. Wagner until evening and he did not seem to be any worse. When I went home, I couldn't sleep that night thinking about Mr. Wagner. Early the next day, I went back to the room and Mr. Wagner was very sick. I knew what I had done to him."

After the ailing Wagner promised not to turn the bank books over to authorities, Anna called two physicians "to try to save the life I had tried to take." Wagner's condition worsened, and Anna had him admitted to Good Samaritan Hospital. "I didn't want what had happened to Mr. Palmer (to happen again)," she explained. "I knew I couldn't stand a thing like that and stay in my right mind. It was another mind that made me do these things. I didn't do them."

Anna claimed that while in the hospital Wagner gave her a check for $1000 for medical expenses but that he had signed the check in pencil. Since the bank would not accept a check so signed, Anna said, she herself signed Wagner's name to the check. Then Jacob Wagner died.

"I cannot describe how I felt when Mr. Wagner died and that I had something to do with his death.... but when I went to (the funeral home) where Mr. Wagner was laid out, it was all I could do to keep from screaming. I felt as though I was bursting, knowing that I was responsible for this terrible thing and that everyone was looking at me and pointing their fingers at me. Here was another one that I had brought death to. I don't know what made me do it, all that I can say is that my troubles were so big that it must have turned my mind. I did not harm Mr. Wagner for his money. I never had such a thought. It was not until Mr. Wagner had died that I wrote the will. I placed it in his room on the afternoon that the man from the Probate came to Mr. Wagner's room.

"The poison that I used is, for all that I know, still in my house. I found it first in the paint cupboard in the basement. If I had never found that poison in the first place I know that I would not be in all this trouble right now.... Finding this poison I guess made me do these things to Mr. Palmer and Mr. Wagner. It changed my whole mind, it made it turn over and I never will know what made me give it to those men.

"When I think of that poison even now, I feel a strange something come over me, something happens to my mind. I cannot say anything about those other cases that came after – Mr. Gsellmann and that last one, Mr. Obendorfer – except that they died of the same symptoms and as I face my Maker I take full responsibility for what happened to them....

"There were times in that courtroom, the times that the newspapers wrote, that I seemed worried, that I was just about ready to cry out. I was just about ready to cry out. I couldn't hardly keep my secret in me. It seemed that I would have to cry out. I wanted to cry out that they were trying the other Anna Hahn and not this one sitting in the court room. But somehow I kept the secret....

"I hope that God will take care of (my son), for I would not want anything to happen to my boy. I tried so hard to keep him from any harm, my boy who has given me the only pleasure in my life. I feel that God has shown me my wrongs in life and my only regret is that I have not the power to undo the trouble and heartache that I have caused.

"(signed) Anna Marie Hahn"

The release of the letters put to rest what few doubts there were as to Anna Marie Hahn's guilt. She had admitted being responsible for four of the murders she was suspected of committing.

Anna Hahn's last wish did not go unfulfilled. A month after her execution Joseph Hoodin told the press that 12-year-old Oskar Hahn had changed his name and was living with a family in the Midwest. "The boy has been assured an education and the utmost secrecy will surround his whereabouts so that he will have every opportunity for rehabilitation. He is with a family who have pledged themselves to bring him up as a normal boy to forget his entire past. There has been no adoption."

Oskar Hahn was able to live as normal a life as possible. Reporters covering the Hahn trial agreed that they would not pry into the boy's new life. He did get an education, paid for by the money from the sale of his mother's confession. It was later reported that he served in the United States Navy during World War Two.

There was an update to the Hahn story in 1953, when the name George Heis appeared in local obituary columns. The "only surviving 'victim' of poisoner Anna Hahn" was found dead in his home at 2922 Colerain Avenue on August 12. He was 78 years old. Heis died in the same house he had lived in when he was poisoned in 1937. He was buried in Spring Grove Cemetery.

In November 1974 the spirit of Anna Marie Hahn appeared again in the Hamilton County court system. This "appearance" resulted from an old habit of the Cincinnati Municipal Court of simply continuing criminal charges if the state did not bring the defendants to trial. The charges against Anna Hahn were being a fugitive from justice and grand larceny. They resulted from her misadventures in Colorado Springs, Colorado. When she was later indicted on the more serious murder charge, these lesser charges went indefinitely into the continuance cycle. In 1974 the Ohio State Supreme Court ordered all state courts to purge their dockets of pending cases which were not likely to be pursued. Some of the cases dated back to 1914. In Hamilton County the court cleared 2262 cases besides those pending against Anna Hahn.

With the purging of these records the Cincinnati was at last officially finished with Anna Marie Hahn. But the story of the poisoning blonde has still lived on as one of the most famous murder cases in the city's history. And Anna Marie Hahn has remained as forever a part of Cincinnati as the German inscriptions that can still be seen on some of the buildings in the Over-the-Rhine neighborhood where she found her victims so many years ago.

Anna Marie Hahn. (*The Cincinnati Enquirer*/Michael Snyder)

**Anna Marie Hahn's first known victim lived in this
Over-the-Rhine apartment building.**

Jacob Wagner lived in this building on Race Street.

Hahn's final victim lived in this Clifton Heights home.

The Pugh Murder Mystery

On Wednesday April 11, 1956, at just after 5:00 p.m., William Worthington Pugh returned from work to his home at 2752 Hill and Hollow Lane in Hyde Park. The home was located at the end of the street, a short cul-de-sac curving down a hill off the north side of Grandin Road. It was, and still is, one of the most prestigious residential areas in Cincinnati. William Pugh lived in the house with his 34-year-old wife Audrey.

After parking his car, William Pugh walked to the front entrance of the house. As he turned his key in the lock he opened not only the door to his house, but also the door to one of Cincinnati's most famous and enduring murder mysteries.

The scene that greeted Pugh when he opened his front door must have shaken any lingering thoughts about work from his mind, for just inside the front door, on the floor of the hallway, was the body of his wife.

Audrey Pugh had been born Audrey Evers in Cincinnati in 1922 She grew up in the neighborhood of Westwood. A friend later described her as pretty, but shy. Born between an older sister and younger brothers, she did not fit in with either, and as a result developed a quiet personality that would last her entire life. She attended grade school at the Mother of Mercy Academy on Werk Road and then went on to The College of Mount St. Joseph. She socialized and dated while in school but still retained the reputation of being the quiet one in the crowd. One of her main interests was religion, and after graduating from college she taught religious classes to poor people. "People really are good," she told a friend. "If only I had more time to help them." When Audrey was in her mid-twenties she met William Worthington Pugh.

Like Audrey, William Pugh was a reticent person. By the time he met Audrey Evers he was a wealthy man, the president of the family printing company. William and Audrey found that they had other things in common besides being reserved. They shared a love of music and reading, and liked to attend social events. After several years their friendship turned into love and the couple were married when they were both 29. Life after the marriage was described as "quiet." While the couple continued to be active in

92

The Cincinnati Crime Book

Cincinnati's better social circles, they spent most of their evenings in the quiet solitude of their home on Hill and Hollow Lane. They were courteous to the neighbors, but did not really develop friendships with them. They only rarely had parties at their home. But because they had not severed their ties with the social set completely, Audrey Pugh would be later described in newspapers as a "society matron."

William Pugh tried to revive his wife with some spirits of ammonia, but the stimulant had no effect. He called the Cincinnati Police Department's District Six. "I've just found my wife lying on the floor," he said.

The first patrolmen on the scene quickly determined that the woman on the floor was dead and called in the homicide detectives. They arrived within minutes. Because of the prestigious address and social prominence of the persons involved, the detectives were soon joined by the Chief of the Homicide Squad and then by the Chief of Police, Stanley Schrotel.

Audrey Pugh was lying on her back. William Pugh told officers that when he found his wife she had been lying on her right side, facing a wall, but he had moved the body while inspecting it. She was dressed in a red and white-trimmed short flannel nightgown and a blue robe. It was obvious that she had been stabbed numerous times in the chest, neck and back. More wounds on her forearms indicated that she had futilely tried to defend herself against her attacker.

Investigators dusted for fingerprints, but found none. Looking for the murder weapon – described simply as "knife-type, or unknown sharp instrument" – or other clues, police searched the entire eight room house, including the roof. They also thoroughly searched the heavily wooded area around the house. They found nothing.

The Pugh house was located on an isolated lot. There were no close neighbors. Detectives questioned what neighbors there were, but the only thing they learned was that there had been a strange car on the street that afternoon.

Neighbors also spoke to the press. "None of (us) here have had any experience with prowlers or strangers coming to the door," said one. "This is a quiet street, a private street, and it seems impossible that such a thing could have happened."

While this initial investigation was going on, William Pugh made a statement to the reporters who had quickly converged on the scene. "My wife was a wonderful woman," he said. "I can't understand why, or who, would do such a thing." He added that although his wife had complained of feeling ill that morning, everything else had been normal when he left for the work. The couple had pancakes for breakfast. The dirty dishes were still in the sink, indicating that Audrey had not felt well enough to wash them as she usually did. "The last thing she said to me as I was leaving the home this morning was 'See you this evening,'" Pugh said.

After the crime scene was thoroughly photographed, the body was removed to the morgue at General Hospital for an autopsy. Referring to the numerous stab wounds, Coroner Herbert P. Lyle commented, "I don't think there is any doubt as to the cause of death." Characterizing the slaying as a "threat to the community," he also said, "This case perturbs me more that the usual homicide investigation. Here, apparently, we have a housewife answering a knock at her front door. Then, before she has time to know what is happening, she is a dead woman. This case is not more important than others because of the neighborhood or the family. It could happen to any housewife in Cincinnati. But it's more important because it places on investigators the burden of proving that this kind of thing will not go unpunished."

Lyle later officially declared that the cause of death was due to stab wounds to the neck and throat. Audrey Pugh had been stabbed more than twenty times. The weapon was described as a small knife.

Other residents of the Grandin Road area were shocked by the news of a brutal murder in their exclusive and presumably secure neighborhood. At least nine of them called police with information they thought might help catch the killer. One reported a pesky traveling salesman who had been in the area on the day of the murder. After the murder became news the man remembered his presence in the area and turned himself in to police in order to clear himself. He admitted that he had been in the area, but denied being on Hill and Hollow Lane. He also admitted being a former patient at a mental hospital in Indiana. The man was held overnight and released.

An investigation into the mysterious car seen on the street revealed that it contained two employees of a contractor who was planning to build a house on Hill and Hollow Lane. They were cleared.

A man scheduled to be interviewed by the Pughs on the day of the murder for a gardening job was checked out and cleared.

A Camp Denison resident, who had allegedly been posing as a police officer in Hyde Park, was detained. Police found an ice pick in this man's car. Still, they could find nothing to connect him with the murder. He later provided a good alibi and was released.

A Cincinnati Water Works meter reader who had been on Hill and Hollow Lane on the day of the murder was questioned and released.

As the investigation continued with no quick apparent progress different theories of the crime were advanced. One theory was that a stranger had committed the crime, some lone psychopathic criminal who had been passing through the area. But neighbors said that the nature of the street, an isolated dead end, would prevent such a stranger from being in the area. "It wasn't the work of a tramp of prowler," a neighbor said.

Another difficulty with the "stranger did it" theory was that there was no evidence of any crime besides the murder taking place. No valuables were missing from the residence, and Audrey Pugh had not been sexually assaulted.

The Cincinnati Crime Book

One obvious suspect, of course, was the husband of the victim. But he could easily establish that he had been at the Pugh Printing Company all day on the day of the murder. Investigators quickly determined that William Pugh had nothing to do with the murder of his wife.

Police seemed to have better luck when they questioned the water meter reader. His account of the time when he was on Hill and Hollow Lane did not match the recollection of neighbors who had seen him there on the day of the murder. The meter reader, Robert Lyons, told officers that he had been at the Pugh residence and was admitted to the house to read the meter by Audrey Pugh at about noon on April 11. "I went to the back basement door," he told police. "When I knocked on the door she let me in. I didn't notice anything strange. She seemed to be in good spirits. I don't recall how she was dressed. I didn't notice."

Neighbors recalled to police that in fact Lyons had been on the street much later in the day. Based on this discrepancy, the meter reader was detained. Police took the shirt he said he had been wearing on the day of the slaying and sent it to a forensics laboratory for testing.

But the Lyons lead apparently was no good. He took a lie detector test and passed. The report from the lab came back and said that while there was blood on Lyons' shirt sleeve it matched neither Audrey Pugh's nor his own blood type. Robert Lyons was released.

Another suspect was picked up, the fourth man to be arrested in the case. He was picked up after a routine investigation into past crimes similar to the Pugh slaying revealed that he had a previous conviction for burglary and assault. When questioned, the man's account of his whereabouts on the afternoon of the Pugh murder did not jibe with other information that the police had. Also, the man lived in O'Bryonville, just a half mile from Hill and Hollow Lane. But this man soon passed a lie detector test and was also released.

Police announced that they were seeking a "mystery car," a 1948 or 1949 black Studebaker with a dented front right fender and grill, that had been seen on Hill and Hollow Lane the afternoon of the murder. They also disclosed that Mrs. Pugh had not been wearing shoes or slippers when she was attacked, that the wallet she usually carried was missing, and that some church collection boxes with change in them had been disturbed. These disclosures indicated that police were concentrating on the theory that a strange intruder, not someone familiar to her, had murdered Audrey Pugh. Still, the presence of two undisturbed purses in the Pughs' bedroom, as well as an easily found wallet with cash in it, caused authorities to be reluctant to state positively that burglary was the motive for the crime.

One week after the murder authorities released details of the autopsy performed by Dr. Frank Cleveland. The victim had received 23 stab wounds, 14 of which were described as "serious." Five of the wounds were classified as fatal in and of themselves. One wound was on the left side of the neck, eight were in the left chest area, and five more were on the left side and back. "It is my opinion," Dr. Cleveland wrote, "that Audrey Pugh died of internal and external hemorrhage resulting from multiple stab wounds of the neck and chest." The wounds were about four inches deep. There were also seven defensive wounds on Audrey's arms and hands. Cleveland said that the knife had a blade four inches long and a half inch wide. Judging from the location of the wounds, Cleveland opined that the assailant was right handed. He said that Audrey Pugh had died in the mid-afternoon of April 11.

Authorities continued to check out leads. Because of the prominence of the victim and the randomness of the crime, a 24 man investigative team of detectives worked the case on a 24 hour basis. This squad was under the direct supervision of Police Chief Schrotel, Detective Chief Lt. Col. Henry Sandman, and Homicide Chief Charles Martin. Chief Schrotel appealed to the public for help. "No matter how insignificant a tip or scrap of information appears in itself, it may take on far greater significance when viewed in context with the total case," he said.

The public did not need much encouragement. The case was already the main news event of the day, and there was no shortage of tips. Authorities received hundreds of phone calls and dozens of letters containing possible leads. Police checked them all out, "and we would like to see them keep coming in," Colonel Sandman said. "One may be the payoff." Police checked and eliminated over 50 cars that people suggested might be the "mystery car." Ex-cons with records for burglary or assault were detained and grilled.

Police questioned four more potential suspects. The number of individuals detained for questioning during the first two weeks of the investigation already totaled twelve. But it was quickly determined that these latest four men had nothing to do with the crime, and police released them.

Authorities then began investigating all of the 1948 and 1949 black Studebakers known to be in the Cincinnati area. There were over 800 of them. Form letters were sent out to the vehicle owners requesting that they bring their cars in for inspection. The contacted motorists began doing so.

But two weeks after the discovery of Audrey Pugh's body investigators had still not made an arrest for her murder. And residents of Hyde Park were nervous about it. An elderly woman resident explained the new post-murder philosophy that neighbors had adopted regarding people coming to their homes. "Just look out the window," she said, "and it you don't know who it is, don't go near the door."

While regular salesmen, mailmen, and delivery persons had no trouble making their rounds, anyone unknown to the residents had difficulty doing their jobs. One man, a substitute meter reader for the gas company, had trouble getting into houses to check the meters even though he was in uniform and had a marked truck parked at the curb. But he acknowledged that the situation could have been worse. "I'm sure glad that water meter reader was cleared in the case, else it would have made it tough on all of us," he said.

The Cincinnati Crime Book

More time went by. Officials continued questioning gardeners, fire inspectors, salespersons, anyone who had any connection with Hill and Hollow Lane. They searched the wooded area behind Hill and Hollow Lane, down the hill to Golden Avenue and to Columbia Parkway and Eastern Avenue, theorizing that a homicidal burglar may have come from one of these areas. Part of this theory was based on the statement of water meter reader Robert Lyons that he had entered the house through the basement door at the rear of the house. If this basement door was left unlocked after Lyons left, police figured, the assailant might have entered that way and surprised Audrey Pugh. (Friends told the police that she would never have answered a knock at the door without wearing shoes. Her body was found shoeless.) The isolated and secluded location of the Pugh residence added weight to this theory. There were at least half a dozen directions behind the house where an assailant could have disappeared into the woods without being seen by any neighbors.

But despite the fact that more officers had been assigned to the case than to any other case in the history of the Cincinnati Police Department, investigators appeared to be getting no closer to a solution to the crime. Cincinnati Safety Director Oris Hamilton called the crime, "the nearest to a perfect crime in the annals of murder cases. (It is) the most baffling murder, bar none (in Cincinnati history). Ellery Queen and Mary Roberts Rinehart together couldn't have written a greater mystery than this one."

Even with some evidence of robbery, not all investigators were convinced that theft was the motive for the crime. Police were still not sure whether the killer was an anonymous prowler or someone whom the victim knew. "We're right back where we started," Detective Chief Sandman said. "We've worked hundreds of thousands of hours. We've run down every possible clue. We've questioned hundreds of people and we just haven't got a thing. It's one of those cases where the killing was either so carefully planned that the killer left no clues or by accident he has left none. We're still digging and we'll keep on."

Keep on they did. And finally, a month and a half after the discovery of Audrey Pugh's body, police announced that the murderer was in custody. On May 26 area newspapers announced the news of the arrest of Robert Lyons, the City of Cincinnati Water Works meter reader.

The arrest of Lyons came as a result of routine police follow-ups of earlier witness interviews. One witness was the maid at the house next door to the Pugh residence. The maid recalled that on the day of the murder Lyons had read the meter in her employers house, but that the reading had taken much longer than usual and that when Lyons was finished he had changed his jacket.

Another witness was a housewife who cast doubt on Lyons' claim that he knew he was reading the meter in her house at a certain time because he glanced at a wall clock in her basement. The housewife told police that she had no such clock.

The Cincinnati Crime Book

On Friday May 25 detectives decided to question Lyons again about his movements on the day of the murder. They picked him up at 1:00 p.m. First they took him to the coroner's office, then to another location where they administered a lie detector test. This went on until about 5:00 p.m. Then the group went to supper before returning to the coroner's office for more interrogation. At 10:00 p.m. they all went to the crime laboratory in City Hall for more questioning. At 2:30 a.m. Lyons confessed. "I want to get it off my chest," he said.

He had been undergoing interrogation of varying degrees for over twelve hours.

After making the confession Lyons was immediately arraigned in Police Court before Judge Gilbert Bettman on a charge of aggravated murder.

According to Lyons' confession, he had gone to the Pugh house at about 1:00 p.m. on the day of the murder to read the water meter. "I went to the basement door and knocked," he told police. "She (Audrey Pugh) came down and when she opened the door she complained, 'That screaming meter man.' She had told me before, 'Don't come to the rear door, I can hardly hear you knock. Go to the front door by the garage.' It was around noon. I knocked at the back. She was pretty mad about it. She told me, 'You're the most insistent of all the people who come to the door. Don't make a fool of yourself.'"

Lyons' remarks that Audrey Pugh had been upset with him for using the back door rang a bell with investigators. They had already learned that Audrey was afraid of people coming to the secluded house and that to alleviate that fear William Pugh had installed a window near the front service door so his wife could see who was there before answering any call. "Gas company meter readers used the front service entrance," Col. Sandman explained. "They said Mrs. Pugh let them in, waited for them to go, and locked the door behind them." If Lyons had gone to the rear door, police surmised, he was doing something he had been specifically asked not to do. His actions may have caused Audrey, who was already not feeling well, to become irritated and abrasive.

Lyons recalled how Audrey Pugh's condescending manner in the basement made him angry. "She got pretty nasty with me down there and I just ain't used to that. I read the meter and came back as she was going upstairs. I decided to go up and find out how I was making a fool of myself. When I got to the kitchen she was standing there with a knife in her hand, a small knife, like a paring knife. I was worried that she would complain about me to the Waterworks."

Lyons claimed that when Audrey Pugh saw him upstairs she became combative. They struggled, and he managed to get the knife away from her. "She slapped me in the face. I stabbed her twice. I don't know what happened after that. I washed off the knife and laid it on the sink. Then I went downstairs to the rear door and picked up the (meter reading) book and flashlight. Then I went out the rear door. It was 1:00 or 1:15 when I left the house. I went up the street to the next house. The maid let me in." Lyons denied taking Audrey Pugh's missing wallet.

Police said that the motive for the murder was Lyons' fear that Audrey Pugh would report him at work and he would lose his job. "His job was his very life – he lived for it," Colonel Sandman told the press. "We tried everything under the sun in our earlier questioning – God, mother and family, all of that. But the only thing that seemed to create any reaction was a reference to his job. When he talked of his job, tears actually came to his eyes."

Lyons had been employed by the Water Works Department for over twenty years. He had an impeccable work record.

After confessing at City Hall, Lyons was taken to the Pugh residence, where he reenacted the crime in front of police movie cameras. William Pugh, startled at the intrusion of his home at 4:30 a.m., refused to view the accused murderer. "I don't want to see the man," he told officers. "I don't want to see any part of him."

Robert Vernon Lyons was 43 years old. He had a ruddy complexion and sandy colored hair which earned him the nickname "Red." He lived on Setchel Street, a short street running south off Eastern Avenue towards the Ohio River. His home was less than half a mile, as the crow flies, from the Pugh residence on Hill and Hollow Lane.

After Lyons confessed, police descended on his house to search for the murder weapon and the clothing the suspect had been wearing on the day of the slaying. Other people living on the street could not believe that their neighbor was capable of such a crime. "When they picked him up the first time, I said, 'I know they can't hold him.' I still can't believe it. (The Lyonses) are really swell people," said one. Lyons was described as an easy-going guy. He was a veteran of World War Two. His main interests seemed to be his job and beer drinking. He was divorced and had a 16-year-old daughter who lived with him on Setchel Street along with a brother named George.

Robert Lyons' worksheets for the day of the murder were sent to the FBI for testing. The tests revealed that someone had made erasures of the entries for the Pugh meter and the ones before and after it. The entry for the Pugh meter read "sweaty dial" and yet a reading had been taken. Police wondered how Lyons could have obtained a reading from a meter with a clouded dial cover.

Further support for Lyons as a suspect came from William Pugh, who told police that nearly a year before the murder, on April 12, 1955, there had been another confrontation between his wife the meter reader. On that day, Lyons had also tried to gain entry to the house via the rear door, and Audrey Pugh had become upset. "There's that water meter man making a fool out of himself again," she told her husband. She then had a confrontation with Lyons over his behavior. His reaction to her complaining unnerved her enough that she had insisted that her husband install the window next to the service entrance at the front of the house. Even so, the next time Lyons came to read the meter, in July, he again knocked on the back door to gain entry, and he again angered Audrey Pugh.

Robert Lyons was held in the maximum security section of the Hamilton County Jail. On Monday, May 29 he requested to see the lawyer who had represented him in his divorce case. Since criminal law was not that lawyer's specialty, he recommended an attorney whose specialty it was – William Foster "Foss" Hopkins.

Foss Hopkins was a good choice. Born in Cincinnati in 1899, he grew up in Norwood. He attended Hughes High School and the University of Cincinnati. After graduating from U.C. he attended law school, received his degree, and went into the practice of criminal law. Over the following years he defended many unpopular clients, and some of that unpopularity rubbed off on him. But while he may have been controversial, and even disliked in some circles, Foss Hopkins was an excellent attorney.

Hopkins went to the jail and visited the accused man. After a brief meeting, the attorney decided that he would take the case. Lyons had made a good choice. Foss Hopkins was the best.

Robert Lyons would need the best. The news media assumed he was guilty from the moment of his arrest. Accounts of his confession included details of him allegedly smiling and laughing when he talked about the crime. On May 30 the *Cincinnati Post* printed a large front page story headlined "The Four Big Lies" which recounted the supposed falsehoods in Lyons' statement to police. "The meter reader did it!" began an article in the *Post*. The *Enquirer* referred to the murder as "his (Lyons') ghastly crime." "Case Closed!" read the headline of an editorial commenting on the arrest. The papers alluded to an unspecified "sexual deviation" in Lyons and remarked that Audrey Pugh was similar in appearance to the wife Lyons had divorced fourteen years before.

On May 30 Robert Lyons was fired from his cherished job as a meter reader with the Cincinnati Water Works. The official reason: discourtesy to the public and failure of good behavior.

With Hopkins in charge of Lyons' defense, the behavior of the defendant suddenly changed. The once easygoing and talkative meter reader, described in one newspaper as "happy-go-lucky," now kept his mouth shut. "Why don't you stop bothering me?" he asked reporters questioning him outside a Hamilton County courtroom. "I've told police everything."

But by now Lyons contended that everything he told police had been a lie. Indeed, he informed his lawyer that he was in fact totally innocent of the crime and had only confessed because he was under intense pressure from the police to do so. Lyons repudiated his confession on June 2.

Foss Hopkins believed him. Based on his interviews with Lyons at the county jail, Hopkins reached the conclusion that Robert Lyons was an innocent man.

The Cincinnati Crime Book

The trial of Robert Lyons began on November 1, 1956. The case was heard by Hamilton County Common Pleas Court Judge Carson Hoy. The defendant entered the courtroom dressed in a blue suit, white shirt, and blue tie and declared, "As God is my witness, I am innocent and wouldn't kill an ant."

The first request from the defense was that the jury be sequestered. Remarking on the large amount of negative press coverage of his client, Foss Hopkins said, "In my opinion, no case since the Anna Marie Hahn trial has enjoyed the publicity that this case has. This case is being reported nationally."

Judge Hoy denied the motion. "While it is true that this case has attracted an unusual amount of public attention, I have full confidence in the integrity and sense of fairness of the people of this community generally and of this jury panel," he said.

With that, jury selection proceeded and by the next day a jury of eight men and four women was selected to hear the case against the accused murderer.

In the prosecution's opening statement Hamilton County Prosecutor C. Watson Hover told the jury that the state would prove that Robert Lyons killed Audrey Pugh.

Defense attorney Hopkins countered that he would show that Lyons' confession was false and was only obtained after hours of intense interrogation. Hopkins characterized the interrogation session as "a 13-hour brainwashing by the police."

The trial resumed on Monday November 5. The first order of business was a trip by the jury to the Pugh residence on Hill and Hollow Lane. Robert Lyons accompanied the veniremen. He was upbeat on the rides to and from the murder scene. "I appreciate this sunshine and air," he said. "I haven't enjoyed anything like this for a long time." At the Pugh house, however, Lyons was silent. He was also handcuffed the whole time. The tour was over before lunch, and court then recessed for the day.

Tuesday, November 6, was election day and there was no court session.

On November 7 the prosecution began its presentation of the case by calling the first police officers who had been dispatched to the scene of the crime. One of them, Homicide Lieutenant Charles Martin recalled how genuinely shocked William Pugh had been. "Several times he asked if he could sit or lie down and I permitted him to do this," Martin recalled. Captain Willard Elbert, head of Police District Six, testified that several women's rings were found in the Pugh residence. The state introduced this fact in order to disprove that robbery was the motive for the murder.

Hopkins' cross-examination of these witnesses was fairly routine. He asked questions about a throw rug that had been in the front hallway of the house and tried to cast doubt on the officers' power of recall by emphasizing a discrepancy over whether a magazine rack had been overturned at the crime scene.

The prosecution then introduced an exhibit that produced an audible gasp from the courtroom spectators. It was a full sized mannikin of a woman. Lying on its back, it had been marked with red paint to indicate the location of the over twenty knife wounds in Audrey Pugh. Assistant Hamilton County Coroner Frank P. Cleveland then testified about the injuries to the deceased, stating that she died of "severe lateral and external hemorrhages of the neck and chest.... Mrs. Pugh would have died in a relatively few minutes, five to ten minutes, with the maximum of an hour." Cleveland put the time of death at about 2:00 p.m. on the day of the murder.

On Thursday November 8 the prosecution called William Pugh to the stand. The husband of the victim was questioned for almost an hour and a half by Prosecutor Hover. Pugh recalled his actions on the day of the crime, going to his office, lunch at the University Club, checking at a jeweler's about a watch, and finally arriving at Hill and Hollow Lane and finding the grisly tableau in the front hallway of his home.

Pugh stated that when he saw his wife lying on the floor he thought she had passed out as a result of the illness she had been complaining about that morning. "I shook her. I called out to her loudly. I thought she had passed out from loss of blood. The day before that she had felt very sick, she had a vomiting spell. I didn't know. I was darned upset. I knew I wanted to get medical help as quick as possible. That's a fact. I thought she was alive. That's why I kept calling doctors all the time, because I thought she was alive. It came as a shock to me when the police or the patrolman told me she was dead. I could not even believe it. It just did not seem possible that she could have died."

The state also elicited from Pugh the fact that there were a number of small knives kept in the house, any one of which could have been the murder weapon.

The state then called a documents expert from the FBI who testified that there had been erasures in Robert Lyons' route book for the day of the murder. The prosecution maintained that these erasures were part of Lyons' attempt to alter the evidence of the time he had read the Pugh meter.

Lyons' supervisor from the Water Works testified that he had read the Pugh water meter on April 16, at the request of police, and that the meter dial had not been "sweaty" as Lyons had noted in his route book. The supervisor characterized Lyons' job performance favorably. "I would put him in the top bracket of my readers," he told the court. Still, the supervisor called Lyons' seemingly erroneous notation of "sweaty dial" a "malfeasance of duty."

Another Water Works employee testified that after the murder he had kidded Lyons about the woman killed on his route. The employee told Lyons that the police would probably pick him up. "They won't bother me," Lyons had replied.

A homicide detective took the stand and testified that on April 16 he had searched Lyons' Setchel Street home and retrieved a shirt that had what appeared to be bloodstains and lipstick smears on it. Lyons admitted that it was the shirt he wore on the day Audrey Pugh was slain, but said he had no idea how the stains got on it.

One of the final witnesses that Friday was the maid from the house next door to the Pugh residence. She testified that a water meter reader had read the meter at her employer's house at about 12:30 p.m. the day of the murder. The woman could not positively identify Lyons as the meter reader she saw that day, but the maid from the house on the other side of the Pughs' was then called to the stand and she did identify him and said that his behavior had been strange. "I heard a loud knock at the door. I walked down to see who it was. I walked up to the door. The meter man was bent over like this (she indicated his posture). I said, 'Who is it?' He said, 'Water man.' I stood there a second. I opened the door. He walked in real fast. I still stood there holding the door. He stayed so long I looked around to see what he was doing. I noticed the furnace room door was open (about two feet). I still didn't see anyone. I still stood there holding the door. When I looked around (again) he had a brown sweater on, and grey trousers and a black leather cap. I waited for him to come out and he didn't come out. I wondered what he was doing so long. Then I saw him come out of the house with a notebook in one hand and something under his arm. He changed the brown sweater and had on a short jacket and walked real slow. I said to myself, 'I wonder what's wrong here?' He just went out. I had a funny feeling. I was just nervous and upset. It was about 1:00, or a quarter after or 1:30."

On cross-examination Foss Hopkins brought out that the witness had not seen any blood on the defendant, and had her re-emphasize that Lyons had been at her employer's house after 1:00 p.m.

Prosecutor Hover then recalled pathologist Frank Cleveland to the stand. Hover showed the doctor several items of clothing and asked him if he had found blood on any of them. The doctor replied that he found traces of blood with Audrey Pugh's blood type (A) on the nightgown and bathrobe she had been wearing when she was slain. He also found traces of blood type A on a pair of trousers that belonged to Robert Lyons. There were bloodstains on Lyons' shirt, but the doctor was not able to determine the blood type. Lyons had blood type O. The source of the lipstick found on the same shirt was never determined.

Doctor Cleveland also testified that in his opinion none of the eight knives recovered from the Pugh residence was the murder weapon. Prosecutor Hover implied that Lyons had brought the knife with him, thus suggesting premeditation.

Hopkins cross-examined the witness and got him to admit that the bloodstains on Lyons' clothing were old and that he had not gotten around to testing them for blood type until May 28, a week after Lyons' arrest. Hopkins also got the pathologist to admit that it was possible to make errors in blood testing, and that the stain on Lyons' clothing had been so small that none of it could be saved for another test.

On November 13 Cincinnati Police homicide detective Eugene Moore was called to the stand. He testified that police had used a "friendly, sympathetic approach" while interrogating the defendant. Moore said that during the questioning of Lyons he had showed the meter reader one of his (Lyons') fingerprints and told him that it had been recovered from an immovable object from the first floor of the Pugh residence. The print had really come from Lyons' fingerprint chart. In explaining this lie to the court the detective said, "We wanted his reaction." Moore also misled Lyons by telling him that his lie detector test indicated he was lying when in fact the results were merely inconclusive.

These lies about the fingerprint and lie detector test came early in the evening of May 25. By 2:00 a.m. the next morning, Officer Moore said, Lyons broke down and confessed. "Yes, I stabbed her," Lyons had said. Moore then went on the recount the details of Lyons' confession.

On cross-examination Foss Hopkins made the most out of the Moore's dishonest treatment of the defendant. Referring to the fingerprint lie, he asked the detective, "Do you call that good police work? Is that following your police duties? Is that being kindly and sympathetic?" Hopkins also got Moore to admit that the murder weapon had never been recovered.

Another detective, Wilber Stagenhorst, under cross-examination by Hopkins, also justified the lie about the fingerprint by saying, "It's a technique used in investigations. Even in poker games you may imply you have a better hand."

"Yes, but you're playing for money then (not for a man's life)," replied Foss Hopkins.

While cross-examining Colonel Sandman, Hopkins brought out that the rug Audrey Pugh had been found lying on in the foyer of her home had been cleaned after it had been examined by the FBI laboratory. Hopkins said that the cleaning had removed clues, "certain things" that would prove that Robert Lyons was innocent. Detective Martin had said during earlier questioning by Hopkins that while he was interrogating Lyons he noticed that the skin on the meter reader's hands was cracked and peeling. "Do you know anything about the disease ichthycosis?" Hopkins asked the detective. Martin replied that he did not. "Well, sometimes it's called 'fish skin,'" Hopkins explained. With this line of questioning Hopkins introduced one of the defense's main contentions, specifically that Robert Lyons suffered from a disorder of the skin which caused him to drop flakes of skin wherever he was present. No flakes of skin were found on the rug in the foyer of the Pugh residence. Therefore, Hopkins contended, Robert Lyons could not have been the killer of Audrey Pugh.

Later that day, Judge Hoy ruled that Lyons' confession, since repudiated, would be allowed as evidence. Hopkins took only a formal exception to the admission of the confession, based on the claim that it was obtained from his client involuntarily. The objection took less than two minutes. Detective Hover then read the 27-page statement to the jury.

The state rested it case on November 16. The defense then called its first witness, William Pugh. Pugh brought with him to the stand the rug that had been in the foyer of his house. Hopkins questioned Pugh closely about the rug and about the length of time, over a month, that police had it in their possession before returning it. Hopkins clearly wanted the jury to know that the police had examined the rug thoroughly and found nothing besides blood that they considered to be evidence – no dirt or leaves from outside, no fibers from an assailant's clothing, and certainly no flakes of dried skin from an individual suffering from ichthycosis.

After Pugh left the stand Hopkins called 14 witnesses who testified to the general good character of Robert Lyons. He then called the two witnesses who had seen the mysterious Studebaker parked on Hill and Hollow Lane between 1:30 and 2:00 p.m. on the day of the murder. Both men said that the driver of the car had worn a hat. (Police had never been able to trace the car to anyone.)

November 19 was the big day for the defense as the defendant himself took the stand. Robert Lyons testified for over an hour and a half. He claimed that he had only made his confession after police officers told him that confessing would keep him from going to Ohio's electric chair.

Recalling the circumstances of his confession, Lyons said that on the afternoon of May 25 he had been picked up by Homicide Detectives Moore and Stagenhorst. First, they stopped for a meal at Schuler's Wigwam restaurant in Cheviot. Lyons claimed that the conversation at the restaurant centered on the Pugh case and that detectives constantly pointed out various women to him and asked him if they resembled Audrey Pugh. After the meal, Lyons said, he was given several lie detector tests at the County Garage before being taken to City Hall. At City Hall the detectives informed him that the results of the tests "looked bad" for him. Then Stagenhorst showed Lyons the blowup of his fingerprint and lied, saying that the print had been found on the first floor of the Pugh residence. Lyons denied ever being on that floor, but Stagenhorst told him that "fingerprints never lie." Then Lyons was confronted with his Water Works meter book and told that FBI tests had determined that he changed the entry and that this further incriminated him. Hopkins asked his client to recall the exchange with Assistant Hamilton County Prosecutor Don Roney.

Lyons remembered, "Roney said, 'It looks like they got you Bob. Found your fingerprint. Looks pretty rough. They are going to send you to the chair. Now, listen to me. We're all one big team. You work for the city. I work for the prosecutor's office. We should all pull together. We should help each other. Just say that you killed Mrs. Pugh.' I said,' I didn't kill Mrs. Pugh.' 'Oh Bob,' he said, 'you're going to the chair.' I said, 'I didn't kill Mrs. Pugh and I can't help that a bit.' He said, 'I can help you. After all, the police bring the charge.' He said, 'I am the one who decides how and what could be brought against you.' He said, 'I represent the state of Ohio. I handle the case in any way I want to handle it.' He asked if I ever heard of George Remus. I said, Yes, I heard my parents discuss this case.' He said, 'Well, if you will make a statement that you killed Mrs. Pugh I can fix it that we will send you to the hospital and after that everything will work out for you just like it did for George Remus. We're all on this one big team and....' Roney said if I didn't play ball with him they were going to fry me."

Hopkins asked his client how he felt during this interrogation session. "Pretty beat up," Lyons replied. Lyons then told how he had decided to confess. "(Roney) said, 'If you don't go along with me you are going to the chair for sure.' There was no alternative but to go along with him."

After agreeing to confess, Lyons was given over to detectives Moore and Stagenhorst. Lyons tried to confess based on the prompting given by Roney, but the detectives weren't satisfied with that version, so they all went over the details until they had a confession that fit with the known facts of the crime.

Now, on the stand, Lyons told Hopkins what he said really happened on Hill and Hollow Lane on April 11, 1956.

Q (by Hopkins): Do you know what time you got to the Pugh house?

A (Lyons): Around noon time.

Q: How do you place the time?

A: The last meter I read on Ambleside (the street next to Hill and Hollow Lane) was 11:30 a.m. Then there is only three homes before I come to the Pugh home, so I figure about half an hour or less to read those three meters.

Q: What did you take out of the car when you entered the Pugh home?

A: My meter book and a flashlight.

Q: Were you carrying a knife?

A: No, sir.

Q: When you got to the basement door, what did you do?

A: I knocked upon the door and hollered "Meter Man."

Q: Did you holler loudly?

A: Yes, sir.

Q: Did anybody answer the door?

A: Not right away

Q: Do you know who answered the door?

A: Mrs. Pugh.

Q: Did she open the door?

A: Yes, sir.

Q: Will you tell whether or not you had any conversation with Mrs. Pugh?

A: I never said a word.

Q: What, if anything, did she say to you?

A: "Don't come down here screaming, water man. Come to the door next to the garage door," she said. "Don't make a fool of yourself."

Q: What did you say?

A: I never said a word.

Q: What did you do?

A: I entered the home, walked through the rumpus room, to the meter room.

Q: Where is the meter room?

A: As you come in the basement door you turn left and walk straight ahead.

Q: As you walked straight ahead, where was Mrs. Pugh?

A: I imagine she was still behind the door where she let me in.

Q: Did Mrs. Pugh say anything to you?

A: She said, "When you leave, pull the door shut."

Q: Did you answer her?

A: No sir.

Q: What did you do next?

A: I went out and pulled the door shut and proceeded on to the next house.

Lyons said that he made the erasures and "sweaty dial" entries in his work book because he thought he noted some peculiarities in the readings he was getting from the Pugh meter but that he was afraid to return to the house to get another reading because of the hostile Audrey Pugh.

After Lyons left the stand, the defense rested its case.

On November 20 the state called Assistant Prosecutor Roney to the stand as a rebuttal witness. Roney denied saying during his interrogation of Lyons that if Lyons didn't "play ball" with the prosecution he would go to the electric chair. "You don't tell suspects (in murder cases) that they might fry," he said. "I urged him to tell the truth, that that is always the wise thing to do. That a man should first be honest with himself and then he can live in peace with himself." Roney denied making any promises to help Lyons if he made a confession and denied mentioning the case of George Remus.

Prosecutors also sought to refute the claims that if Lyons had been in the Pugh house his skin disease would have caused him to leave flakes of skin at the scene. Assistant Prosecutor Melvin Rueger, in his cross examination of the defendant, tried to get Lyons to admit that he had been wearing long underwear on the day of the slaying. (The temperature on April 11 had not gotten out of the forties.) Several pairs of long underwear had been recovered from Lyons' Setchel Street home. If the underwear had been tucked into the defendant's socks, Rueger claimed, it would have been impossible for him to drop skin flakes at the crime scene. Lyons denied that he wore long underwear that day.

More witnesses were called in an effort to clarify the time frame of Lyons' meter reading on April 11. Lyons insisted that he had been finished at the Pugh residence by noon or shortly thereafter. That meant he couldn't have been the killer, since the coroner testified that the attack on Audrey Pugh had occurred no earlier than 1:00 p.m. Two neighbors from Hill and Hollow Lane testified that they were sure their meters had not been read by 12:30.

The state began its final summation on November 21. Calling the defendant a "trickster" and referring to the defense case as "Operation Big Lie," Prosecutor Rueger asked the jury, "Are you going to believe (the defendant) or the men of the Police Department, Colonel Sandman, Lieutenant Martin, Moore, Stagenhorst, Donald Roney and the others who testified against him?" Rueger said that Lyons lied during the investigation and that he lied again during his testimony in court. Referring to the defense's contention that Lyons had a skin disease which would have left skin flakes at the crime scene he said, "This is Operation Big Lie, or The Case of the Red Herring. That is what we have here, a deliberate, planned attempt by one of the most capable criminal attorneys in this section of the country to lead you down a cold trail." Rueger asked for a verdict of guilty without mercy. If Robert Lyons was given that verdict, he would be sentenced to death.

The next day it was Foss Hopkins' turn. He told the jury "Robert Lyons signed the confession in the greatest fear he ever felt in his life: fear of the electric chair." Hopkins said that the coroner said that Audrey Pugh was slain between 1:00 and 2:00 p.m. and reminded jurors of the witness who said that Lyons was reading her water meter at that time. He displayed the long underwear the prosecution claimed Lyons wore on the day of the murder and pointed out that they were several sizes too small for him. He ended with an apology to his client. "You have been arrested and thrown in jail. You have been indicted for a heinous crime and you are standing trial for your life. You have borne your cross, mental anguish and ridicule, and you have somehow withstood the pitiless spotlight of public condemnation. You have somehow withstood the torture of the damned.... I don't know if you can find it in your makeup to forgive society for this terrible and despicable wrong. I, at least, as a member of society, can humbly apologize and beg your forgiveness."

Now there was nothing to do but wait for the jury's verdict. They were given the case late in the afternoon on November 23. Seven hours later they announced the verdict: Robert Lyons was found not guilty of the murder of Audrey Evers Pugh.

Courtroom spectators cheered as the verdict was read. Supporters and newsmen rushed to the defense table. Robert Lyons said, "This is the greatest moment of my life. Now I hope they get the real murderer of Mrs. Pugh. (That) would take any doubt out of all the peoples' minds."

An obviously disappointed Prosecutor Hover said, "The jury has the final word in these matters. The state has no choice other than to accept its decision."

Defense attorney Hopkins said, "I am utterly humble."

Jurors later said that they believed from the beginning that Lyons' confession had been obtained under duress. While some of the jurors had wanted to convict the meter reader of first degree manslaughter, when the judge explained the elements of that charge they voted to acquit instead.

As Lyons gathered up his belongings at the county jail he said, "I am going home now to see my Dad. I am going back to my old normal way of living." He said that he would contact the Water Works about getting his old job back, but added, "I don't want my old meter reading job back until the real murderer of Mrs. Pugh is brought in. I want to have any doubts that remain in some people's minds that I am the killer eliminated."

Robert Lyons returned to his home on Setchel Street, where he initially celebrated his acquittal with family, friends, and neighbors. But the whole experience had taken a toll on him, and after the excitement over the verdict died down he settled into a quiet and reclusive life.

Lyons remarried in 1958. He got his job back at the Water Works and worked there until he retired in 1976.

At 11:35 p.m. on May 18, 1977 Robert Lyons was found dead in the hallway outside his apartment at 3712 Eastern Avenue in the East End. Nearby was a paper bag containing almost $10,000. There were no signs of foul play. He was 65.

The Hamilton County Coroner later established that Lyons' death was due to liver failure. Investigators determined that he had withdrawn the money in the paper bag from his savings and loan, but they never learned what he planned to do with it.

A neighbor of the dead man said, "You're not going to find anybody around here who'll say anything bad about him. He never bothered anybody. If you spoke to him, he spoke to you. If you didn't, he left you alone. (The murder trial) just made a recluse out of him. I guess he felt the public was afraid of him."

William Pugh said, "I'm naturally sorry that anybody has died. I feel sorry for the man and his family. Other than that, I have no reaction."

Retired Police Colonel Henry Sandman spoke for many when he said, "This (murder case) was an incident that happened a long time ago. This man was accused, investigated, tried and acquitted by his peers. I think the whole question (of whether Lyons really was the killer) should be laid to rest with him. May he rest in peace."

The secluded Pugh residence on Hill and Hollow Lane.

Robert Lyons (left) and Foss Hopkins say the underwear don't fit.
(*The Cincinnati Enquirer*/Michael Snyder)

The Stories Of Edythe Klumpp

Early on the morning of Saturday November 1, 1958 two duck hunters piloted their small boat through the fog and mist on the waters of Cowan Lake, a man-made recreational lake located about seven miles south of the town of Wilmington, Ohio. Suddenly, the boat's motor stalled.

The men were unable to restart the engine, so they rowed to the nearby shore to pull the boat up out of the water and decide what their next move should be. It turned out that their next move would have little to do with duck hunting. As soon as the men walked a short distance away from the lake they almost literally stumbled upon the badly burned body of a dead woman.

The discovery of that body was the beginning of one of the most sensational and controversial murder cases in Cincinnati's history.

Naturally, the men reported their grisly find to authorities. Clinton County Sheriff Floyd Foote arrived on the scene and began supervising the investigation. "You couldn't tell much," the sheriff said, "because the body was burned so much. The body hadn't been there very long, though, because workmen were in that lake area all week." The remains were taken to Cincinnati for a forensic examination.

A preliminary inspection of the corpse by pathologist Dr. Frank Cleveland revealed that the dead woman had probably died from a blow from a blunt instrument on the back of the head. Cleveland added that the fire that consumed the corpse must have been kept going for over two hours to achieve the degree of burning that had occurred.

The same day the body was discovered at Cowan Lake, a William Bergen reported to Cincinnati Police that his wife was missing. Bergen said that his wife, Louise, 32, had last been seen the previous Thursday at 5:00 p.m. when she left her place of employment, the Stillpass Transit Company on Spring Grove Avenue. Neither she, nor her car, had been seen since.

Authorities quickly correlated William Bergen's missing person report with the body found at Cowan Lake. One reason for the connection was that the description of Louise Bergen closely matched that of the burned body. Also, half a necklace, some red cloth, a penknife, and a key chain had been found under the body of the dead woman. Louise Bergen had been wearing a red jacket on the day she disappeared. Further investigation determined that the penknife was the same kind that had been presented to employees of Stillpass Transit by its president. One of the five keys on the chain was for a General Motors car. Mrs. Bergen drove an Oldsmobile. (A few days later her missing car was found in the parking lot of the Swifton Shopping Center at Reading Road and Semour Avenue.)

Other personal effects found on the body, including engagement and wedding rings, when viewed by William Bergen, cinched it that the corpse was that of Louise Bergen.

In order to determine how Louise Bergen had ended up burned to a crisp on the shore of Cowan Lake, police began investigating her background. When they did, they discovered a scenario that seemed more like something out of *Peyton Place* than from staid and conservative Cincinnati Ohio.

The dead woman did not live with her husband. She had an apartment on Langdon Farm Road, in Cincinnati near Golf Manor, while he lived in a house at the end of Bloomingdale Avenue in Mount Washington. And William Bergen did not reside alone in the house on Bloomingdale Avenue.

The other residents of the house were 40-year-old Edythe Klumpp and her four children. Mrs. Klumpp was a recent divorcee. When authorities questioned her, she explained her current living situation by saying that she was planning on marrying William Bergen. In fact, she already referred to her live-in lover as "my husband, Bill."

On Tuesday, November 18, William Bergen was given a lie detector test. Results of the test indicated that he was not involved with the death of his wife. Relieved to be cleared, he told the press, "I'm glad it's over. I knew all the while police had me down as a suspect." Bergen also said that he had been wanting to get back together with his wife for some time, although he admitted that "we had some things that had to be worked out first. Naturally, Edythe was opposed to (any reconciliation)." The Bergens had separated the previous June.

After his session with police, Bergen went back to the house on Bloomingdale Avenue. Edythe Klumpp then went downtown for her own interrogation session. Police asked her to drive her car to the session.

Police questioned Edythe Klumpp thoroughly. As part of the questioning, they asked her to take a lie detector test. She agreed. The lie detector test indicated that she had information about the death of Louise Bergen.

While one set of officers questioned Edythe, others were examining her automobile. They noticed what appeared to be blood on the front seat. The car was then taken to a forensics laboratory where testing detected a "large amount" of blood on the front seat as well as evidence of blood being cleaned up.

Edythe was confronted with the evidence of blood in her car and the results of her lie detector test. She then admitted that she had been involved in the death of Louise Bergen.

Edythe gave her first formal statement to police at 1:30 a.m. on November 19, 1958. In that first version of her actions she said that she met Louise Bergen at the Swifton Shopping Center on October 30. "Louise called me a little before 5:00 p.m. that October 30 and said she wanted to talk to me – it was important," Edythe recalled. "I agreed to meet her at the Swifton Center." When the two women met at Swifton they got into Edythe's car. Then they drove off to have their meeting in a more private location than the crowded shopping center. Edythe drove to Caldwell Park, located off North Bend Road in Hartwell, where "we could talk." The location she drove to in Caldwell Park was frequently used as a lovers lane.

According to Edythe, when the two reached Caldwell Park a fight ensued during which "something happened and Mrs. Bergen was injured." Edythe said that, contrary to the coroner's report, Louise Bergen had been shot when the two women struggled with a gun that Louise found in the car. Edythe was vague about what happened next, but she remembered struggling to get Louise's body into the trunk of the car.

Then, she said, she drove home, cleaned up, and went to the Woodward Evening School at Woodward High School to teach an adult class in sewing.

The next morning, Edythe continued, she bought a gallon of gasoline and drove 45 miles north to Cowan Lake, where she set fire to the body.

Based on the results of the polygraph test, the blood in the car, and Edythe's own statements, police placed her under arrest.

The murder of Louise Bergen and arrest of Edythe Klumpp immediately dominated the local news, and would continue to do so for years to come. It was yet another sensational story added to the annals of Cincinnati crime. The press dubbed the crime "The Torch Slaying."

A second examination of the body of Louise Bergen revealed metal residue in the neck which suggested that she had indeed been shot. Edythe told police she disposed of the murder weapon during the trip to Cowan Lake. When police took her there to look for it, she changed her story and said that the gun actually belonged to William Bergen, not to his dead wife. She also said she hadn't really thrown the gun away. It was a .22 caliber target pistol that officers had already confiscated during a search of her home. Bergen admitted that he owned the gun.

Edythe now said that she had the gun in the glove compartment of her car when she went to meet Louise Bergen at the Swifton Center. It was not her intention to use the gun, she insisted. It was in the car because she had taken it out target shooting two days earlier. Upon seeing it in her glove compartment on the way to Swifton, she said, she placed it on the front seat "so I wouldn't forget to return it to the bureau drawer (when I got home)." As

Edythe and Louise drove away from Swifton, the gun sat on the front seat between them, wrapped in a piece of cloth.

When the car got to Caldwell Park, Edythe got into the back seat of the car because she had been uncomfortable in the front. The two women began arguing. Edythe later said that Louise Bergen refused to divorce her husband. "Louise told me she loved her husband and wanted him back. I told her I would fight for him." The meeting grew more acrimonious. Then, while sitting in the back seat, Edythe noticed a pop bottle wedged under the front seat. Thinking that the bottle had been what was making her uncomfortable, she reached down to remove it. "I reached down to get it and when I straightened up Louise had a gun in her hand and pointed at me. I was startled – I thought it was a joke. I grabbed for the gun, I got a hold of her hand – the one with the gun – and her arm. We kind of wrestled around and the gun went off. It was pointed up under her chin. I can't recall that a thing was said while we were struggling."

That was Edythe Klumpp's story. The shooting was self-defense.

Then, Edythe said, "the blood gushed out. I was panic stricken. Something would have to be done."

Edythe went on to describe her actions after the crime. After placing Louise Bergen's body in the trunk of her car, she drove back to her home, arriving at about 6:30 p.m. She then drove to Woodward High School where she taught her sewing class until after 9:30. Students in the class noted that she was fifteen minutes late. "We asked her what was the matter," one student later said. "She just said she had some car trouble."

Edythe acted completely normal during the class. "She seemed just the same as always," another student recalled. "She helped us with our sewing and dismissed class the same time as usual, about 9:45 p.m."

After the class, Edythe said, she called William Bergen at the home of a friend but was unable to reach him. So, she went home. When she got home she attempted to clean out the car and disposed of a bloodstained skirt and sweater. She kept Louise Bergen's body in the trunk of her car overnight, parked outside her house.

Edythe said she did not tell William Bergen what had happened.

The next day, Edythe told stunned investigators, she got into the car with three small children she was babysitting at her house and drove to Cowan Lake. She said she picked the lake because she was familiar with the state park there. She drove around until she found a deserted spot. Then, while the children, aged between two and four years old, sat in the backseat oblivious to what was going on, she removed the now "very stiff" body of Louise Bergen, poured gasoline over it, and set it on fire. She said she burned the body "not so much to destroy it, but because I was afraid of fingerprints or some evidence that might point to me."

On the way back from Cowan Lake, Edythe said, she disposed of Louise Bergen's purse, shoes, and glasses by tossing them out the car window. (These items were found a few days after the discovery of the body.)

She arrived back at Bloomingdale Avenue at about 2:00 p.m. She did a more thorough job of cleaning the car. She also burned Louise Bergen's wallet.

Upon learning of her arrest, relatives of Edythe Klumpp immediately sought legal help for her. And they started at the top of the local legal roster by contacting William Foster "Foss" Hopkins. Hopkins was one of the best-known defense attorneys in Cincinnati. He had won much acclaim two years earlier for winning an acquittal for his client in the Audrey Pugh murder case.

Edythe had already been held in custody for over 24 hours without being charged, so Hopkins' first act was to inform police that if they had not charged his client by 3:00 p.m. on November 20 he would institute a writ of habeas corpus to obtain her freedom.

Police obliged. On the 19th they filed first degree murder charges against Edythe Klumpp. She was arraigned in Police Court the next morning. The first degree qualification to the charge, implying premeditation, indicated that police did not believe Edythe's story about an accidental shooting. This surprised the defendant. "I thought it (the charge) was supposed to be manslaughter," she said. "It was accidental, you know. (Police) said yesterday (the charge) would be manslaughter." She added that she had not been allowed to see her attorney when she requested him. "(Detectives) told me I would have to make a statement before I could see him," she said.

Those detectives immediately denied that they had promised Edythe a lesser charge or kept her from meeting with her attorney. Foss Hopkins, however was not convinced. "I am utterly amazed at the way in which police obtain these statements (from accused persons.). I've argued for years that a public defender or other neutral person be present during the entire time a suspect is being questioned and that during the entire time a tape recording should be made of all that is said."

Because there was some confusion over where Louise Bergen had actually died, Edythe Klumpp was charged with murder in both Hamilton and Clinton Counties. But Hamilton County officials were confident of their claim of jurisdiction since they were certain that the attack had commenced in Caldwell Park in Hamilton County. On Monday, November 22 Edythe Klumpp was arraigned before Criminal Court Judge Simon L. Leis. She entered a plea of not guilty. She continued to be represented by Foss Hopkins.

While Edythe Klumpp sat in jail, her estranged husband Richard returned to the property on Bloomingdale Avenue to take care of the house and children. William Bergen had moved out to an undisclosed address. He had also lost his job as a result of the publicity surrounding the death of his wife.

More details began to emerge about the background of Edythe Klumpp. She was born Edith Reis forty years earlier at Deaconess Hospital in

Cincinnati. Her father was a steam fitter, and he also played some professional baseball with the St. Louis Cardinals. Edythe spent her early years on Victor Street in Corryville. She attended several different high schools in Norwood, Springdale, Glendale, and Mt. Healthy before finally graduating from Hartwell. After graduating she went to work as a playground supervisor and assistant teacher for the National Youth Administration.

She had first been married, at age 18, to George Montgomery in Lawrenceberg, Indiana. This first marriage lasted four years before Edythe filed for divorce. She had a son from that marriage who was now 20 years old and in the Air Force in Oklahoma.

On December 28, 1940 Edythe married again, to Richard Klumpp. Richard Klumpp worked as a printer. Her marriage to him eventually produced four more children, one of which died at age six months.

At about this same time, in the mid 1940s, Edythe started a foster home. In the beginning she would sometimes have as many as 15 children at her house. After World War Two that number went down to six or eight.

Edythe had always worked during her adult life, sometimes holding two or three jobs at once. "I've always worked," she explained. "Somebody had to support the kids. I've done it for years. I needed the money."

Co-workers gave differing views on the reasons for Edythe's work ethic. Some said she was simply a devoted mother working hard to support her children. Others claimed that she worked solely to get money for clothes, make-up, and partying.

Since 1947 Edythe taught evening classes for adults at several Cincinnati high schools. She also provided day care for children at her home. Over the years she would take care of more than twenty children. She also worked as a driver tester for the Ohio State Patrol at Lunken Airport and as a waitress at Lunken's Sky Galley Restaurant. It was at the Sky Galley that she met William Bergen.

She had lived in the Mount Washington house for six years, but had not become friendly with her neighbors. "I can't say any of them are friendly," she said later. "Maybe I was too busy to make friends."

The murder trial of Edythe Klumpp began on June 8, 1959 in Courtroom 316 of the Hamilton County Courthouse. The case was heard before Judge Frank Gusweiler. The defendant appeared in court wearing a dark blue dress with the light blue initials "EK" on the front. She had made the dress herself on a sewing machine in the Women's Detention section of the Hamilton County Jail. (She would wear a different jail-made dress nearly every day of the trial.) She wore little make-up.

It took four days to select a jury. The panel who would judge Edythe Klumpp consisted of six men and six women. The men's professions ranged from transmission repairman to postal clerk to Procter and Gamble employee. Most of the women listed their profession as "housewife."

The Cincinnati Crime Book

The trial started off with the jury and other trial principals going on a tour of the crime scenes. The first stop was the Courthouse's basement garage for a look at Edythe Klumpp's 1956 sedan. Then everyone went to Swifton Shopping Center. Edythe began crying when they reached the scene of her fateful rendezvous with Louise Bergen. The jury next went to a house in the East End where Edythe had picked up two small children on the way to Cowan Lake. The jury also went to Woodward High School and Caldwell Park. At the park Edythe stood on the sidelines sobbing while the jury viewed the location of the fatal fight.

Then, after a break for lunch, the jury rode up to Cowan Lake. Edythe did not accompany them on this leg of the tour. Hopkins had objected to the inclusion of Cowan Lake in the tour since, he said, the burning of the body was not relevant to the charge of first degree murder. "We do not believe Lake Cowan has anything to do with this case," he said. "Our client did take Mrs. Bergen's body there in an auto trunk, poured gasoline on it and did try to cremate and disfigure the body. We are not denying it. It is a horrible, despicable situation. (But) this is a first degree murder case and something that happened afterward, such as taking the body to Clinton County (and burning it) I don't believe has anything to do with premeditation or deliberation." As they viewed the scene of the cremation of Louise Bergen the jurors could not help but notice that the vegetation in the area was still charred by the fire. Ironically, the location was just off a small lane named Cemetery Road.

After viewing a quarry near Clarksville where Louise Bergen's personal effects had been found, the jury returned to Cincinnati and the company of Edythe Klumpp for a look at her house on Bloomingdale Avenue. The house was occupied by her second husband and her three young children, but the jury did not see them. Edythe cried again.

On June 15 the prosecution began presenting its case. Assistant Hamilton County Prosecutor Harry C. Schoettmer said that the state would prove that this was a case of carefully premeditated murder rather than being a spontaneous act of self-defense as Edythe claimed. Edythe had purchased the gasoline used to incinerate Louise Bergen the day before the murder, Schoettmer said. He said that the motive for the murder was that Edythe Klumpp had used the name "Mrs. Bergen" to get a loan on a new home. Schoettmer said that Edythe had lied and told bank officials that she and Bergen were married on June 14, 1958. Because bank officials were investigating the loan and making inquiries at the residence of the real Mrs. Bergen, the real Mrs. Bergen had to be gotten rid of. "October 30 was the trigger day," Schoettmer said. "Louise Bergen had to die because of that loan." The prosecutor said that Edythe had persuaded William Bergen to cooperate with the loan fraud by telling him she was carrying his child. He also said that Bergen had been tiring of his live-in situation with Edythe and hinted that the feeling may have been mutual. Schoettmer said that Edythe was familiar with the lovers lane in Caldwell Park because she had been there on several occasions with a man other than William Bergen.

Defense attorney Hopkins countered that it was Louise Bergen, not Edythe Klumpp, who had arranged the meeting at the Swifton Shopping Center on October 30. Edythe "didn't even realize she had the gun with her," he added. At Caldwell Park "she looked up, and there, with a grin on her face, was Louise Bergen pointing a .22 pistol. There was an argument. Edythe Klumpp grabbed the gun, there was a struggle and the gun went off. The blood gushed from (Louise Bergen's) mouth and my client sank in the back seat. You can call it shock, panic, or fright.... (but) then she panicked and made the worst mistake any person ever made. Through fear that (authorities) would never believe her story.... she did this very terrible, despicable thing (burning the body)." Hopkins asked for a verdict of not guilty or, at most, guilty of manslaughter.

The state called over a dozen witness as it presented its side of the case. One witness was a man, supposedly another paramour of Edythe Klumpp, who said he had spent time with her at the lovers lane in Caldwell Park, thus making her familiar with the eventual crime scene. Another witness was a Mount Washington gas station employee who claimed he sold a gallon of gasoline to the defendant on the day before the killing. Louise Bergen's supervisor from Stillpass Transit testified that she had received a telephone call on the afternoon of October 30. This testimony buttressed the claim of the prosecution that it was Edythe Klumpp who arranged the meeting with Louise Bergen, not the other way around as the defense claimed.

One key witness for the prosecution was Mel Abrams. Abrams was a fleet superintendent at Stillpass Motors who also socialized with the Bergens. Abrams testified that he sold the murder weapon to Louise Bergen in 1956. She then gave the pistol to her husband as a Christmas present. Abrams said that he and William Bergen went target shooting together about once a month. He said that on the night of the murder William Bergen had been at his Golf Manor home from about 7:30 until 11:00. He said Bergen frequently waited at his house while Edythe taught her sewing classes at nearby Woodward High School. Abrams said that his wife had taken a phone call for Bergen from Edythe Klumpp at about 10:30 p.m. He admitted that he knew Bergen and Edythe were seeing each other "every night," but said he knew of no marriage plans between the couple.

On June 17 Dr. Frank Cleveland testified about the two autopsies he performed on the victim. Cleveland said that Louise Bergen died from three skull fractures caused by "multiple impacts." He said he thought the fractures were caused by blows from the muzzle of the murder gun. Hopkins suggested that the fractures were caused when Edythe Klumppe moved Louise's body from the front seat to the trunk of the car. Under cross-examination by Hopkins the doctor admitted that he had done a second autopsy after Edythe said she shot the victim. He denied that he was careless in missing the metal fragments during the first examination.

"Isn't it almost a religion in thorough autopsies to take an X-ray (to reveal metal bullet fragments)?" Hopkins asked.

"I don't believe that has to be done," the pathologist replied. Cleveland did not even concede that the metal fragments found in Louise Bergen's neck were bullets. He said that the head and neck area of her body was too badly burned for him to detect a bullet entry wound. He added that the second autopsy had revealed traces of gasoline residue in Louise Bergen's lungs, implying that she may still have been alive when she was set on fire.

On June 18 the prosecution introduced as evidence a credit card receipt from a gasoline station in Mt. Washington. The imprint of the card on the receipt read "William M. Bergen Jr., 1851 Bloomingdale Avenue." The receipt, dated October 29, 1958, was signed "Mrs. Edythe H. Bergen." Prosecutors said the receipt proved Edythe purchased the gasoline used to incinerate Louis Bergen the day before she was killed, thus indicating that the murder was premeditated.

After the testimony about the gasoline receipt, the state called Richard Klumpp, Edythe's estranged second husband, to the stand. Klumpp testified that he had married Edythe in 1940 and that they had three children together. They separated in August, 1956 and a divorce was granted a year later. Edythe got custody of the children while Richard got weekly visitation with them. Klumpp said he found out that William Bergen had moved into the Bloomingdale Avenue house in June, 1958. He said he did not know whether his ex-wife and Bergen were married, but said that in October 1958 Edythe told him William Bergen was planning to leave her.

But the main prosecution witness that day was William Bergen, the husband of the murder victim. Tall, gaunt, and with a receding hairline and sunken eyes, he hardly looked like a man who could wreak havoc on the love lives of women. Bergen had to be subpoenaed from Washington DC, where he had moved after the murder, to get him to testify at the trial. He was on the stand for just over an hour. Edythe Klumpp watched him intently as he testified. Some courtroom observers thought she was wearing a little more makeup than she usually did. Bergen did not meet her gaze.

Bergen began his testimony by recalling how he met Edythe Klumpp at Lunken Airport's Sky Galley Restaurant in March of 1958. He said their relationship was intimate by April. As he related how Edythe had wanted him to cosign on a loan application he said, "I was hesitant. I didn't want to get involved. I was afraid she might not be able to keep up the payment and it would come back on me."

After 65 minutes Bergen was excused from the stand and court was recessed for the day. Commenting on her former lover's testimony, Edythe remarked, "He's the same old Bill."

The Cincinnati Crime Book

The next day Bergen was back in the witness chair. He admitted that he had given Edythe an informal "engagement ring" and had even taken her on a three day "honeymoon" at the Spring Mill State Park near Indianapolis in the summer of 1958. But he insisted that he had always intended to return to his wife. He said Edythe told him twice in 1958 that she was pregnant by him. He claimed this news "came as a surprise. You just don't expect those things to happen." Bergen said that Edythe claimed the first pregnancy had ended in a miscarriage. The second time she said she was pregnant was in the fall of 1958 after he told her he wanted to return to Louise. Bergen also said that Edythe was upset by the possibility of him returning to his wife. "She said, 'Oh, what would happen to me? How would things look? Folks think that we are married and you (would be) running out.'" Bergen admitted cosigning the $9000 loan application six days before his wife was killed. He said that he kept the murder weapon in the house on Bloomingdale Avenue and that the gun had a "hair trigger." He also admitted that even after Edythe told him she had killed his wife and burned her body he continued to live with her for more than a week before moving out.

On June 21 Assistant Hamilton County Prosecutor Melvin Rueger called Cincinnati Homicide Detective Eugene Moore to the stand. Moore's purpose was to introduce into evidence the statements Edythe Klumpp made to police about the slaying of Louise Bergen. Foss Hopkins objected to the introduction of the statements in a three hour argument, but Judge Gusweiler ruled that they could be admitted.

Moore testified that after Edythe was arrested on November 18 she had remarked, "I can't think. I can only think of my kids. I know how Louise met her death." Moore said that Edythe told police of four other meetings with Louise Bergen before the fatal one. During one of these meetings, Moore claimed, Edythe said that Louise had changed her mind about permanently separating from her husband. "I didn't think that was fair," Moore quoted Edythe as saying. "She knew we had already agreed to our marriage plans." But in a subsequent meeting, Mrs. Bergen had supposedly changed her mind again and decided to grant Bill Bergen the divorce because "she had a boyfriend, a big hillbilly truck driver who wanted (her) to go away with him."

On June 21 the two sides in the case argued over the gasoline credit card receipt. The state claimed that the receipt proved that Edythe bought the gasoline used to incinerate Louise Bergen on the day prior to her murder, thus showing that the murder was planned in advance. To support this argument, they called an employee of Standard Oil of Ohio (Sohio) who testified that Edythe Klumpp had been the only person to use William Bergen's gas credit card between October 29 and November 11. Foss Hopkins countered this testimony by pointing out that the receipt showed a purchase of 11.3 gallons and only proved that Edythe had gassed up her car, not that she had bought the single gallon used in the cremation attempt. Hopkins also noted that a gasoline purchase made with cash would not show up on any records.

Several other witnesses were called that day. A customer of Edythe's babysitting service testified that on the day after the murder Edythe had picked up her and her children as usual. Edythe routinely gave the woman a ride part way to her job before she returned with the children to 1751 Bloomingdale Avenue. "When we got on Beechmont Avenue," the woman said, "there was sort of a funny odor like a dead animal. I asked Mrs. Klumpp if she noticed that. Mrs. Klumpp answered, 'I noticed it when we got in the car this morning.'" (According to Edythe's confession, Louis Bergen's body was in the trunk.) When Edythe dropped the woman's children off at their house later in the day she told the woman that she had been burning leaves and that her children "might smell like smoke."

Edythe's confessions to the murder were read to jurors on June 23. Foss Hopkins fought vainly to keep them from being heard. He said that Edythe had only made the statements after law enforcement officials promised her she would only be charged with manslaughter. In support of this contention he called Edythe herself to the stand. "They promised it would be manslaughter," the defendant said. "and they told me I could get out on bond. (They said they would) go before the Judge and I would probably get probation." Edythe added that the police had ignored her repeated requests to have legal counsel present. "I believe I asked to see my lawyer, and they said I couldn't until after I had made a statement. I kept insisting I wanted to see (my lawyer). There were three of them in there and they kept pounding questions after me, one after the other."

To rebut Edythe's testimony the prosecution called Homicide Detective Moore, who denied that any such deal had been offered. He also said that no one had kept Edythe from contacting Foss Hopkins or violated any other of her rights. "We had a nasty crime on our hands," Moore explained. "and we knew we had the guilty person and as I understand Ohio law you don't have to tell a suspect his rights during an investigation. She didn't ask for a lawyer and we didn't press the matter."

Judge Gusweiler ruled that since the confessions were made voluntarily they would be read to the jury. Thus they heard Edythe's first two versions of the crime. The first was given to police early in the morning on November 19; the second twelve hours later. The only major difference in the statements was that in the first Edythe said Louise Bergen brought the murder gun to their meeting and in the second she said that the gun was already in the car, left over from a target practicing session some days previous.

The state rested its case just after noon on June 24.

The defense began presenting its case the next day. More than 100 spectators scrambled to get seats in the crowded courtroom. One would-be spectator collapsed on the steps of the courthouse and had to be taken to a hospital. Those who did get in the courtroom were rewarded for their efforts. June 25 was one of the most emotional days of the trial.

The Cincinnati Crime Book

(That the trial had something of a carnival or picnic atmosphere was reflected in the behavior of some of the spectators – they had taken to bringing refreshments to eat in the courtroom. Judge Gusweiler ordered a halt to this disrespectful behavior. "No eating," he intoned. "If you want a picnic, go outside." The judge also banned spectators under the age of 12 from the proceedings, explaining that the trial's themes of adultery and murder were inappropriate for their young sensibilities.)

The first witness called on June 25 was Edythe Klumpp's 11-year-old daughter Jo Ann. Edythe wept as the girl approached the witness stand. Foss Hopkins called the youngster to the stand to prove that Louise Bergen had made a telephone call to set up the meeting at Swifton Center, not the other way around as the prosecution claimed. His questioning of the young girl was tender. "Do you know the difference between right and wrong? Do you know it's a sin to tell a lie? Do you believe in God?" Jo Ann answered "yes" to every question, then went on to describe how her mother had received a phone call between 4:45 and 5:00 p.m. on the afternoon of October 30. "My mother answered it," the girl said. "We went outside and played."

The next witness was Edythe Klumpp herself. As an aid to her testimony, Foss Hopkins had the front seat of her car wheeled into the courtroom on a dolly. Edythe then re-enacted her version of the shooting. She described Louise Bergen as "very friendly" at the beginning of their meeting. According to Edythe, Louise said she planned to divorce her husband and said, "I hope he does not make life as miserable for you as he did for me." Edythe said that Louise confided that she had been seeing other men and "going with her boss. She was afraid Bill would find her with him."

But suddenly Louise Bergen's mood changed and she was pointing a gun at Edythe. A struggle ensued and the gun went off. "I was dazed when the blood came out of her," Edythe said. "I felt her pulse and heart to see if there were signs of life." Panicked, Edythe bolted from the car. "I started running, I don't know why," she said. "I ran up the road and then I came back and felt the pulse and heart again. I started shaking her." Then, she thought, "I'd better put her in the trunk." She described, almost comically, her frantic efforts to get the body in the trunk. "When I got the head in the feet would fall out, and when the feet were in the head would fall out." Foss Hopkins had earlier alleged that the fractures to Louise Bergen's skull occurred when Edythe struggled to place her body in the car trunk. To support this Edythe now testified that the head had, indeed, been bumped. "I don't know what it (hit), but it made an awful sound."

Edythe also gave more details on her relationship with William Bergen. They had met in late February or early March of 1958 in the Sky Galley Cafe at Lunken Airport. Edythe worked there as a waitress. One Sunday a friend came in and introduced Edythe to another man: William Bergen. Not much happened during their first meeting, but Bergen returned to the cafe several times in the next few weeks. Edythe barely noticed him. Finally, he asked if

122

he could call her and she said yes. A few days later he called from a bar in Mount Washington. He asked if he could come over, and Edythe again said yes. "We just sat around and watched television and talked," Edythe recalled. Talked about what? "I don't remember too much exactly. My kids, partly, and his little girl I asked if he was married when he mentioned his little girl. He said, 'In a way, but I won't be for long. I'm getting a divorce.' I figured the divorce was already filed, the way he said it." After that first date, Edythe and Bergen were together almost every night. In June Bergen moved into the house on Bloomingdale Avenue. Edythe said her kids were "crazy about him." But Edythe noted that Bergen had lied to her about his age. "The first night he was there we were talking and I asked him how old he was and he said 36. I said, 'I'm older than you.' He said (their mutual friend) had told him I was around 40. Later, after I told him I'd marry him, he got his pilot's license and showed it to me and I saw his birth date was 1928 and I began figuring his age. He got real white-faced and said he was going to tell me when we were married. He said he was afraid I wouldn't marry him if I knew he was that much (ten years) younger."

In May Bergen began to have doubts about the relationship, though, and he took a week off and went to Norfolk, Virginia to decide what to do. But, Edythe said, "he called me every night. He would tell me how much he missed me and that he loved me." When Bergen returned from his soul-searching trip "he said that if there had ever been a doubt in his mind it was gone now. He said that he would not leave me for any reason."

Edythe described an informal "wedding ceremony" that Bergen had performed in Ault Park on June 14, 1958. "We had dinner and we went to Ault Park. There he put the ring on my finger. We exchanged vows. He made quite a long speech. He said I was his wife, that the ring was the thing. He said the ring will not come off until he took it off, and that would not happen." (It did happen. The ring was one of the state's exhibits in the trial.)

That summer, Edythe and Bergen spent all their time together, "flying, we had picnics, swimming." The couple decided to buy a house and had settled on one in Forest Park. "Every chance we had we went to what we called 'our house.' My son came home (from the service) and we took him to see the house." (It was fraud on the loan application for this house, the prosecution contended, that had been the motivating catalyst for the murder of Louise Bergen.)

But by the fall both Bergen and Edythe seemed to be tiring of their relationship. "Bill had got kind of cool toward me and, well, I found out quite a few things about him and changed my mind about him," she said. "I was just drifting along, waiting for him to make up his mind (about us)."

Edythe also said that at this time she had begun a friendship with Louise Bergen, based on their common problems with Bill. "She called me to meet her. She wanted to talk about Bill.... We went to Walgreen's and had a Coke. I made a remark that no one would believe this. We were two wives. She kind of laughed and said she felt close to me, like there was a bond between us....She asked me to meet her someday at her home for dinner. We never got around to that...."

On Friday, June 26 Prosecutor Harry Schoettmer began his cross-examination of Edythe Klumpp. His interrogation of the defendant was relentless, but she stuck to her version of events. While Edythe had frequently wept during her direct examination by Foss Hopkins, she maintained her composure as she responded to the prosecutor's questions. Describing the shooting, she said, "My hands never touched the gun. I was frightened. I grabbed for the gun – her hand was on the trigger, not mine." If the shooting was an accident, Schoettmer asked, why hadn't Edythe tried to seek help for the unfortunate Louise Bergen? "I was afraid (the authorities) would say I killed her. You're not believing me now. You're calling me a liar." After the killing, back home at Bloomingdale Avenue, Edythe looked at the body in the trunk. "(I) just couldn't believe it possible that it happened," she said. Asked whether she had any remorse for the death of Louise Bergen, Edythe replied, "I feel anything I have done God has forgiven me for. He is the one to judge." She had always felt friendly towards Louise Bergen, she added.

"How did you feel toward her when you poured gasoline on her body?" the prosecutor asked.

"When I did that I didn't have much feeling toward anyone. I was upset, scared."

Despite the prosecutor's strong questioning, Edythe was unruffled on the stand. She frequently interrupted Schoettmer with shouts of "That's a lie!" The only time she appeared affected was when Schoettmer showed her a color photo of Louise Bergen's incinerated corpse.

At one point Schoettmer handed her the murder pistol and said, "Load that gun." As Edythe did so, there was temporary excitement in the courtroom.

"Don't point that at me!" a juror exclaimed.

Schoettmer reassured everyone that the bullet was a fake. Edythe loaded the gun with difficulty. Then she unintentionally pulled the trigger. The resulting "click" was heard throughout the courtroom. Edythe said she didn't know she had pulled the trigger.

Cross-examination of the defendant was concluded on Monday, June 29. After that there was follow-up testimony regarding the receipt for the gasoline purchase. Then each side made its closing arguments.

Prosecutor Schoettmer called Edythe Klumpp "a mistress with certain physical charms and wiles. (She) went on the stand and said she was a religious woman. And yet she admits she burned the body and lived in adultery. She claims to be a truthful woman, yet she admits lying to her mother, her daughter, Bergen, the community, the police. How many more? Now, as to her appearance (in court). On Thursday Mrs. Klumpp testified for three and a half hours under direct examination. She had a meek, reticent appearance. Her counsel literally screamed at her to keep her voice up. She had the appearance of a fragile woman. That was her role on Thursday. But on Friday (under cross-examination) she came out of that role. She was fighting. She even asked the prosecutor questions. (And) when she said, 'The Lord has forgiven me,' she didn't mean it at all. She was never close to tears. She wanted to be a fighting cat, and that is what she is. Yesterday she again played the meek, fragile role. Well, was she meek and mild on October 30? Or (was she) a fighting wildcat?"

Foss Hopkins did what he could in his closing statement, but with Edythe admitting to the shooting and burning there was little he could do. He tried to shift blame for the killing to Bill Bergen, suggesting that Bergen's philandering was really responsible for the circumstances that led to the death of his wife. "I have come to the conclusion that we are trying the wrong party," Hopkins said. "The man – and I use the term loosely – who caused this tragedy has been allowed to go scot free. This target-pistol Romeo, this aviator of sorts, by his deceit, subterfuge, and honey-dripping promises and vows has brought about the death of his wife and the trial of Edythe Klumpp upon the charge of murder.... Surely there must be some way for the law to clip Bergen's wings so as to protect other women he will come into contact with. From the stand he is a confessed adulterer. The State of Ohio would be remiss in its duty if it did not prosecute on this charge and give a warning that such conduct will not be tolerated. But maybe because he testified against Edythe Klumpp they will give him a gold medal. I don't know. All I know is, until this happened, Edythe Klumpp was a decent woman."

Then, after over three weeks of testimony, the case went to the jury.

The panel deliberated just one day before it returned with its verdict. Edythe Klumpp was guilty of first degree murder. The jury did not recommend mercy, which meant a mandatory sentence of death. Formal sentencing was set for August 28. Court was dismissed, and Edythe Klumpp returned to her cell.

But within a month of her conviction a rumor began circulating that the convicted murderess had changed her story of the killing again. According to this rumor, Edythe now said that while she had knowledge of the shooting of Louise Bergen, her only role in the crime had been to burn the body. The rumor did not explain who the actual murderer of Louise Bergen was.

But by the time of her formal sentencing Edythe was ready to tell who the shooter really was. At the August 28th hearing, Foss Hopkins read a new statement from his client that named William Bergen as the real killer.

Edythe had started telling her new story shortly after the jury found her guilty of murder. There were two reasons for the change. First, the reality of the mandatory death sentence sunk in and Edythe realized, perhaps for the first time, that her life was at stake. The second reason was that William Bergen had completely turned his back on his former lover. After her conviction he returned to Washington DC. Soon Edythe heard that he had a new girlfriend.

The Cincinnati Crime Book

The new story differed from the earlier versions in many important ways. Now Edythe said that she had not met Louise Bergen at Swifton Shopping Center, but that William Bergen had brought his wife to Mount Washington in his car on the afternoon of October 30. As she told Hopkins, "Louise Bergen called me on October 30.... and said she wanted to see me and it was important. I called Bill and suggested that he pick her up and I would meet them behind the Mount Washington Theater as soon as I could get there. I guess I got there about 5:45. They got out of his car and got into mine. They were arguing.... Bill slapped her.... They were arguing about more money.... I started driving and I told Bill that I wanted to look for a gas station because I wanted to go to the restroom.... He said, 'Just pull back in that new subdivision and you can go there.'" The subdivision was located on Stratton Drive, off Four Mile Road in Anderson Township. Edythe got out of the car and went into the bushes. When she got back, "(Louise) was on the front seat and he was leaning over her. I don't know what he was doing. Her head was all bloody. I started running down the road. I said I was going for help. Bill told me to get back there or I would get some of the same thing.... He said they were arguing.... and then she leaned over and opened the glove compartment. She opened it and pulled the gun out and he reached over and grabbed her arm and the gun went off under her chin and shot her." After the shooting, Edythe helped Bergen place Louise in the trunk of the car. Then she took him back to his car and he told her to go to her sewing class. "It would look funny if I didn't go, is what he said." After her class, she called Bergen and they decided to take the body to Cowan Lake and burn it. They got there at about midnight. "He is the one that poured gasoline on the body," Edythe recalled. "I had the car started and I glanced back. It made a terrific blaze." After igniting the corpse, Edythe said, she and Bergen returned to 1751 Bloomingdale Avenue.

Authorities had a quick response to Edythe's new story. They announced that they would not reopen their investigation of the case. "There isn't anything left to check," said Detective Colonel Henry Sandman. Responding to Edythe's claim that Bill Bergen was the real killer, Sandman added, "We checked Bergen out thoroughly at the time Mrs. Bergen was killed. He took two lie detector tests and we thoroughly checked his alibi."

Judge Gusweiler agreed. On sentencing day, moments after Hopkins presented Edythe's new version of events to the court, the judge formally sentenced Edythe Klumpp to death in Ohio's electric chair. The execution date was set for December 15, 1959.

Foss Hopkins appealed Edyth's conviction and sentence to the First District Court of Appeals. That appeal postponed her execution, but the court denied it on February 1, 1960. Hopkins then appealed to both the Ohio and United States Supreme Courts. Both courts refused to hear the case. Next he tried an appeal to Ohio's parole board.

By now Hopkins was fully convinced of Edythe's innocence. He told the parole board that he himself would pay for the administration of a truth serum test to prove that she was innocent. But the board was unswayed, and they also turned him down.

Now the only chance of saving Edythe Klumpp from the electric chair was a direct appeal to Ohio's Governor.

In 1960 that Governor was Michael V. DiSalle. DiSalle had been Ohio's chief executive for just over a year. A democrat, he was personally opposed to the death penalty. Only one person had been executed in the state since he took office.

Governor DiSalle had an obvious official interest in the Klumpp case. When the parole board turned down Edythe's last appeal, he began looking further into it. The further he looked, the less he liked.

DiSalle discovered that Edythe's original confession to authorities, the one the prosecution had based most of its case on, could not be reconciled with many of the indisputable facts of the case. For example, it would have been impossible for Edythe to drive from Mount Washington to pick up Louise Bergen at Swifton Center, drive to Caldwell Park in Hartwell, argue with and kill Louise, stuff her body into the trunk, drive back to Mount Washington, and then drive to her sewing class at Woodward High School in the ninety minutes she said it took to do all that. Also, there had been workmen at Cowan Lake near the spot where the body was burned at the time Edythe said she burned it. Those workmen could not have helped but notice the large and long-burning funeral pyre. But they didn't. Finally, a witness had found Louise Bergen's discarded shoes two hours before Edythe said she threw them out of the car window after the burning. All of these discrepancies, DiSalle noted, were cleared up if one followed the chronology in Edythe's new version of events.

The Governor went to the Ohio Women's Reformatory at Marysville and visited Edythe Klumpp several times. After talking to her he was sure that the new version of the story was true.

Governor DiSalle then took an unprecedented step. He decided to administer a truth serum test to Edythe Klumpp, just as Foss Hopkins had suggested. On January 4, 1961 he went back to Marysville with Dr. Milton Parker, an expert in the administration of sodium amytal, the so-called "truth serum." Sodium amytal works on the brain to suppress an individual's conscious inhibitions, thus making them unable to lie. Governor DiSalle had set up an appointment to administer the drug to Edythe Klumpp.

Edythe was injected and soon succumbed to the influence of the drug. Both Governor DiSalle and Dr. Parker questioned her extensively for two hours. When the session was over, both men were convinced that her new story was the truth. Two days later, DiSalle announced that he would commute Edythe's sentence from death to life in prison.

Reaction was immediate and mostly negative. DiSalle was widely criticized for making a legal decision based on the use of "truth serum."

The whole affair of the sodium amytal test was widely reported in the press. Two Cincinnati newspapers even printed complete transcripts of DiSalle and Parker's session with Edythe. One reader read the transcripts with particular interest. He was a deputy with the Hamilton County Sheriff's Office.

The deputy recalled that on the night of October 30, 1958 he had been given a pair of glasses, pieces of a necklace, and some bloody children's clothing by an Anderson Township Ranger. The glasses, necklace, and clothing had been found on Stratton Road, right at the spot where Edythe Klumpp now said Louise Bergen had been shot.

The evidence was turned over to the Hamilton County Prosecutor's Office at the time it was found, but since there was no known crime to connect the items to they were placed in a miscellaneous file. At the deputy's urging authorities now looked at the items again. The glasses were traced to an optometrist who checked his records and confirmed that he had made them for Louise Bergen. The pieces of the necklace matched the portion of the necklace found under Louise's body at Cowan Lake. Here was proof positive that at least one part (and a major part) of Edythe Klumpp's revised story was true.

But even with this new revelation and the likelihood that Edythe was now finally telling the truth, many citizens of Ohio still disagreed with Governor DiSalle's decision to spare her from the chair. When he was voted out of office in the next election many observers said it was partly because he had commuted Edythe Klumpp's death sentence.

And despite the light the new developments cast on William Bergen's possible role in the killing of his wife (the timetable of Edythe's second story completely wiped out his alibis), he was never charged with any complicity in the crime. Both Foss Hopkins and Governor DiSalle invited Bergen back to Ohio to answer questions that had arisen as a result of Edythe's new statement, but he politely declined to return to the Buckeye State. He never came back. (After leaving Ohio shortly after Edythe's conviction, Bergen settled down in Maryland with a new nineteen-year-old wife.)

Edythe Klummp remained at the Ohio Women's Reformatory at Marysville, where she became a model prisoner. On May 12, 1971, after serving 11½ years, she was paroled. She left the prison without making any statement to the press and returned to the Cincinnati area to begin a new life of much-desired and deserved obscurity.

The Mount Washington home shared by Edythe Klumpp and Bill Bergen.

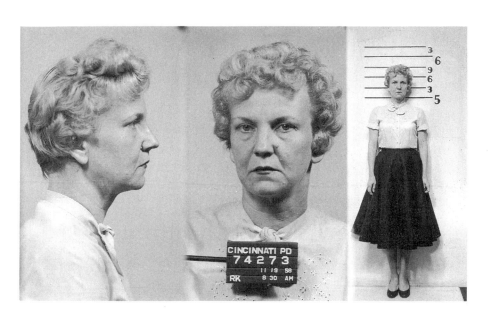

Edythe Klumpp.
(Courtesy Hamilton County Sheriff's Department)

Louise Bergen was murdered on this
isolated road in Anderson Township.

Cowan Lake, in Clinton County, Ohio, where
Louise Bergen's body was burned.

The Cincinnati Strangler

Nothing affects a city quite the way that a serial killer does. All other civic issues take a back seat as the panic of the citizenry rises in proportion to the body count. In some cases, as when the victims are prostitutes or drug addicts, the horror is muted by the feeling that the dead, being "lowlifes," somehow deserved what they got. But when the covered corpses on the evening news are children or other presumably innocent people the reaction is much broader, and much more terrible. Perhaps most people don't consort with drug addicts or prostitutes, but almost everybody knows a child that they love.

For just over a year in the mid-1960s Cincinnati was held in the grip of this type of killer. A beast prowled the streets. His victims were women, most of them middle-aged or older. And because the killer selected this type of victim not only did older women dread the unknown monster, but so did everyone who had a wife, mother, or grandmother.

By the first week of December, 1965, Cincinnati was well into autumn. Temperatures ranged from the 30s to the 50s and the leaves were long gone from the trees. Later in the week there was a threat of rain, but otherwise it was dry and mild.

Thursday, December 2 was a typical fall day in the Queen City – cloudy and cool. On that day Mrs. Emogene Harrington, an East Walnut Hills housewife, was brutally murdered. Her death would be the first attributed to the killer who became known as "The Cincinnati Strangler."

Emogene Harrington lived with her husband, Dr. R. Paul Harrington, in a top floor unit of the Clermont Apartments at 1404 East McMillan Street. Dr. Harrington was an internationally recognized authority on aerodynamics and was head of the Aerospace Engineering Division at the University of Cincinnati. His 56-year-old wife was a cultured and well-educated woman, a holder of a Phi Beta Kappa key. She was also a Deaconess at the Knox Presbyterian Church in Hyde Park. The couple had three grown daughters who lived in other cities.

131

The Cincinnati Crime Book

Thursdays were routine shopping days for Mrs. Harrington, so after a morning of visiting with friends over the telephone she climbed into her late-model station wagon and drove to the Kroger store in Hyde Park Square. She arrived at the store around noon and bought four large bags of groceries for $33.48. She gave the checkout clerk checks totaling $55.00 and thus received $21.52 in change. After loading the groceries into the front passenger seat of her car, Mrs. Harrington headed back to her home.

Parking was tight in her busy neighborhood, so Mrs. Harrington was forced to park in a space on the street about 200 feet from her apartment building. The slightly built woman cautiously locked the groceries in the car and walked toward the Clermont to find the janitor. The janitor lived in the building's basement and often helped the tenants with small chores like carrying groceries.

Indeed, the janitor was in another part of the building performing a maintenance service for a tenant at the time Mrs. Harrington returned from Krogers. He did not get back to his subterranean quarters until about 1:25 p.m. At that time he prepared for one of his regular Thursday chores, the cleaning of a doctor's office also located in the basement. As he approached the office, he glanced down one of the basement's dimly lit side corridors and noticed that a restroom door was slightly ajar. When the janitor went to investigate the open door, he found the body of Emogene Harrington.

Mrs. Harrington was lying face up on the restroom floor, with her legs extending just outside the door. Her clothing was in disarray. A length of yellow plastic clothesline, knotted into nooses at each end, was looped around her neck. Her purse, minus the billfold and money, was lying nearby.

The janitor immediately summoned police to the scene. They sealed off the basement and searched for clues, but were quickly frustrated. Aside from the strangling chord and the discarded purse suggesting robbery as a motive, there were no useful leads to be gleaned from the dark, trash-strewn cellar.

The next information on the crime came from outside the Clermont.

First came the discovery of Mrs. Harrington's empty wallet. It was found at the corner of Elm and Findlay Streets, downtown, at 1 p.m., actually about half an hour before the body was discovered. The person finding the wallet was unable to get through when he called the Harringtons' phone number until the police finally answered at 3:00 p.m.

The second clue came when the Hamilton County Coroner reported after an autopsy that the victim had been beaten and raped before being strangled to death. The rape aspect provided an additional motive besides robbery.

Finally, and perhaps most disturbing, the police noted that the modus operandi (MO) of the slayer matched that used by the unknown assailant in a series of attacks on women in the same general area of town.

On the previous October 12 a 65-year-old woman had been beaten and raped in the basement of the Verona Apartments on Park Avenue, about four blocks away from the Clermont. In that incident the rapist had attempted to strangle his victim with a length of rope with nooses knotted on the ends, nooses identical to those in the clothesline found around Emogene Harrington's neck.

The Park Avenue woman survived the murder attempt and described her attacker as a black man between 35 and 40 years old, about 5 feet 4 inches tall, and of medium build. This description matched very generally with the assailant descriptions given in the other reported attacks.

Police questioned all known violent sex offenders. They canvassed the neighborhoods around the attack scenes and where the wallet was found. Deliverymen and taxicab drivers who may have been in the areas were questioned about anything they might have seen. Material from the crime scene in the Clermont, including the strangler's cord, was sent to be analyzed by the FBI in Washington, DC.

On the Thursday after Mrs. Harrington's murder a memorial service was held for her at the Knox Presbyterian Church. By that time the news of her murder had already disappeared from the front pages of the city's newspapers.

But the story, and the mystery, about what happened in the basement of the Clermont Apartments on December 2 was really just beginning.

Winter came and went. By April 1966 few people in Cincinnati thought much about the attacks on women in East Walnut Hills the previous fall. But that would soon change.

Frank and Lois Dant were a devoted and loving couple. At age 66 Frank Dant was a retired purchasing agent for the Cincinnati Union Terminal. He had been married to his 58-year-old wife for 29 years. Since shortly after their marriage the Dants had lived on a ground-floor apartment at 1210 Rutledge Avenue in Price Hill. There they raised a daughter, Sue Ann, who in 1966 was a member of the Sisters of Charity Convent in Albuquerque, New Mexico. Sue Ann was due to take her final vows as a nun the next year, and the Dants were excited about a visit she planned to Cincinnati, her first in six years. The Dants were active in their own church, St. William's, which was located near their home on West 8th Street. The couple was well-regarded by their neighbors.

On Monday April 4 Frank Dant went to the early mass at St. William's. Ironically, Monday mornings were virtually the only time that he left his wife home alone.

While her husband was at church that day, Mrs. Dant busied herself with chores around the apartment building. She washed a load of clothing in the basement laundry room and chatted with a neighbor there. At about 10:00 a.m. she spoke on the phone with her cousin. The two women happily discussed Sue Ann Dant's upcoming visit.

Suddenly, the conversation was interrupted when Mrs. Dant said, "There is somebody at the front door." She put the phone down, spoke briefly with the person at the door, and then returned to her phone call. She told her cousin that the person at the door had been looking for the caretaker of the building.

The Cincinnati Crime Book

The two women were back into their conversation when Mrs. Dant said, "There's the front door again. I'll talk to you later."

Lois Dant hung up the phone, but she never called her cousin back.

(This telephone conversation has an eerie parallel in the Boston Strangler case of a few years earlier. On June 30, 1962 Nina Nichols, a 68-year-old Boston widow, was on the phone with her sister discussing a dinner date the two women were planning for later that evening. Mrs. Nichols abruptly interrupted the conversation. "Excuse me Marge, there's my buzzer. I'll call you right back." She hung up the phone and opened her door to admit Albert DeSalvo, the man who later confessed to being the Boston Strangler.)

When the mass ended at St. William's, Frank Dant stayed late at the church to oversee the counting of the previous Sunday's collection money. He then took the money to the bank and deposited it. He arrived back at 1210 Rutledge at about 10:40 a.m. He parked his car in the lot behind the building and looked into the laundry room window to see if his wife was there. She wasn't, though their laundry was still hanging up, drying on the lines. He tried the rear entrance to the apartment but discovered that it was locked. He rang the buzzer and got no response. Then he walked around to the front entrance of the building, walked in, and unlocked the front door to his apartment. When he opened the door he found his wife dead on the living room floor.

Lois Dant was lying on her back. Her black and white polka dot dress was pulled up under her armpits and had been torn with such force that its buttons were scattered around the room. Her underwear had also been torn off. Her shoes lay on the floor next to her. A stocking was knotted tightly around her neck. Police later said that it was obvious that Mrs. Dant, a large and strong woman, had put up a terrific fight for her life. Her head lay in a pool of blood, evidence of the blows to her face that the assailant had to inflict in order to subdue her. It was later determined that she had been raped after her death.

The similarities between the murder of Lois Dant and the attacks on the Walnut Hills women were immediately apparent. The *Cincinnati Enquirer's* headline read "Killer Strikes Again." The *Post Times-Star* printed a chart on page one showing the like patterns in all the attacks.

All of the victims were either middle-aged or elderly white women who lived in large apartment buildings. All had been attacked during the day. All had been raped, strangled with a ligature, and left for dead. The first two victims had been robbed. Mrs. Dant had not, but police theorized that her slayer had been frightened from the scene by the return of Frank Dant before he could ransack the apartment.

Unfortunately the main similarity between all of the incidents was a lack of solid clues. The stocking around Lois Dant's neck was her own; its mate was found in the bathroom. The object used to bludgeon her into submission was not found. Neighbors could recall no strangers lurking in the area, though one woman said she heard a door slam at 10:00 a.m. Clothing and hair samples were sent to the FBI, but testing turned up nothing that could be used

The Cincinnati Crime Book

as evidence. Grilling the usual suspects bore no results. By April 10 rewards in the case from local businesses and civic organizations totaled over $800, but this produced no leads either.

The days went by and the case of Lois Dant followed that of Emogene Harrington off the front pages. But a nagging question remained. How long was Cincinnati going to be terrorized by the maniacal repeat killer? Was the city in for an extended reign of terror similar to that experienced in Boston Massachusetts a few years before?

The city's worst fears were realized just over two months later.

On June 10 a young man was walking his dog in Burnet Woods, a city park located near the University of Cincinnati in Clifton. It was just after 6 o'clock in the morning. As the man approached the steps at the bottom of the park's Chipmunk Hollow Nature Trail, he noticed a black and white dog tied to a tree there. The dog was barking. The man's own dog ran ahead of him on the trail, and when it got to the steps' first landing it went off into the woods about 25 feet to the left. When the man got to the landing he could see what attracted his pet's attention. It looked like, he would later say, "a bum sleeping in his underwear." Knowing that the police frequently patrolled near a bandstand farther along the trail, the man leashed his dog and proceeded there. He quickly found an officer, who followed the man's directions back to the "bum."

The figure lying in the overgrown bushes was not a bum, but a 56-year-old woman named Jeanette Messer. She was dead. She had been raped and strangled.

Jeanette Messer was a widow who lived alone in an apartment over a bar on nearby Jefferson Avenue. She had a son in the Navy who was stationed in Europe and a daughter who lived elsewhere in Cincinnati. It was Mrs. Messer's habit to walk her dog Judy every day as soon as she got up in the morning. Her neighbors often warned her about walking alone in Burnet Woods, but the obstinate woman wouldn't hear of abandoning her morning ritual.

On the last morning of her life Jeanette Messer left her apartment as usual and walked northwest on Jefferson Avenue into Burnet Woods. She turned left on Brooklyne Avenue, crossed it, and walked down a hill and between a picnic shelter and a set of swings to the steps of the Chipmunk Hollow Nature Trail.

Her killer caught up with her on the first landing.

The strangler was improving his technique. With an object like a 2 by 4 piece of lumber, he struck Mrs. Messer in the face with such force that the blow shattered both of her cheekbones. The assailant then dragged the semiconscious woman into the woods and finished his deadly attack.

When police arrived on the scene Mrs. Messer was nude. Her clothing had been torn off and was bundled under her body. A blue and red paisley necktie was tied tightly around her neck. Her purse lay on the ground nearby. It had

135

been rifled and the wallet was missing. Police learned the victim's name from a tag on the collar of the dog that the killer had apparently tied to the tree after the murder.

Police again applied all of their usual investigative techniques. They searched the woods around the body for clues. They were convinced that Mrs. Messer's slayer was the same man who had killed Emogene Harrington and Lois Dant. "The man is a maniac," said Crime Bureau Chief Jacob Schott. "There cannot be three of them."

Unlike the previous victims, Jeanette Messer had been slain outside. Police theorized that because of the publicity in the earlier cases women in apartment buildings had been made wary enough that the killer had to vary his MO.

Mrs. Messer's clothing and hair samples taken from her body were sent to the FBI to be analyzed The only information learned from this effort was that some of the hairs found on the body were apparently those of a black man.

Psychiatrists consulted by the police theorized that the killer chose older women to attack because he had at one time been dominated by a woman in her fifties (overlooking the more practical fact that older women are easy to subdue). They said that the strangler was a young man of considerable strength who had an active, although possibly paranoid, mind. They also said that the man probably held a responsible position but may not have been regularly employed. But despite these tentative conclusions, the doctors stressed "anything is possible."

By now the phantom-like murderer was becoming a pervasive part of Cincinnati's consciousness. He was *The* Strangler, or, as the *Cincinnati Enquirer* headlined, the "Mad Strangler." The paisley necktie was added to the ever-growing catalog of Strangler clues. Numerous theories abounded and were constantly discussed by an increasingly worried public.

Also, for the first time, the crimes made the transition from the front page to the editorial page. An editorial in the *Post Times-Star* headlined "If you know something...." implored the public to assist the police in capturing the madman. "Somewhere in this city of half a million there must be somebody who knows something... It could be that just a little bit of information would be just the information police need to find the killer and end the killings.... Any citizen who has some facts has an obligation to tell the police... Every citizen is involved – because the life of someone he knows or loves may be involved. We have no sound reason to believe that there may not be a fourth or fifth heinous killing if this strangler is not arrested......"

The city settled back into an uneasy calm.

Then, in a seemingly unrelated incident, sometime during the second week of August a taxicab was stolen from the Yellow Cab Company lot, located on Kenner Street in Cincinnati's West End neighborhood. Police would later determine that the cab had been stolen so the thief could use it to make money by picking up fares and delivering them to their destinations. It was really an ingenious scheme on the thief's part.

The Cincinnati Crime Book

The stolen cab, number 870, was a 1963 Checker model that had been left on the lot as a reserve vehicle. It had some unresolved mechanical problems. It was relatively easy for someone to steal the car off the lot since all Checker model cabs used the same ignition key and all cabs were filled up with gas and oil at the end of each shift.

Police would eventually recover the stolen Yellow Cab in the early morning hours of August 14. They would find it, disabled by a broken tie rod, abandoned on a secluded Price Hill street about ten feet away from a dying young woman.

Barbara Bowman had lived in Cincinnati for most of her life. The only child of Mr. and Mrs. John Bowman, she spent the first 25 years of her life in their home on Western Hills Avenue. She attended Western Hills High School before being graduated from Woodward. In 1962 John Bowman's company transferred him to Indianapolis. He moved there with his family, but Barbara didn't like it and returned to Cincinnati after six months.

For the last year and a half of her life she lived in a "bachelor girl" apartment in a large house at 2909 Warsaw Avenue in Price Hill. There she was remembered by her fellow tenants and her landlord as a sensible, conservative woman. But she was also remembered as a lonely person. Although she went out almost every weekend, nobody ever met any of her supposed dates. "She was a very lonesome person, I know this," her landlord later said. "She wanted affection."

Barbara Bowman was employed as a secretary at the Mehl Manufacturing Company on Reading Road. She was 31 years old when she died.

Saturday August 13 was a rainy summer night. That night Barbara Bowman shared a drink of whiskey with a downstairs neighbor before going out for an evening on the town. Two friends picked her up at about 7:00 p.m. "Have fun!" her neighbor called to her as she bounded down the steps and through the rain to her friends' waiting car. From Warsaw Avenue the trio drove to the Lark Café, located at 3001 Vine Street in Corryville. They spent the entire evening at the Lark, drinking, socializing, and occasionally dancing to the music on the juke box.

It was almost 2 o'clock in the morning when Barbara decided that she had had enough of the evening's revelry. Since her friends wanted to stay on and close the bar she called a cab for a ride home. The dispatcher at the Yellow Cab Company put out a call regarding the fare at the Lark. Shortly after that a short black man in his late twenties entered the bar and called "Cab!"

Barbara gathered up her purse and a Sunday edition of the *Cincinnati Enquirer* and went out the door with the man. She did not know that he was not a legitimate cab driver or that the cab he was driving had been stolen earlier that week. The patrons of the bar, at such a late hour, did not pay too much attention to the driver.

The Cincinnati Crime Book

It was pouring down rain as Barbara settled into the back seat of the cab for what would be her last ride. She may have ruefully contemplated the loneliness that awaited her back at her small apartment.

The cab left Clifton, crossed the Mill Creek Valley, and climbed up into Price Hill before passing through the intersection of Grand and Glenway Avenues for the final leg of the ride to 2909 Warsaw. After that intersection the street was dark, mostly wooded, and devoid of residences. Barbara Bowman was only a few hundred feet from her home when her deadly nightmare began.

Suddenly the cab stopped and the driver was over the seat and on top of her. He produced a rope and wrapped it around her neck, breaking the necklace of cheap beads she wore. The tightening noose cut and burned into her neck. But Barbara was a strong woman and managed to break free from her attacker. She jumped out of the cab and into the wet night. She began running up Ring Place, a side street. The attacker put the car in gear and followed her up the street, striking and running over her a few yards later.

Then, as Barbara Bowman lay in the street, unable to move because of a broken right ankle, her assailant jumped out of the car and plunged a paring knife into her throat six times. He then quickly rifled her purse and, since the cab had been permanently disabled by all of this activity, fled on foot into the rainy darkness of Ring Place.

Just a few minutes later, at about 2:30 a.m., another driver happened by the scene. Thinking that the woman lying in the street had been hit by a car, he called the police. They soon arrived at the location.

The police found Barbara Bowman lying on top of a manhole cover, clutching a five dollar bill in her hand. She was immediately rushed to St. Mary Hospital, but she died shortly after her arrival there without ever regaining consciousness.

Because of the downpour at the crime scene, police had little luck coming up with any useful physical evidence. Any fingerprints on the abandoned and open cab had probably been washed away by the driving rain. The victim's shoes and earrings, as well as her empty purse, were nearby. The only other real piece of evidence found in the vicinity was the rope used to choke Barbara. It was found a couple of blocks away, at the corner of Ring Place and Underwood Street. The rope had some beads from Barbara's necklace imbedded in its fibers. The rope's location indicated the general direction that the killer had headed when fleeing the scene of his crime.

Soon after the murder police at the scene stopped a passing taxicab and had its driver call his dispatcher to find out who was scheduled to drive the abandoned Yellow Cab number 870. As a result of the ensuing radio traffic other cab drivers quickly became aware of the situation. One driver came to the authorities to report an incident that had occurred shortly after the killing. The driver, who worked for the Parkway Cab Company, told police that at about 3:15 a.m. he had been hailed by a black male at the corner of (ironically)

Bowman and Mistletoe Streets, about a mile from the scene of the murder. The man was drenched, and he appeared agitated and out of breath. He requested to be taken to Brighton Corner, downtown, and as the cab headed east over the Western Hills Viaduct he handed the driver two rain-soaked dollar bills. As the cab slowed down near Baymiller and Bank Streets, the man jumped out of the car and ran down an alley. The Parkway Cab driver gave police a description of his passenger, and said that he was sure he would recognize the man if he saw him again.

But this description, along with a vague one given by some of the patrons of the Lark Café, was not the only clue to be gleaned from this latest slaying. It was apparent that whoever the killer was had extensive knowledge of cab driving operations. He knew how to operate the cab's meter, and indeed the meter indicated that the murderer had driven eleven fares before picking up the hapless Miss Bowman. The killer had even used the cab's radio to tell the dispatcher that he could accept fares, using the phony cab number 186. The cab had been driven 63 miles since it was last officially used by the Yellow Cab company.

Edith Bowman, Barbara's mother, told police that Barbara had been saving money for an upcoming vacation and that she kept that money in her purse. Since the purse was found empty at the murder scene and there was no obvious evidence of any sexual assault, police decided that robbery was the killer's primary motive.

Because of the killer's familiarity with cab operations, police began the laborious task of questioning hundreds of present and former cab drivers licensed by the city. Most drivers cooperated enthusiastically, angered that their profession had been sullied by a murderer posing as one of them.

Police artists produced a composite sketch of the suspect from descriptions given by the Parkway Cab driver and patrons of the Lark Café. Both drawings showed a young black male and were amazingly similar except that the description given by the cab driver included a jacket and duncil cap not seen by the bar customers. The drawings were widely circulated and were published in both city newspapers, but no one came forward to say that they recognized the man.

Whether there was a connection between Barbara Bowman's death and the three previous rape-strangulations was not immediately clear. There were reports that a cab had been sighted in Burnet Woods the night Bowman was attacked, cruising the area near where Jeanette Messer had been found on June 19. Burnet Woods was not far from the Lark Café. The bizarre method of killing and the lack of any apparent sexual assault indicated that this killer might be a different person. But that may have just been wishful thinking on the part of some who would rather have believed that Cincinnati had already seen the last of its Mad Strangler. Any such delusion, however, would not last very long.

The Cincinnati Crime Book

Like something out of a bad TV script, the Strangler struck next on precisely the first anniversary of the rape and attempted murder in the basement of the Verona Apartments on Park Avenue.

Alice Hochhausler lived in a house in Clifton on the corner of Cornell and Evanswood Places. She was the wife of Dr. Carl Hochhausler, a surgeon at nearby Good Samaritan Hospital. Mrs. Hochhausler was 51 years old. The Hochhauslers had nine children ranging in age from nine to twenty-four. Their oldest daughter, Beth, was a nurse who also worked at Good Samaritan Hospital, doing a shift there one night a week. Beth lived away from home, though not far away, in an apartment on Ludlow Avenue across the street from where Cornell Place intersected it.

As midnight approached on October 11, 1966 things were winding down inside the Hochhausler home. All of the children were already in bed. Mrs. Hochhausler had attended a PTA meeting at the Annunciation Church at Clifton and Resor Avenues and returned home at about 10:30 p.m. As Dr. Hochhausler drowsily watched television, his wife changed into a nightgown and bathrobe and prepared for one last chore for the day. It would prove to be the last chore of her life.

Because a couple of months earlier Barbara Bowman had been killed by a homicidal cab driver, Alice Hochhausler was wary of daughter Beth taking cabs home when she got off her evening shift at Good Sam. So occasionally the protective mother would drive to the hospital herself to make sure that the young woman got home safely.

At about 10:45 p.m. Mrs. Hochhausler went out into the driveway behind her house, climbed into one of the family's two station wagons, and made the eight block drive to Good Samaritan Hospital. Picking up her daughter as planned, she drove immediately back to the Ludlow Avenue apartment building. As they approached the building the two women noticed a man in a car behind them. They got the impression that the man was following them. As Mrs. Hochhausler pulled over at the curb to let her daughter out the other car pulled over behind them. "I wonder what he wants," the mother said. "I wonder if he's going to pull around me?"

Beth got out of the car, crossed the street to her building, and safely let herself inside. As she looked back at the street she noticed that the second car had pulled around her mother and turned right onto Cornell Place. Somewhat relieved, she then watched her mother also turn right onto Cornell Place for the final short drive to her own home.

Alice Hochhausler pulled into her driveway and parked the station wagon near the family's separate garage. The family dog, sometimes left overnight in the garage, was instead locked in the basement of the house that night. Inside the house the weary Dr. Hochhausler had already gone upstairs to bed. Outside the sounds of a party a few doors away could be heard through the dark, gaslit night. Alice Hochhausler never got to her house.

The Cincinnati Crime Book

The next morning Carl Hochhausler roused himself at about 7 o'clock. He was surprised not to find his wife in bed. He looked in the basement to see if she might be doing laundry, but found no sign of her. Noting that all the family cars were in the driveway, he went out to the garage to have a look around. There, in a corner among the tools, bicycles, and other garage debris, he found his wife's body. Her nightgown, bathrobe, and topcoat were in disarray. The belt from the bathrobe was tied around her neck. Dr. Hochhausler hurried back into the house and called the police.

The Homicide Squad arrived on the scene and cordoned off the area. It didn't take long for them to reconstruct what had happened. Mrs. Hochhausler had been struck hard on the head from behind. The force of the blow had knocked out her false teeth, which lay in the driveway. Her set of keys had flown out of her hand and landed in a nearby hedge. The killer had then dragged her back into to garage, probably by the ankles. She was raped in the garage. When the assailant was finished with the rape he used the bathrobe belt to strangle his victim to death.

Police questioned Beth Hochhausler extensively about her last moments with her attentive mother. The daughter described the car that seemed to be following them as a cream and bronze colored 1959 Chevrolet Bel-Air. The person driving the car, Beth said, was a black man. Police revealed that a similar car had been reported cruising in the vicinities of the Dant and Messer homicides when they occurred. (Police eventually checked out over 5000 cars similar to the model described.)

Another witness came forward and said she saw a black man walking erratically on Ludlow Avenue at 12:20 a.m. on the night of the murder. Later police would state that hairs found on the deceased's body were definitely those of a black person. In addition, they were able to determine the blood type of the killer. That blood type apparently matched that of the person who killed Emogene Harrington ten months earlier.

The news of Alice Hochhausler's murder sent the city into headlong panic. It didn't help matters that the Gerald Bricca family had been slaughtered in their Bridgetown home just a few weeks earlier.

Convinced that relatives or friends were covering up for the Strangler, acting Police Chief Guy York attempted to get these people to come forward. "I wish there was some way to appeal to these individuals to make them realize the harm they are doing in not reporting (the Strangler) to police," he said. "I'm sure someone knows."

In an open letter "To the Citizens of Cincinnati" City Manager William C. Wichman sought to comfort the fearful public: "We wish to take this means of assuring all citizens of our city that your administrators are aware of the apprehension gripping our community. We want you to know that every resource at our disposal is being brought to bear on our crime problems to assure an early solution...."

The Cincinnati Crime Book

The city set up a Strangler Line called "Station X," displaying the phone number prominently on both city newspapers' front pages. Station X's 22 phones were manned full time by six police officers. More than 800 calls came during the first eight hours that the line was set up. Fourteen prowl cars manned by officers working double shifts were added to those already on the streets. All twelve members of the Police Department's Vice Squad were transferred to Homicide for the duration of the emergency. $100,000 in additional city funds were allocated to the police to assist in the manhunt.

Other groups also contributed to the search. Mail carriers, gas and water meter readers, and even garbage collectors were enlisted for help in locating the suspect's vehicle. The Kroger grocery company announced that it would acquire and give out 100,000 police whistles to those women who requested them. An Evanston karate school offered free classes in self-defense. Deliverymen for laundries and other businesses worked out series of passwords for drivers to use to convince terrified women to open their doors. Pet stores and the Pound were unable to keep enough watchdogs in stock. Demand for teargas pens, locks and bolts, and guns soared at an unprecedented rate. Rewards for the Strangler from businesses and civic organizations now totaled over $10,000.

In another example of how the stranglings affected the community it was urged that the year's Halloween holiday either be restricted to daylight hours or be banned altogether. Some people also wanted to ban Halloween masks. One parents group in Colerain Township planned to have an afternoon parade instead of evening trick or treating. One of the organizing mothers admitted that the parade would "be a little more work, but maybe there will be a little less strangling, too."

The city's paranoia heightened. The Station X lines were kept busy with people reporting anyone they knew who owned a 1959 Chevrolet Bel-Air or wore paisley neckties. City officials called in leaders from the black and white communities to ask their cooperation in capturing the killer. A desperate and ugly mood of vigilantism was beginning to develop. A handwritten sign on a telephone pole in Mount Healthy warned, "Beware! Prepare to account for your presence in this area!"

The story was becoming more than just a local concern. It received coverage in both *Time* and *Newsweek* magazines. Cincinnati's image as a serene place to live was being cruelly demolished. Something had to happen, and it had to happen fast.

Unfortunately, when something did happen it was entirely the wrong thing.

Like everyone else in Cincinnati 81-year-old Rose Winstel knew that a maniac was on the loose raping and strangling the city's women. "She was definitely aware of the other stranglings and quite concerned. So was I," her nephew later said. "'Rose', I told her, ' be sure to use the double locks on your door....'"

The Cincinnati Crime Book

Rose Winstel was a native of the Queen City. She spent most of her early years in Price Hill but lived the last 14 years of her life in a house at 2289 Vine Street, a few blocks south of McMillan Street. She had never married.

Rose Winstel was a very religious person and had moved to the Vine street house to be near her church, St. George's in nearby Corryville. Originally the aged woman shared the house with two relatives, but her bachelor brother died on June 30, 1966, and a sister-in-law, who had lived on the second floor of the small, imitation brick house, had been in a hospital since April of that same year.

By the mid-1960s the neighborhood had witnessed better days. The racially mixed conglomeration of homes, groceries, and cafes had seen its share of violence and crime. Reports of prowlers were common, and the local bars often exploded into violence. In October 1966 a man was shot to death on the sidewalk in front of the Peyton Place Café, located directly across the street from Rose Winstel's home. Over the years Miss Winstel herself had called the police several times regarding prowlers.

At 81 years of age the elderly spinster was pretty much housebound due to failing health. She had cataracts which allowed her to see only three or four feet in front of her. Nevertheless she could get around well inside the house, even though she only used the first floor. When she did go out, about once a month to the bank or a beauty parlor, she used a taxi. In recent years the priest from St. George's had come to the home to administer to her religious needs. Concerned relatives tried to make arrangements for her to enter a nursing home, but the headstrong woman refused. "She didn't want to be crowded in with other women," a relative said.

On Tuesday October 18 at about 6:00 p.m. neighbors of Miss Winstel watched the old woman carry her garbage can down to the curb and then go back into the house. She was never seen alive again.

Throughout the next few days concerned relatives phoned the house on Vine Street but got no answer. Finally, early in the evening of October 20 Miss Winstel's nephew called police. They agreed to meet him at the house.

Everyone arrived there at about 7:30 and entered the kitchen through a door on the south side. Ominously, the chain lock had been ripped out of the door frame. While the distraught nephew waited in the kitchen the two policemen began to search the house. They didn't have to search long.

Rose Winstel was lying on the floor of her downstairs bedroom, partly under the bed. Her clothing below the waist was in disarray. She had been savagely beaten around the face and head. The chord of an electric heating pad was drawn tightly around her neck. Because the bedclothes were also disheveled , police theorized that Miss Winstel had been asleep when the deadly assault began. An autopsy later determined that she had been dead for 15 to 24 hours and verified that the 81-year-old churchgoer had been raped. Nothing had been taken from the home.

The Cincinnati Crime Book

"She was a lovely old woman.... as kind a woman as ever lived," the nephew tearfully recalled. "The murderer just has to be a maniac. It's a completely senseless crime."

As word of the fifth strangling spread throughout the city curious onlookers flocked to the latest murder scene. Soon a crowd estimated at 1000 persons clogged Vine Street, hindering police, buses, and other traffic. The neighbors, used to family arguments and barroom brawls, stood around shaking their heads in shock.

"I'm moving out," one woman said.

"Out of the neighborhood?" a companion asked.

"Honey, I'm going to leave this town!"

Coming just over a week after the murder of Alice Hochhausler, the strangling of Rose Winstel forced the Cincinnati City Council into an emergency session to approve special measures to deal with the ever-escalating crisis. Retired police, firemen, and even ex-servicemen were requested to register at their local police stations in case they would be needed for the manhunt. Uniformed policemen had their shifts increased from eight to twelve hours. Some city firemen were transferred to the police department and cruised neighborhoods in radio-equipped cars.

Although one City Council member proposed that citizens patrol their own streets, the City Manager quickly vetoed that idea. He also begged citizens not to arm themselves and tried to discourage any trend towards vigilantism. One local pawnshop advertised "as a public service" tear gas pens and pistols along with the admonition "Protect yourself." The ad included the phone number of Station X.

If the public was teetering on the edge of mob justice the reaction was understandable. Not only was the latest murder too fast on the heels of the one which preceded it, but for the first time it appeared that robbery was not a motive. Worse, for the first time the killer had actually forced his way into a residence, ripping two locks out of a door frame in the process.

Five women, maybe six, had been slain by the same man over a period of eleven months. One more had been assaulted and left for dead and had never fully recovered. The police had some clues to go on, blood types, hair samples, ligatures, vague descriptions of suspects and vehicles, but despite the largest manhunt in the city's history they had no solid leads and no real suspects. Unless someone stepped forward and confessed, or turned a viable suspect in, all the authorities could do was wait for the next attack and hope that when it happened the killer would finally make the mistake that would lead to his capture.

Another month and a half passed.

At 12:30 a.m. on Friday December 9, Mrs. Sandra Chapas clocked out after working the swing shift at the Kenner Products factory at 9th and Sycamore Streets in downtown Cincinnati. Mrs. Chapas was only 22 years old, but like every other woman in town she was wary of the Mad Strangler. So, as she stepped out onto the sidewalk to begin the walk to her home, located on Court Street near Vine, she noticed a man sitting in a car in a nearby parking lot.

The man was black, and his car was cream and tan.

A few minutes later, as Mrs. Chapas walked west on Court Street, she turned around and was alarmed to see the man following her. "I kept turning and looking at him and he turned off. I guess he realized I was looking at him," she later said. The frightened young woman entered her apartment building at 14 West Court Street and hurried up to her third-floor unit. "When I got home, as I was walking up the stairs I heard someone coming up behind me on the steps." She quickly entered her apartment and locked the door behind her.

Fortunately for Mrs. Chapas, and possibly for the entire city, a downstairs neighbor was also returning from his second-shift job at the same time. The neighbor's wife, waiting up for him, had heard Sandra Chapas' hurried footsteps and glanced out of her doorway in time to see the frustrated pursuer quickly exit the building. As the stranger left, he passed the husband in the building's hallway. Alerted by the man's strange behavior, the husband followed him out onto the street and watched him get into a car. The husband wrote down the car's license number and called the police.

When the police ran a check on the license number it came back registered to Posteal Laskey, a 28-year-old laborer who, according to the registration, lived at 1820 Freeman Avenue. Further checking revealed that Laskey had a record of assaults on women, and had even been among the hundreds of suspects already questioned in the year-long Strangler probe. It seemed that the police might finally have gotten the break they needed. They quickly descended on the Freeman Avenue address to pick the suspect up.

Laskey was not there, and no one at the house could say where he was. Police learned that Laskey was employed by the Adam Wuest Mattress Company, at 911 Evans Street in the West End, so they made plans to arrest him there when he showed up for work.

Police did not know that Laskey had recently moved from Freeman Avenue to an apartment building at 2201 Reading road. Had they known this fact they might have been able to apprehend him earlier than they eventually did. And they might have prevented yet another woman from dying a terrible death.

Miss Lula Kerrick, at 81 years of age, was frail and often ill. Even so, her advanced years did not keep the devoutly religious woman from attending the early mass every day at downtown's St. Peter in Chains Cathedral. She had lived for years in downtown's Over-the-Rhine area until one day, while returning home from mass, she was mugged in her apartment building hallway. That incident convinced her to move closer to her church and in December of 1966 she lived in a fourth floor unit at the Brittany Apartments at 9th and Race Streets. Still, her family was concerned about her welfare, and in a few weeks she was scheduled to move into the home of relatives in Price Hill.

The Cincinnati Crime Book

On Friday December 9 Miss Kerrick left her apartment and walked west on 9th Street to St. Peter in Chains, where the early mass began at 6:30 a.m. It was warm and slightly raining on that late fall day. After receiving communion she stayed on after the service to offer some additional personal prayers before leaving for the slow walk back to her apartment. It was now 7:30 a.m., just seven hours after the incident in Sandra Chapas' apartment building two short city blocks away from the Brittany.

At 8:20 another tenant of the Brittany rang for the elevator to go down to the lobby to get his mail. When the elevator door opened, the man saw Lula Kerrick lying on the floor. A stocking was knotted around her neck. The man ran back to his apartment and frantically dialed Station X. In the meantime, another resident of the building also rang for the elevator and was confronted with the same macabre sight. That person called police as well, and officers quickly converged on the scene.

Lula Kerrick lay slumped on her side. Her hat was pulled over her eyes. Her glasses were still in place, but her false teeth were out of her mouth and on the elevator floor. One of her shoes had fallen into the elevator shaft when the killer removed her stocking to strangle her to death with it. Her clothing was disturbed, but the Coroner later determined that she had not been raped.

At around 9:00 a.m. that same day Posteal Laskey was taken into custody at the Adam Wuest Company. He was charged with assault stemming from the incident with Sandra Chapas. The next day he appeared in Criminal Court and, after being identified by witnesses as the man who followed Mrs. Chapas into her building, was sentenced to six months in the Workhouse and given a $200 fine. He was remanded into custody at once and denied bond because he was already on three years probation for the beating of a girl on October 9, 1965. Also, he had previously served time in the Kentucky Reformatory in La Grange, from February 1964 to August 1965, for snatching a purse from a Covington woman.

Homicide detectives began trying to link Laskey with the stranglings of the women the previous year. He quickly became a prime suspect in the death of Barbara Bowman when it was learned that he had been employed at the Yellow Cab Company for six months in 1962. While driving for Yellow he had been assigned cab number 186, the same number used in radio transmissions by the phantom cab driver who killed Miss Bowman.

Laskey was put into a lineup where six persons who were present in the Lark Café that fatal night said he resembled the "cab driver" Barbara Bowman left with. More importantly, the Parkway Cab driver who gave a lift to the rain-soaked man shortly after the Bowman murder positively identified Laskey as his passenger. Additionally, Laskey was identified as her assailant by a woman who had been robbed of $28 on September 21, 1966 at her office in the New Thought Unity Center on East McMillan Street, directly across the street from the Clermont Apartments where Emogene Harrington had been murdered ten months earlier.

146

While Laskey waited in the Workhouse police continued to consolidate their evidence against him. One week after his arrest they presented that evidence to a grand jury which returned indictments against him for the murder of Barbara Bowman, the robbery at the New Thought Unity Center, and for assault and robbery in connection with the theft of $130 from a 69-year-old Walnut Hills housewife in the hallway of her home on October 4, 1966.

Posteal Laskey's trial began on March 27, 1967 and lasted three weeks. The first week was spent selecting a jury of six men and six women who were acceptable to both the prosecution and the defense.

In his opening statement, Prosecutor Melvin Rueger said he would show that Laskey murdered Barbara Bowman in the course of committing a robbery. Rueger asked for the death penalty.

Laskey's lawyers said that they would prove that the defendant was home in bed asleep when the murder occurred.

The prosecution then presented its case, first calling the woman who had discovered Barbara Bowman lying in the street at Ring Place. Policemen who first arrived on the scene of the crime followed the female witness and testified to what they found. Rueger also produced two patrons of the Lark Café who positively identified Laskey as the man who entered the bar, shouted "Cab!' and left with Miss Bowman.

Then, three days into its case, the state produced a surprise witness, a woman who had stopped at Ring Place and Grand Avenue at about 2:30 a.m. on the murder night to ask directions of the driver of cab number 870. "I asked directions....and a man raised up in the back seat but didn't answer. Then I noticed something else move in the back seat. I noticed it was a lady." The witness positively identified Laskey as the man in the cab.

This woman was followed on the stand by the driver of the Parkway Cab who picked up the rain-drenched man that night. He positively identified Laskey as his fare.

The next day three employees of the Yellow Cab Company were called to testify. The first two were dispatchers who said that they sent cab number 186 to pick up a passenger at the Lark Café on August 14, 1966. 186 was Laskey's old cab number. The third employee positively identified Laskey as a man he saw loitering on the company's Kenner Street lot on the day before the murder.

The state rested its case.

After a weekend recess the defense began its phase of the trial.

Laskey's lawyers quickly produced six witnesses, all friends and relatives of the defendant, who testified that Laskey was at the Freeman Avenue residence all evening on the murder night except for several hours when he went to the Soul Lounge on Madison Road in Madisonville. A patron of the Soul Lounge testified that he saw Laskey there that night. Laskey's mother testified that she saw her son at 5:00 a.m. on April 15 and that his clothing was not wet, mud-splattered, or bloody. All defense witnesses testified that Laskey always wore a mustache and goatee, a point never mentioned in any of the descriptions given by prosecution witnesses.

On April 11 Laskey took the stand in his own defense. He testified that he had been home in bed when Barbara Bowman was slain. He said that earlier that evening he had gone to the Soul Lounge because he thought his band, The Outlaws, was scheduled to play there that night. Discovering that he had the schedule mixed up and that his band would not be playing, he stayed for a few beers before returning home. He said he arrived home at 1:30 a.m., watched television for about an hour, and then went to bed. He denied ever meeting Barbara Bowman or going to the Lark Café. He claimed that he was the victim of mistaken identity. After 25 minutes on the stand he was excused, and the defense rested its case.

The jury got the case just after noon on April 12. During the afternoon they asked that the testimony of two of Laskey's alibi witnesses be read back. They took a break overnight and resumed deliberations the next morning. At 11:00 a.m. they asked to have the judge's instructions reread. At 12:10 they announced that they had reached a verdict: guilty on all counts, with no recommendation for mercy, meaning that Laskey would automatically be sentenced to death.

As the verdict was read the defendant's mother rose from the row of spectators and began to scream. "Oh my God," she cried hysterically, "Why did they do it?"

Posteal Laskey was never tried for any of the six slayings attributed to the Cincinnati Strangler. Police still consider him the prime suspect, though, and there is much circumstantial evidence that links him to some of the crimes. The Strangler-type murders ceased after he was apprehended. Nevertheless, there are many people in Cincinnati who believe to this day that he was just a convenient scapegoat sacrificed to take the heat off a beleaguered city government. Indeed, the "injustice" of Laskey's conviction has been cited as one of the causes of the race riots that occurred in Cincinnati the summer after his trial.

Laskey was sentenced to death, but appeals delayed the execution and finally, when the United State Supreme court ruled Ohio's death penalty law unconstitutional, his sentence was commuted to life in prison. Eligible for parole since 1980, he has been turned down every time he has appeared before the parole board. His last denial was in February 1997.

In 1982 Barbara Bowman's mother, then 80, bitterly ruminated on Posteal Laskey's parole eligibility. "I don't think he should ever be paroled. I think he should have been executed. My daughter was executed. She was sentenced to death. I think he should be in jail as long as he lives."

John Bowman died in 1971 and was buried next to his daughter in the family plot in Indiana. "He never got over Barbara's murder," Edith Bowman said. "Barbara was all we had."

A man believed to be the Cincinnati Strangler attacked an elderly woman in the basement of this apartment building on Park Avenue. The victim survived.

Emogene Harrington was slain in the
basement of the Clermont Apartments.

Lois and Frank Dant lived in this Price Hill apartment building.

**The trail in Burnett Woods where
Jeanette Messer was strangled to death.**

Barbara Bowman. (Author's collection)

The site of the Lark Café, 1989.

Barbara Bowman was murdered at this intersection in Price Hill.

Alice Hochhausler was murdered in this Clifton garage.

The first-floor hallway of the Brittany Apartments.

Posteal Laskey. (Author's collection)

The Soul Lounge, 1997.

The Bricca Family Murders

In September of 1966 Cincinnati was a city besieged. The Strangler hysteria hadn't hit its peak, but it was getting there. Everyone was aware of the mysterious killer on the loose and citizens tried to be alert and aware. People watched over their own families with extra care and neighbors kept tabs on their neighbors. Anything out of the ordinary was regarded with suspicion and concern.

On Greenway Avenue, a quiet residential street in the western Cincinnati neighborhood of Bridgetown, the neighbors were getting very concerned.

It was Tuesday, September 27. The concern on Greenway Avenue was due to the fact that no one had seen the residents of number 3381 since the previous Sunday. The cars had not been moved in the driveway, garbage cans had not been taken in from Monday, and the newspapers were beginning to pile up. Lights inside and outside the house were never extinguished. Pet rabbits had been left in an outside pen during a rainstorm. The neighbors phoned the house, but got no answer.

3381 Greenway Avenue was the home of Gerald Bricca and his young family. Jerry Bricca was a 26-year-old Project Engineer with the Monsanto Chemical Company. His beautiful wife Linda, 23, was a former airline stewardess. The couple had a daughter Deborah, aged 4.

Jerry Bricca was born into a prominent family in San Francisco. In San Francisco he attended St. Ignatius High School, and then went on to Stanford University. A short, muscular man, Bricca was a good athlete and had accumulated a good number of swimming trophies while in school. He left Stanford with a graduate degree as a chemical engineer and joined the Monsanto Company. They sent him to work at their facility at Seattle, Washington.

Linda Bricca was born Linda Bulaw in the fashionable western Chicago suburb of Barrington, Illinois. A fast learner, she graduated from Barrington High School two years ahead of schedule and, by attending summer school, completed three years of academic work in two years at Evanston's National College of Education. In 1959 she lied about her age by adding two years,

156

entered the United Airlines School for stewardesses at Cheyenne, Wyoming, and became a stewardess at age 18. Her first assignment for United took her to Seattle, Washington where she met the up and coming Jerry Bricca. After a brief courtship the attractive young couple was married. Linda gave birth to daughter Deborah in 1962.

In 1963 Jerry Bricca was a rising star at Monsanto, and the company transferred him from Seattle to their installation at Addyston, Ohio. There, as Project Engineer, he oversaw in-plant operations. To accommodate his family he purchased a ten-year-old house at 3381 Greenway Avenue in nearby Bridgetown.

The Briccas fit right in with the suburban lifestyle of Greenway Avenue. They were friendly and popular and attended many neighborhood activities like parties and barbecues. Because they were the youngest family on the block they were known as "the kids." Jerry was regarded as a hard worker who was dedicated to his job. Linda was well-known for her love of animals. (The family had two mongrel dogs, Thumper and Dusty, as well as rabbits in a hutch in the back yard.) Linda once told a neighbor that as a child she had briefly joined a circus just to be able to feed the animals. In the summer of 1966 she started working part-time as a receptionist for a veterinarian in Western Hills. Daughter Debbie was a favorite in the neighborhood. She was later recalled as "a beautiful child," well-behaved, "who talked like an adult." Sometimes, for childish reasons, she would asked to be called "Carole."

The Briccas' home was as well-maintained as any on the street. It was a brick and wood tri-level house with a playroom and garage on the first level, a kitchen, living room, and dining room on the second, and three bedrooms and a bath on the third. A cement walkway led from the sidewalk to a stone front porch. The backyard had a patio and a brand new swing set and slide that Deborah loved to play on. The backyard was enclosed by a four foot cyclone fence. It was only about fifteen feet to the neighbors on either side.

Thus, for all outward appearances the Briccas were the archetypal American family of the 1960s – young, energetic, and bright. The Briccas had it all, and they had nowhere to go but up. And nothing indicated that anything was wrong with this picture. Nothing, that is, until the newspapers started piling up in late September 1966.

September 25, 1966 was a Sunday, but Jerry Bricca went to work anyway. He was a hard, perhaps overzealous, worker who frequently worked at night and on weekends and holidays. Often he was only home for a few hours at a time for weeks. The day before, Saturday, he went to the Monsanto plant in the morning and worked straight through the night. On Sunday Bricca, a devout Catholic, went to the 10:00 a.m. mass at St. Aloysius Church in nearby Bridgetown. He then stopped at 3381 Greenway where a neighbor chatted with him briefly. After a quick stop at his house he returned to his duties at Monsanto, working there the rest of the day. Finally in the early evening he checked out of work, climbed into his gray Volkswagen, and headed for home.

The Cincinnati Crime Book

He stopped at a dairy on Glenway Avenue and purchased three half-gallons of milk for his family. He continued on to Greenway Avenue and parked on the street in front of his home between 8:30 and 9:00 p.m. Garbage collection was the next day so he walked into his garage and carried the full cans down to the sidewalk. A neighbor walking her dog exchanged greetings with the tired young man, who then trudged up the walk to the front door and went inside. The neighbor woman was the last to see any of the Briccas alive.

Late summer rainstorms had passed through the Cincinnati area that day dumping almost half an inch of water on the region. Because of the rain more people were not outside on that cool, dark night. Another thing keeping people inside was the well-publicized television premiere of the Academy Award winning film *The Bridge on the River Kwai*, being broadcast as a "three hour plus movie spectacular" on local ABC affiliate Channel 12. The film attracted 72 percent of the people watching television that night. With a good movie to watch on a rainy evening, no one on Greenway Avenue noticed whether anything unusual was going on at number 3381.

At 6:30 the following morning Monsanto officials phoned the Bricca residence to find out why their dutiful plant manager had not shown up for work. They got no answer. Later that day a helpful neighbor tossed the Briccas' newspaper from the sidewalk to the front porch. The paper was never taken in.

By late evening of the next day the neighbors were becoming gravely concerned. Besides the obvious and unusual lack of activity at the house, all phone calls went unanswered. The two dogs could be heard inside, barking wildly. At just after 10:30 p.m. the neighbor men from next door and across the street met on the front porch of the Bricca home. Trying the front door, they found it unlocked. This was not an unusual circumstance for the neighborhood before that night. The men pushed the door open and shined a flashlight into the darkness.

Because of the layout of the house it was possible to see into the master bedroom from the front door. Shining the light up that way, the men could see a woman's leg. Then, the smell. "I knew what it was as soon as I opened the front door," one of the men later said. "Nothing smells like that. I remember it from World War Two."

The men quickly closed the front door and went to call the police.

Officers arrived soon and entered the residence. They found the Briccas dead in the upstairs bedrooms.

The parents were lying on the floor of the master bedroom between the bed and a wall. Jerry was wearing a dark brown, long-sleeved sport shirt and black trousers, but no shoes. He was lying face down. He had been stabbed four times in the back, three times in the neck, and twice in the head. Linda was lying face up, slightly on top of her husband. She wore a negligee and a housecoat. Her clothing was in disarray. She had been stabbed six times in the chest and side, twice in the neck, and twice in the head. There was a considerable amount of blood on the floor and on the wrinkled bed.

Debbie Bricca was found on the floor of her bedroom. She wore a terry cloth robe, panties, and one sock. She had been stabbed four times in the back. On three of the strokes the blade had passed completely through her body.

The Briccas' two dogs were found confined in the ground level playroom. The television set there was still on, its volume turned up loud enough to be heard throughout the whole house. The set was tuned the Channel 12, the channel that had aired *The Bridge on the River Kwai.*

The neighbors who called police were taken into the house to identify the bodies. When they came out, their faces mirrored disbelief and shock at what they had seen. "My God, what they did to that baby," one said.

More police arrived on the scene. They strung a crime scene rope around the house, both to secure possible evidence and to keep away the growing crowd of onlookers.

In the master bedroom police found Jerry Bricca's billfold, with no money in it, lying on the bed. All of the drawers in the house had been pulled open, but their contents did not appear to have been disturbed. There was wet laundry in the washer and dryer, and some towels had been folded and left on the playroom couch. Jerry's missing shoes were found in the playroom. Both front and rear doors of the house had been closed but were not locked. A carving knife was missing from a set in the dining room. The absent knife had a carved teakwood handle and a 6 ½ inch blade with "Rajba Bros., India" engraved on it. There was some indication that Jerry and Linda had been bound and gagged with adhesive tape but that the tape had been removed sometime before the killer left the house.

The murder of the Bricca family immediately dominated both of the city's newspapers. In 1966 the murder of a family was still very big news.

"FAMILY OF THREE KNIFED TO DEATH; RAPE IS SUSPECTED" was the headline in the next day's *Cincinnati Enquirer.* The city was in the middle of the Strangler case and was rape conscious. Rape was suspected due to the fact the Linda Bricca's negligee was in some disorder, though police said that the dishevelment could have been caused when she rolled off the bed onto the floor. But the coroner would not say that Linda Bricca was raped. All he could confirm was that she had engaged in "recent sexual intercourse."

But it seemed unlikely that a homicidal sexual deviate would be out prowling the close-knit residential neighborhood on such a dreary, rainy night. Rape was soon discounted as the motive.

The murderous burglar theory also seemed less and less plausible as the investigation continued. For one thing, the ransacking of the house seemed to have been done as a diversion. Nothing of value (other than possibly the contents of Jerry Bricca's wallet) was missing. There were no signs of a struggle. The neighbors noted that the dogs usually had the run of the house and that they were known to be violently aggressive towards strangers. Who had locked them in the ground floor playroom, and why?

In such a horrific case as this people would much prefer to think that the act was committed by a mentally unhinged stranger than by anyone known to the victims. An editorial in the *Enquirer* three days after the discovery of the bodies compared the crime to the senseless killings committed by strangers depicted in Truman Capote's *In Cold Blood*. (Capote's book about the mass murder of a Kansas farm family was published that year and remained on bestseller lists for many months. Coincidentally, the *Enquirer* had begun printing a serialization of the book on the Sunday a week before the Sunday the Briccas were slain.)

But police know that the large majority of homicides are committed by people known to the victims, either family or friends. That the victims could have been killed by someone known to them only added a new dimension to the shock of their deaths.

The character of Greenway Avenue changed literally overnight. Doors that had never been kept locked were now doubly secured. Children who before had the run of the street were now never out of their parents' sight. As word of the crime spread, crowds of morbid sightseers began to clog the narrow street. Young mothers drove by with their children to show them the infamous death house where another young mother and her child had been killed. There was so much extra traffic that some of the cars almost ran into each other.

But by far the worst impact on the street was the nagging possibility that the killer was someone the residents knew, or was maybe even one of them. "You just can't feel secure anymore," one woman said. "Even when your husband is home you still have doubt. Jerry was home when his family was killed and he was young and strong. It gives you the creeps."

The Monsanto Company donated $5000 to the Hamilton County Sheriff's Department to be used to aid the investigation. The Hamilton County Board of Commissioners offered a $5000 reward for the killer. WCPO-TV and a Mount Healthy dentist each contributed another $1000.

The investigation continued. Officers checked the surrounding sewer system for the murder weapon, without success. (It was never found.) They checked out known burglars, sex offenders and people prone to violent behavior, but got no useful leads.

About thirty items, including bed sheets, fingerprints, hair samples, and bloody towels were sent to be analyzed by the FBI in Washington DC. When the FBI report came back, police disclosed that fingerprints not belonging to any of the victims were found in the master bedroom "on items that would not be touched by the ordinary visitor." Cops were mum about the rest of the report.

Investigators probed links between the crime and similar murders around the country, including the murder of the daughter of Illinois Senator Charles

Percy and the stabbing death of a 12-year-old girl in Nitro, West Virginia. A 22-year-old employee at the Monsanto plant in Nitro was the lead suspect in that case.

In addition to looking for suspects who were unknown to the Briccas police questioned family members, friends, and neighbors for any leads they might provide. In this area the investigation made more headway.

Speaking with Linda Bricca's family, the officers learned some "interesting things" about life on Greenway Avenue. One of the things learned was that Linda Bricca had a male friend whom she had been seeing since shortly after the family's arrival in Cincinnati in 1963. Other witnesses placed Linda and the man together several times on a secluded lovers lane. Jerry Bricca, the devoted workaholic for the Monsanto Company, apparently wasn't taking care of business at home.

Mrs. Bricca's friend was questioned for about ten minutes by officers regarding his familiarity with the Briccas' family situation. Later the man was questioned for 45 minutes by Cincinnati Police Lieutenant Herbert Vogel, who was heading the murder probe. Vogel tape recorded this interrogation at the suspect's place of business. Listening to the tape later, he was puzzled by some of the man's replies. But when Vogel contacted the man's wife regarding another meeting she informed him that her husband had been so upset by the original questioning that he had hired an attorney. The attorney refused police any further access to his new client.

Police had seven questions they wanted to ask the man, questions which clearly indicated the direction of the investigation. The questions were the same that police had asked over 400 other people:

When did you last see Linda Bricca alive?

Did you see Linda Bricca on Thursday, September 22, 1966?

When did you last visit the Bricca residence?

For what reason did you last visit the Bricca residence?

Did Linda Bricca ever discuss with you any of her personal problems?

Were you ever out with Linda Bricca socially?

Where were you on Sunday night, September 26, 1966, between 9:00 p.m. and midnight?

On the advice of his attorney the man exercised his legal rights and refused to answer these questions. He also refused to submit samples of his hair, bodily fluids, or fingerprints for comparison to those found at the crime scene.

Police were confident that the alleged lover was the killer. A year after the crime, Hamilton County Prosecutor Melvin Rueger told the press that he knew who killed the Briccas but couldn't make an arrest.

"Here is a case where a man kills three persons, there are no living witnesses and he doesn't leave any clues behind," Rueger said. "The only chance the law enforcement official has is to talk to the suspect because we have to have sufficient evidence to go to the grand jury. But we can't question the man because the Supreme Court says that would be infringing on his

Constitutional rights. We have always informed suspects of the rights before questioning them, but (before) we could use psychology and sales talk to get them to confess. Now we have been deprived of those tools by the Supreme Court, and men are walking around free who should be behind bars."

Police theorized that when Jerry Bricca came home from work that rainy Sunday evening he surprised the man and Linda in the act of making love. Daughter Debbie was probably playing elsewhere in the house, oblivious to the grownups' games.

Details are imprecise, but in the ensuing explosion the killer probably grabbed the carving knife from its place in the dining room drawer. Perhaps in self defense, or to protect Linda Bricca, the man stabbed Jerry Bricca to death.

In defense of her stricken husband Linda may have then turned on her knife-wielding lover. (It is common in domestic violence that whatever acrimony exists between a husband and wife can dissolve in a crisis, and a spouse will defend a stricken mate.) The killer may have stabbed Linda to death defending himself. Or, he may have simply had to eliminate her as a witness to the murder of Jerry. In any case, Linda Bricca was the next to die, falling on top of her husband's body.

That left only young Debbie. She was only four years old, but that was old enough to recognize and identify the killer of her parents. The murderer may have looked away as he held her down on the floor and stabbed her four times.

Then, after an attempt to make the house look like it had been plundered (or perhaps to look for things that might connect him to the crime), the killer slipped out into the dark, drizzly night.

He was never caught.

Jerry and Linda Bricca. (*The Cincinnati Enquirer*/Michael Snyder)

Debbie Bricca. (*The Cincinnati Enquirer*/Michael Snyder)

An officer from the SPCA leads Thumper from the Bricca house after the discovery of the bodies there. (*The Cincinnati Enquirer*/Michael Snyder)

The house on Greenway Avenue in 1997.

The Easter Sunday Massacre

At about 9:40 p.m. on March 30, 1975, Easter Sunday evening, the phone rang at the headquarters of the Hamilton Ohio Police Department. Hamilton is a city of about 60,000 souls located twenty miles northwest of downtown Cincinnati. The caller told the dispatcher that he wanted to report a shooting at 635 Minor Avenue.

"A man has been shot," the caller said.

While the call sounded bad enough, police responding to it had no idea that they would soon arrive at the scene of the worst mass murder in the history of Cincinnati area crime.

Officers arriving at the location, a small wood frame house with white and green shingle siding in the Lindenwald neighborhood on Hamilton's south side, were naturally apprehensive. They were met at the door by James Ruppert, 40. Ruppert lived in the house with his 65-year-old mother Charity.

Ruppert appeared alert. He calmly told the officers that he was the one who had called them. Then he let the police inside his mother's home. What they found was a charnel house.

Just inside the front door was the living room. Scattered about the room, like discarded dolls, were the bodies of five children. Beyond the living room, in the kitchen, were six more bodies   three children and three adults.

All of the dead had been apparent victims of gunshot wounds. There were four guns in the house. Three revolvers – a .38 and two .22s – were found on a table and chair arm in the living room. A rifle was leaning against the refrigerator in the kitchen. All of these weapons appeared to have been fired recently. Spent shell casings of both calibers were scattered around the rooms.

It did not take police long to identify the victims. In addition to Charity Ruppert, the owner of the house, the eleven dead were her son Leonard, 42, his wife Alma, 38, and the couple's eight children – Leonard III, 17; Michael, 16; Thomas, 15; Carol, 13; Ann, 12; David, 11; Teresa, 9; and John, 4.

James Ruppert, the only living person at the house, was taken into custody.

The Cincinnati Crime Book

Police spread out through the neighborhood and scoured the house to try and get a grip on what happened on that bloody Sunday.

They found out from neighbors that the house was occupied by Charity Ruppert and her younger son James. Leonard Ruppert and his family were visiting in celebration of the Easter holiday.

Leonard Ruppert was an engineer with General Electric. He lived with his family on Walter Avenue in Fairfield, about a mile and a half south of Minor Avenue. Neighbors on Minor Avenue told police that Leonard and his family arrived at number 635 at about 2:00 p.m. That afternoon the children had an Easter egg hunt in the front yard of the house. That was the last time any of the neighbors saw the murdered family. No one heard any gunshots.

The fact that no one heard any shots was one of the most unusual aspects of the unfolding case. Minor Avenue is a crowded street. The houses are close together and people frequently come and go from those houses. Yet nobody heard any of the over 40 gunshots that police later determined had been fired inside Charity Ruppert's house.

Investigators from the Ohio Bureau of Criminal Identification arrived and combed the house for clues that might tell them what had happened to cause the carnage. The house showed the trappings of the holiday, with Easter baskets and a large Easter Lily in the living room. Also in the living room was a group portrait of the Leonard Ruppert family. On the stove in the kitchen were the remains of a meal that was started but never served. Police discovered 31 spent shell casings in the two downstairs rooms. Five of these cartridges were .38 caliber; the rest were .22s. In addition to these spent rounds there were more empty shells still in the guns. The only possible sign of a struggle was an upset waste basket. Nothing related to the massacre was discovered on the second floor.

A preliminary examination of the bodies revealed that all of the victims but one had been shot in the head. The exception was Leonard Ruppert, who had been shot in the chest. The bodies were taken to a funeral home to have autopsies performed on them.

James Ruppert was held at Hamilton Police headquarters. By 1:30 a.m. he had been charged with eleven counts of aggravated murder. It seemed apparent the he had slain his family members. But why?

The investigation of James Ruppert began with his neighbors on Minor Avenue. They described the 40-year-old man as a "loner" and "gun freak" who did a lot of target shooting. His skill with firearms was well-known in the community. "It's no secret Jimmy had guns," a neighbor told police. "He used to do a lot of hunting and trap shooting. He loved to hunt." But, the neighbor added, "Jimmy was a peaceful man, very quiet and reserved."

At the time of the shootings James Ruppert was an unemployed draftsman. His last employer recalled that "He did fine work, and as far as we're concerned we never had a problem with him." Ruppert had been living with his mother on Minor Avenue off and on for several months.

166

The Cincinnati Crime Book

James Ruppert was born near Wapakoneta, Ohio in 1934. His father supported the family by farming and by working at the Mosler Safe Company in Hamilton. James was the youngest of three sons born to the Rupperts. The first son died as an infant. Then came Leonard, in 1932, then James. At age two James contracted bronchial asthma and suffered from the disease until he was twenty years old. As a teenager, he was hospitalized for a month with spinal meningitis.

As a result of these afflictions Ruppert was unable to participate in physical education classes or any form of school sports. He kept to himself and developed a reputation as a loner. His grades were average and there were no disciplinary reports from his days as a student at the Hamilton Catholic High School. Although Ruppert was born left-handed, his teachers tried to teach him to write with his right hand. They were unsuccessful.

After high school Ruppert took night courses at the University of Cincinnati and Xavier University before dropping out after two years. He then worked at the Evendale General Electric plant for seven years. After that he worked part-time as a draftsman and invested some of his earnings in the stock market. When he didn't work he spent his time in Hamilton's library and in various bars and cafes. He would usually sit by himself and mind his own business.

And, as mentioned, James Ruppert loved to target shoot.

In addition to investigating James Ruppert, police also looked into the backgrounds of the victims.

Charity Ruppert, a neighbor recalled, was "a very nice, kind person. She was quiet and minded her own business, but she would always speak or stop and talk with you. And she was devoted to her sons and her grandchildren. She always hired the children to do her yard work." Charity had lived at the Minor Avenue address for over twenty years.

Charity's husband Leonard died when their sons were 12 and 10. "She said her kids were never allowed to be children," a neighbor said. "They were always the men of the house because their father died at that early age. They were very responsible."

Leonard Ruppert was well-regarded in his Fairfield neighborhood. He and his family were called friendly and outgoing. Alma was active in the parish of the Sacred Heart of Jesus Christ Church. "She was a very sweet woman," a neighbor said.

The eight Ruppert children were described as typical kids with no problems.

At 8:00 p.m. on Thursday, April 3, 1975 a funeral mass was held for the victims at the Sacred Heart of Jesus Christ Church. James Ruppert was not allowed to attend the service for his murdered family. The eleven caskets were kept closed. After the service the victims were buried in the Arlington Memorial Cemetery on Compton Road in Mount Healthy.

The Cincinnati Crime Book

James Ruppert continued to be held at the Butler County Jail. He was arraigned on eleven counts of aggravated murder and held on a $200,000 bond. His trial was scheduled for the following June. He quickly obtained an attorney, who advised him to say nothing about the slayings.

James Ruppert's trial for murder began on June 15, 1975. Many people wanted to witness the proceedings for this historic crime, and they started lining up for seats as soon as the courthouse opened each day. The courtroom was packed every day of the trial.

Everybody wanted to know why James Ruppert killed eleven members of his family.

Ruppert entered a plea of "not guilty and not guilty by reason of insanity." Instead of having the case tried before a jury, he decided to have his fate determined by a three-judge panel. He was defended by attorneys Hugh Holbrock and Joseph Bressler.

In its opening statement the state, led by Butler County Prosecutor John Holcomb, claimed that James Ruppert coolly slaughtered his entire family because he felt that he was a failure and resented his brother's comparative success in life. Ruppert, said Holcomb, also planned to inherit the estates of his brother and mother.

James Ruppert was guilty, Holcomb said, "and only deserves to be put to death."

The defense waived its opening statement, reserving the right to make it at the conclusion of the state's case.

After the prosecution's opening statement the jury was taken to view 635 Minor Avenue. Ruppert chose not to accompany them to the house.

Back in court the first witnesses for the state were the officers who initially responded to Minor Avenue on March 30. They described the locations of the eleven bodies and the four firearms.

Then Holcomb called technicians from the London England-based Bureau of Criminal Investigation who testified that fingerprints found on one of the weapons matched those of the defendant. The technician also was able to determine that 30 of the 42 bullets submitted for comparison testing had been fired from the three revolvers found in the house. The .22 caliber rifle, apparently, was not used. Another technician testified that he recovered Type O blood from trousers belonging to James Ruppert. Ruppert's blood was Type B, but eight of the victims were Type O. The Butler County Coroner testified that of the 40 bullet wounds in the bodies all "except one or two" were fatal in and of themselves.

James Ruppert's aunt testified that Ruppert seemed puzzled and confused when she went to visit him in the Butler County Jail shortly after the killings. "He broke down and cried like a baby and everything seemed to be a blank to him," the aunt said. When she asked him what happened on Easter Sunday he would only reply, "I don't know." Hoping to buttress the insanity defense, attorney Holbrock questioned the woman about mental illness in the Ruppert family. She replied that another aunt and a cousin of the defendant had been in mental hospitals, another cousin committed suicide, and still another cousin had tried to.

An employee of a gun shop on Dixie Highway near Hamilton testified that in January or February of 1975 James Ruppert had asked him "very casually" where he might obtain a firearms silencer.

Another witness, who coincidentally lived on the same Fairfield street as the slain Leonard Ruppert family, testified that he had witnessed James Ruppert's crack marksmanship while target shooting at a public shooting area along the banks of the Great Miami River. The man said that Ruppert, shooting simultaneously with two pistols, could "walk" a tin can along the ground. "It's not difficult to fire and hit the can," the impressed witness said, "but to keep it moving.... He was definitely far superior at shooting than I was."

To bolster the claim that money was the motive for the murders, prosecutors presented employees of various area banks who testified as to the financial status of James Ruppert and the slain family members.

The president of a Hamilton bank testified that the defendant had a balance of $3373 in an account there until he withdrew it for attorneys' fees shortly after the shootings. The bank president also said that Ruppert had opened an account with $10,000 in May of 1974 but that he withdrew the money a month later. This testimony was supposed to demonstrate that James Ruppert was not doing too well financially.

An employee at General Electric testified that Leonard Ruppert's automatic life insurance coverage with that company amounted to $52,400 and that additional coverage he had obtained for his wife and children brought the total to $94,000.

An officer from a savings and loan association testified that Leonard Ruppert had an account there worth $7870. An officer from another bank stated that the slain members of Leonard Ruppert's family had combined deposits of $18,008.16 at his institution. An insurance company employee said that Leonard Ruppert had two life insurance policies worth $7356 and $3966. Alma Ruppert was the beneficiary. A real estate broker testified that the value of what Leonard Ruppert owned of his house on Walter Avenue was $19,500.

All of these policies, combined with the worth of Charity Ruppert's estate (including the $14,000 value of the house on Minor Avenue and another house in Hamilton) meant that if James Ruppert was found innocent by reason of insanity he would, by law, inherit a total of $343,000 upon the death of his entire family. That, said the state, was a pretty good motive for murder.

The prosecution concluded its case on Wednesday, June 18 after just three days. It had called 29 witnesses and presented almost 200 exhibits. The defense moved for an acquittal, claiming that the prosecution had not proved the "prior calculation" required to support the aggravated murder charge or that James Ruppert had any knowledge of the financial status of either his mother or his brother's family. The three-judge panel denied the motion.

The defense began presenting its case on Friday June 20. Joseph Bressler immediately conceded the obvious and confirmed that the defendant had killed the eleven members of his family, but added that Ruppert had been insane for at least ten years and was "unable to control his own being."

Bressler revealed that Ruppert had seen a psychiatrist when he was in his early twenties but that he had discontinued the sessions. "This (discontinuation) was the worst thing that could have happened. It led to the biggest tragedy in the history of our state, perhaps the nation." Bressler claimed that Ruppert's mental illness began in his childhood, when his character was affected by the poverty of his surroundings, sibling rivalry with his brother Leonard, and the belief that his parents had wanted a girl and instead got him. Years of brooding on these circumstances had led James Ruppert to believe that his family was conspiring against him.

To substantiate this claim, Bressler called Dr. Lester Grinspoon, a professor of psychiatry at the Harvard Medical School.

Grinspoon had examined James Ruppert for several hours at the Butler County Jail on May 9. Calling Ruppert "a classical case of paranoia," Grinspoon said that the conspiracy idea first entered Ruppert's mind after he was questioned by Hamilton Police regarding an obscene telephone call in 1965. By 1975, Grinspoon said, Ruppert "was absolutely obsessed with his conspiracy. It's the most important thing in his life." The conspirators by now included the FBI. The purpose of the conspiracy, Ruppert supposedly believed, was to label him as a Communist homosexual.

Ruppert also claimed, according to Grinspoon, that as a child he had been frequently beaten by his mother and brother, that his mother hated men yet tried to seduce him when he was 15 years old, that he "had never been successful with a woman," and that "my mother has destroyed me." Lately Leonard had been thwarting his attempts to find gainful employment and was also sabotaging his Volkswagen.

According to Grinspoon it was a question about the car that touched off the slayings. James Ruppert was in the kitchen of the Minor Avenue house on Easter Sunday, getting ready to go out target shooting, when Leonard asked him, "How's your Volkswagen?" That remark, said Grinspoon, caused Ruppert to become "overwhelmed with rage" and he responded by shooting his brother. Shot in the chest, Leonard Ruppert cried for someone to call the police. James then shot Leonard again, then shot his sister-in-law and his mother, and then his eight nieces and nephews. "In fact, if there had been more people in the house they might have been killed also," Grinspoon concluded.

Another psychiatrist, appointed by the Court to examine the defendant, testified that when Leonard Ruppert asked about the car James felt a "surge of hatred and rage" and shot him. "There was a lot of gunfire. Someone from the next room asked 'What's going on?' (Ruppert) doesn't remember too much. There was a lot of shooting – and then silence."

After the shootings, according to attorney Bressler, James Ruppert lay on the couch in the living room, just feet from the bodies of his victims, and contemplated suicide. Finally, after three hours of soul searching, he decided that it would be a mortal sin to kill himself. So, after changing out of clothing he considered "too effeminate," he called Hamilton Police and said, "Hello. A man has been shot."

After the psychiatrists, the defense presented a female witness who said that she had seen Ruppert in a Hamilton coffee shop a few months before the murder and that when she tried to speak to him he said, "Shhhh, I'm listening to Castro." The woman said that Ruppert had no radio or other equipment that would enable him to hear the Cuban leader, who was not in the coffee shop. "I thought he was either using ESP or something," she said.

On June 23 another defense psychiatrist reiterated that Ruppert believed himself the victim of a conspiracy and that this belief caused him to keep his feelings to himself and thus appear to be fairly normal to those around him. "The nature of his illness was such that everyone was suspect," Dr. Philip Mechanick testified. "Surrounded by a sea of enemies, who could he tell?"

Mechanick said that Ruppert could not determine right from wrong on Easter Sunday, and said the defendant told him that when he heard his wounded nieces and nephews moaning he shot them again to put them out of their misery. "How wrong can anything be?" Mechanick asked. "He's treating a child as though it were an injured horse." The psychiatrist added that, in his opinion, it would be impossible for Ruppert to be faking his mental illness.

The first three defense psychiatrists who testified had only examined Ruppert after the shootings. To bolster the claim that Ruppert's mental illness was longstanding, on June 24 his lawyer called Dr. Glenn Weaver, a Cincinnati psychiatrist who had treated James Ruppert 23 times between 1961 and 1965, to the stand.

Dr. Weaver recalled a 1961 dream in which Ruppert had visualized himself in a courtroom where he was "condemned to death for no known reason. He even drew a sketch of the court. He showed where some of his friends were sitting almost as you see the courtroom today." Ruppert voluntarily ended these psychiatric sessions in 1965.

Weaver had visited the defendant in jail since his arrest and found him profoundly changed from 1965. "This wasn't the same man," Weaver said. "It was quite apparent that he had become paranoid." Weaver also concluded that it would be impossible for Ruppert to be faking his mental illness. "He's not faking. This is too well organized."

Dr. Leigh Roberts, from the University of Wisconsin medical school examined Ruppert in early May and now testified for the defense that the defendant was "grossly preoccupied" with the conspiracy against him. "The major thing we talked about was the conspiracy and way it affected him,"

Roberts said. On the day of the shootings Ruppert had been calm until "the situation changed markedly at the point where his brother asked him a question about his automobile. There suddenly flashed through his head a series of particular ideas, preceding experiences he felt were perpetrated by his brother. Everything came together. All of this resulted in loss of his ability to reason and loss of his ability to engage in purposeful thinking or to refrain from violence." Had Leonard Ruppert not asked about the Volkswagen, Roberts opined, James "would have left and remained away until his brother had departed and the incidents of that day would not have occurred."

The defense rested its case on June 25. The state then began calling its rebuttal witnesses and responding to the defense's case.

A Hamilton Police detective who had grown up near the Ruppert family testified that James' upbringing was not as traumatic as the defense claimed. The detective conceded that Ruppert grew up in a house with no indoor plumbing, but said, "I've been in houses in lots worse condition today," and added that Charity Ruppert always kept the house neat. The witness recalled Leonard Ruppert protecting his younger brother from neighborhood bullies.

Other witnesses to James Ruppert's sane behavior included Hamilton residents and stock trading acquaintances of the defendant. "I thought he was normal. (He) seemed like a nice guy to me," said one.

"In my opinion, he was sane," said another.

"To me he is of very sound mind; more sound than I am," admitted a third.

A Hamilton bar maid testified that she knew James Ruppert well because he frequented the bar she worked in. After she stopped working in the bar, the woman said, she returned there several nights a week to be with him. "I was in love with him," she said. She testified that on March 29, the day before the shootings, Ruppert confided in her that he had a problem "and had to take care of it right then and there." The bar maid said that Ruppert's mother had given her unemployed son an ultimatum: "If he could drink seven days a week, he could help pay the rent. Otherwise, he would have to leave home."

To rebut the defense's psychiatric testimony, the state called Dr. Robert McDevitt of the Butler County Forensic Center. "From the things (Ruppert) related to me, he certainly did know right from wrong," McDevitt said. But the doctor conceded that Ruppert was mentally ill, a "schizophrenic reacting paranoid." McDevitt said that Ruppert "probably knew he had some kind of chronic mental disease." He said that the shooting of Charity Ruppert was "psychotically motivated" and the shooting of the others "was a spillover of that psychotic rage. He was not able to explain why he shot the others." But even considering these factors and opinions, McDevitt was "not prepared to make a decision whether (Ruppert) was sane or insane when he committed the acts."

Another state psychiatrist said that before the shootings Ruppert "(functioned) in a lonely, self-contained way. (His) whole social relationship seems to involve visiting a bar, discussing stocks, or going to the public library." The doctor concluded that while Ruppert existed in a "paranoid state" he "did know right from wrong and could have adhered to the right and resisted the wrong."

Another doctor who examined Ruppert for the prosecution doubted that he actually believed in a conspiracy against him since he seemed willing to discuss it so freely. "A paranoid never asks if you believe him," the doctor explained. "He is hostile and very guarded."

(When the battle of the dozen "hired gun" psychiatrists from each side was concluded – some were paid up to $600 per day for their testimony – the scorecard was: Ten said Ruppert was a seriously mentally ill psychotic, two said he was not. Eight said Ruppert couldn't control himself during the Easter shootings, three said he could have, and one said he wasn't sure but that he probably couldn't have.)

The defense called rebuttal witnesses to counter the testimony of the Hamilton bar maid. The woman's estranged husband testified that his wife was home with him the night she said she had been at the bar having a conversation with Ruppert about "taking care of a problem."

A woman who also worked in the bar said she had never seen the witness with the defendant and characterized her as a "trouble causer," adding, "She doesn't have a reputation for truthfulness at all as far as I know."

Testimony in the trial ended on Wednesday July 2.

In the state's closing arguments Prosecutor Holcomb said the motive for the murders was the "first recorded motive in the history of mankind; from the book of Genesis – jealousy, hate, and greed toward his brother." Holcomb said that Ruppert planned to kill his family and had not acted spontaneously in a fit of rage while on his way to target shoot. "The only target shooting he had in his mind was on the members of his family." He reminded the judges of the monetary motive. "Money – that is what this case is all about. It's the gold at the end of the rainbow." As to the defense contention that Ruppert was mentally ill, Holcomb called the various psychiatric descriptions of Ruppert – psychotic, schizophrenic – "labels" and added "Men invent labels to facilitate thinking, but the thinking sometimes ends up enslaved to the label. The state has introduced an abundance of evidence as to his sanity from responsible, reputable people. The defense has not produced any lay people to say he was of unsound mind – not a single person."

Holcomb concluded, "Is the defendant's condition such that he deserves to avoid responsibility or accountability for what he has done? Do we consign this case to the homicide reports of the Hamilton Police Department? Do we wrap up 600 years of human life into eleven police reports and throw it into a waste basket and say he is not accountable? I ask you – what is sanity? The issue is clear and pay day is now. The question is – does the defendant pay or does he get paid?"

Defense attorney Bressler called the case "one of the greatest human tragedies ever to occur in the history of the United States. This isn't the act of a sane man. This was the act of an insane man, and some very capable witnesses have told you it was." Discounting the monetary motive, Bressler reasserted the defense claim that James Ruppert did not know how much money his family was worth. "The court is being asked to infer that Ruppert knew a lot of things that he did not."

The final words for the defense came from attorney Hugh Holbrock. Invoking the spirits of the dead family, he said, "If those people could arise from the dead and stand before you today, one by one they would say, 'Judges, acquit him, for you have heard the psychiatric testimony. He was insane at the time and knew not what he did.'"

The three-judge panel deliberated for three hours before announcing their verdict: guilty of eleven counts of aggravated murder. The judges concluded that Ruppert was "sane at the time of the offense" and that the state had "proved beyond a reasonable doubt each of the specifications contained in each of the eleven counts of the indictment."

But this decision of the judges was not unanimous. Two of the jurists voted for the conviction; the third dissented. Although another hearing would be held within thirty days to determine Ruppert's punishment for the crime, the lack of unanimity in the verdict meant that he could not be given the death penalty.

On July 14, 1975 James Ruppert was formally sentenced to serve eleven consecutive life sentences in the Ohio prison system. Under Ohio law he would have to serve 16 years on each of the sentences before becoming eligible for parole, virtually assuring that the 41-year-old man would never get out of prison. He was ordered transferred to the Ohio State Reformatory at Lucasville.

Ruppert's attorneys then appealed the verdict on the grounds that their client had misunderstood the consequences when he waived his right to a jury and had his case heard by a three-judge panel instead. He believed, they contended, that a unanimous verdict of guilty was required for a conviction instead of simply a majority of two to one, as had happened at his trial.

The case ended up in the Ohio Supreme court, where the justices ruled that the defendant had indeed been misinformed and that the resulting error was great enough to warrant a new trial. The justices also ordered a change of venue for the new trial based on the extensive coverage of the first trial in Butler County. The second trial was scheduled to begin on June 14, 1982 in Findlay, in Hancock County, Ohio. Retired Ashland County Common Pleas Court Judge A. Ross Silvering would preside over the case.

The jury for the second trail, seven men and five women, was selected by June 18.

Execpt for the new location and the substitution of a jury for the three-judge panel, there was not much new in James Ruppert's second trial. The prosecution, again handled by Butler County's John Holcomb, characterized the defendant as "consumed with greed, envy, hatred, anger, and jealousy" and again contended that he had killed his family for money. The defense, again handled by Hugh Holbrock, claimed Ruppert was a "very, very sick man... not guilty by reason of insanity" who committed the murders during an insane episode.

One new bit of testimony possibly answered a question that many people had asked from the very beginning. How could a person fire over forty shots and kill eleven people and not be heard by anyone in a crowded residential neighborhood? The Reverend Kenneth Baker was the former pastor of St. Anne's Church, located just a half block away from Charity Ruppert's house on Minor Avenue. Reverend Baker testified that the church's bells were ringing at 6:00 p.m. that Easter Sunday, the estimated time of the shootings. That· ringing may have been loud enough to prevent anyone in the neighborhood from hearing the shots. (Also, March 30 had been a cloudy and chilly early spring day. Most of the people on Minor Avenue, including Charity Ruppert, had their windows closed that Sunday.)

Shortly after the trial session began on July 1, a juror collapsed and was rushed to nearby Blanchard Valley Hospital. He died a few hours later. It was later determined that the man had suffered a heart attack. An alternate juror moved into his place and the trial was recessed until July 6.

Both sides in the case rested on July 21. The prosecution summed up by saying "Hate, envy, jealousy and greed.... all came together. (James Ruppert) coveted all that was his brother's, and that is where he got into trouble." Holcomb called the defense's psychiatric testimony "artistic speculation, guesswork. (Ruppert) didn't think he was Napoleon. He didn't think he was a dog (a reference to New York City's "Son of Sam" killer) and when he shot his family, he didn't think he was shooting at a tree stump."

Hugh Holbrock disagreed and summed up his client's mental state by declaring, "It is what you believe that makes you what you are, and James Ruppert really believed his mother and brother were conspiring against him."

The jury got the case on July 21. They could choose from any of four verdicts: guilty of aggravated (premeditated) murder, guilty of non-premeditated murder, not guilty, or not guilty by reason of insanity. Since the indictment contained counts for each of the murders, a separate verdict was required for each of the eleven counts. Judge Silvering announced that the jury would be sequestered at a hotel in Findlay while they deliberated.

Two days later, the jury announced its verdict, finding James Ruppert guilty of two counts of aggravated murder for the deaths of Charity and Leonard Ruppert and not guilty by reason of insanity for the deaths of Alma Ruppert and the eight children. As he had throughout the trial, James Ruppert showed little emotion as the verdicts were read. Judge Silverling immediately sentenced him to two consecutive life terms for the murders of his mother and brother.

Defense attorney Holbrock said that he was "extremely pleased to know there are jurors that still respect their sacred oath and possess the courage to do what they think should be done."

But Holbrock's partner, Joseph Bressler, said, "How they arrived at the two guilty verdicts I don't know unless they were concerned about the money issue."

Prosecutor Holcomb was outraged. He called the entire insanity defense "a farce," and said, "There needs to be some common sense written into the law of insanity. Although Ruppert was mentally ill, he was not insane. He could distinguish between right and wrong and he could control his conduct.... It is almost immoral, in my opinion, that a criminal defendant uses the crime itself as a means to avoid punishment.... It's like a defendant killing his mother and father, then asking the court for mercy because he is an orphan.... Psychiatrists do not speak the language of the law. They apply the language of certainty to a discipline of ambiguity. A change is long overdue." Holcomb said that Ohio should include a "guilty but mentally ill" option as one possible verdict in future criminal cases.

The prosecutor wasn't the only person puzzled and angered by the verdicts. Edna Allgeier, Alma Ruppert's mother, told the press, "I really can't accept it. The crime is so enormous.... It's (been) seven years of living with agony, and you're just dying by the inch." She believed that James Ruppert was responsible for thirteen deaths, not just the eleven he was charged with. She blamed him for the death of the juror who had collapsed during the second trial. "He (the juror) couldn't take it," she said. "Those pictures (of the dead bodies at the crime scene) must have gotten to him." The thirteenth victim was Edna Allgeier's husband, Frank. Unable to handle his depression over the murders, he shot himself to death on March 30, 1978, three years to the day after the murder of his daughter and her family.

On July 29 Judge Silverling ruled that James Ruppert should begin serving his two life sentences in the Columbus Ohio Correctional Facility.

James Ruppert disappeared from the newspapers until March 31, 1985, when the enormity of his crime made it a subject of "tenth anniversary" coverage. Law enforcement officials and others recalled the worst mass murder in the history of the Cincinnati area. An officer who responded to the first call that night ten years earlier said, "It was a scene I don't believe you could blot out of your mind if you lived to be a thousand. I can close my eyes and tell you where everyone was lying and what the inside of the house looked like, even down to the utensils."

"It never goes away," said Edna Allgeier. "I can still see that funeral procession with eleven hearses in a row...." She recalled the last time she had seen her daughter, son-in-law, and grandchildren. They had visited her home before going to their deaths on Minor Avenue. "That day (Easter Sunday, 1975) was like an unplanned farewell dinner. We had such a nice time. The children were all dressed up in their best clothes, hunting Easter eggs. Who would have known it would have ended that way?" She had nothing but contempt for James Ruppert. "How could (he) do such a thing? I would have made him suffer, but nothing I could do to him would ever make him suffer as I have. I have often thought if I had a gun when I saw him I could have shot him. At the trial in Findlay he was like a stone. He never shed a tear."

There was no media coverage for the twentieth anniversary of the murders, but on Friday June 23, 1995 the Ohio Parole Board announced that it was denying parole to James Ruppert and ordered him to serve at least another 40 years in prison. That meant that his next chance for freedom would come when he was 100 years old.

Was James Ruppert insane when he killed his family? A three judge panel and twelve psychiatrists could not agree on whether he was or not. The jury seemed to think, "Well, yes and no."

Did he kill in hopes of gaining a fortune, or was he reacting to an imaginary conspiracy?

The only person who really knows is James Ruppert.

Charity Ruppert's home in south Hamilton, Ohio.

James Ruppert. (Courtesy Butler County Sheriff's Department)

Charity Ruppert's grave.

Leonard and Alma.

Leonard III and Michael.

Thomas and Carol.

Ann and David.

Teresa and John.

The Devil In His Eyes

Serial killers have plagued mankind for centuries. And, as witnessed by the cases of Anna Marie Hahn and The Cincinnati Strangler, Cincinnati has not been without its share of these repeat offenders.

But while these killers were once considered criminal anomalies, in the decades since the 1950s (and especially in the United States) their methodically committed murders have reached almost epidemic proportions. Depending on which source one chooses to believe, there are currently between thirty-five and five hundred of these of killers active in this country alone.

In the early 1980s Cincinnati was visited briefly, albeit fatally, by three of the more vicious of this new breed of killing animal. In this chapter and the next we will meet them.

On January 14, 1982 an attractive Anderson Township housewife disappeared after completing a day of shopping at several Cincinnati area malls. The abduction and subsequent murder of 30-year-old Jerilyn Stanfield was tragic enough in itself, but it also set into motion a chain of events that escalated into one of the most brutal and senseless serial killing sprees ever visited upon the eastern United States.

Jerilyn Mysonhimer's main interests in life were fashion, sewing, and homemaking. The daughter of a veteran Cincinnati police officer, she had attended the College of Design, Architecture, and Art at the University of Cincinnati, emphasizing her studies in the field of fashion design. Upon leaving the school, she was employed by the McAlpin's department store until she quit after becoming frustrated with the retail clothing business. She returned to school to get a license in hair design and then, in 1973, got a job at the Beechmont Mall Shillito's department store. In the store's University Shop she met another employee, David Stanfield.

David Stanfield had also been a student at the University of Cincinnati. A 1972 graduate with a degree in Education, he was supplementing his income as a math teacher by working part-time in the department store. He and

Jerilyn Mysonhimer struck up a friendship, began dating, and were eventually married in June of 1974 at the Hyde Park Community Methodist Church.

After the wedding, the couple bought a Cape Cod-style house on Coral Sea Drive in Anderson Township. David decided to leave the teaching profession and become both a real estate agent and life insurance salesman. Jerilyn modified her career also, quitting her job at Shillito's to become a sewing instructor in a Montgomery sewing center and a hair stylist in a beauty shop in Hyde Park's Madison House. The childless couple were happy and very devoted to each other. They were active in church affairs and had many friends.

On January 14, 1982 Jerilyn Stanfield was enjoying the last day of an extended Christmas vacation from her jobs. During the first part of the day she left her home to shop at the nearby Beechmont Mall. After noon she drove to the Eastgate Mall in Union Township where she browsed through the shops and purchased a small quantity of cosmetics. She returned to her car in the mall's parking lot at about 2:30 p.m.

Then, she vanished.

Unsure of his wife's plans for the day, David Stanfield did not start to become worried about her absence until well into the evening. Finally, at 10:30 p.m., he called the Hamilton County Police and reported her missing.

David told authorities that Jerilyn might have gone mall hopping, so Hamilton County asked the Union Township Police to check the Eastgate Mall. It was there, several hours later, that they found Jerilyn's 1974 Volkswagen parked near the main entrance.

The car was covered with a blanket of snow that had begun to fall at 7:00 p.m. Tossed around inside the car were Jerilyn's purse and wallet, $20 in a bank envelope, and the purchases she had made that afternoon. The car keys, and Jerilyn herself, were missing.

Police immediately went to work on the case. Although there were no signs of violence, officials assumed that there had been foul play. The Stanfields were a happily married couple and there was nothing to indicate that Jerilyn would have taken off on her own.

Search parties started working on the areas around the mall but they found no clues. As the days went by the search widened. Helicopters were used to cover some of the more remote areas. Since the case was considered a kidnaping, the FBI was called in. It, too, came up empty.

Numerous rapes and attempted rapes had recently been reported at various shopping centers in southwestern Ohio. Police thought that these attacks might be connected to the disappearance of Jerilyn Stanfield. Area law enforcement agencies compared notes on the attacks and came up with several different descriptions of assailants, but published composite drawings produced no leads or arrests.

More time went by with no apparent progress. Despite increasingly dismal odds, relatives of the missing woman tried to maintain some optimism.

The Cincinnati Crime Book

"She'll be back," said David Stanfield. "We'll get our lives reorganized, get our family started again. She was a super lady."

Jerilyn's father was slightly less positive. "You always have hope," the ex-cop said, "but my experience tells me different."

In Hyde Park members of the Community Methodist Church planned a special prayer service for Jerilyn and her family. Groups of parishioners had already assisted police in their fruitless searches in Anderson Township. The prayer service was scheduled for the Thursday evening exactly two weeks after Jerilyn's disappearance.

Sadly, the service would not be held.

On Wednesday January 27, just before noon, a farmer entered an abandoned barn located just off US Route 50 about 14 miles east of the Eastgate Mall. The farmer stored hay in the barn and had gone there to check on it. After entering the barn, he soon forgot about his hay.

Just inside the barn's main door was the body of Jerilyn Stanfield. She was propped up against a bale of hay in the center of an aisle. Her hands were tied behind her back with baling twine. She had been stabbed once in the chest. Her fully clothed corpse was frozen solid by the wintry temperatures. An autopsy later determined that she had been raped.

The discovery of Jerilyn's body was a crushing emotional blow to her family and friends. In despair, the prayer service at her church was canceled.

As news of the discovery of the body spread, panic seized the rural areas near the barn where it was found. A rape prevention program in nearby Milford drew a huge response. "The whole Clermont County area is panic-stricken," said a deliveryman who worked in the area. "You talk to these people, they are scared and don't want to go out alone. It isn't like it used to be around this area. People never used to lock their doors."

The murder also had its effect on the patrons of Cincinnati area shopping centers. Women who before would not have hesitated to go shopping alone now preferred to be accompanied by male relatives or friends.

Due to the murder and reports of other attacks and rapes, eleven area police departments formed a multi-agency task force to deal with the string of crimes. Initially the task force had a list of six suspects, but the list soon doubled in size. "We're playing a game of catch up with so many leads to cover," said a task force spokesman on January 29. "We're moving as fast as we can to work on them."

The spokesman could not know that the perpetrator of the Stanfield slaying was at that very time moving faster than even he himself could probably imagine. Barely a week and a half after the discovery of Jerilyn Stanfield's body her killer would be in custody. But he would not be in jail because of the law catching up with him. He would be apprehended because of his own burnout and inability to continue on a multi-state spree of murder and mayhem which left eleven more people dead.

The Cincinnati Crime Book

Robert Dale Henderson, Jr. was seemingly a loser all of his life. He was never able or willing to fit into society.

He was born in Irontown, Missouri in 1946. His father was a policeman, and the two seldom got along. Later Robert Jr. would claim that his father was an alcoholic who beat his wife and children. Young Robert never used his given first name out of intentional disrespect for his father.

Dale Henderson spent his early years in the mining country near Esther, Missouri before moving to nearby Poplar Bluff when he was a teenager. There was nothing distinguishing about his early years. He attended Poplar Bluff High School, sat in the back of his classes, and got mostly Cs and Ds. He was not involved in any school activities.

When he was 16 years old Dale dropped out of school and joined the army. He was stationed in Korea as a jeep driver. While there he got into a fight with his sergeant and was given a dishonorable discharge. On his arrival home he traveled the country on a motorcycle from the fur trapping regions of Canada to the coastal fishing towns of Florida and the Gulf Coast. Along the way he developed a taste for alcohol and an aversion to steady employment.

In 1976 Henderson was sentenced to eleven months in jail in Tennessee for burglarizing a home. He blamed the crime on his drinking. Before the sentence was completed he went out on a work release program and never came back.

In 1977 he was jailed for a year in Florida for possession of a stolen driver's license. Released on parole, he skipped the state and thus became a fugitive from Florida as well as from Tennessee.

Henderson hid for a while in some of his Canadian haunts before ending up in Laramie, Wyoming. One night in 1978 he met a woman in a cowboy bar there. The woman liked Dale and invited him to her home. When they got to her place he held a knife on her, tied and gagged her, and fled with less than nine dollars. The woman called police and he was soon arrested.

Convicted of armed robbery, Henderson was sentenced to three to five years at the minimum security farm at the Wyoming State Prison at Rawlins. In prison he did his time well. He got along with staff members and other inmates. "He was a cutup," a fellow prisoner remembered, "Just being around him made you feel comfortable."

While at Rawlins Henderson earned his high school diploma and worked in the prison upholstery shop. He joined an Alcoholic Anonymous group. His record was clean and he was a model prisoner. The only possible problem was that as the sentence wore on his fellow convicts noticed that he was becoming withdrawn.

Because of his good record, Henderson was let out of prison after just three years. He went on parole and stayed in Rawlins, where he got a job as a maintenance man at the Ramada Inn. It was there that he met Donna Barnett.

Donna Barnett was 22 years old and had just been divorced. She had two small children.

The Cincinnati Crime Book

Donna and Dale struck up a friendship. Soon after, to the surprise of many of their friends, they got married.

In October 1981 Henderson suggested to his young bride that perhaps it would be better for them if they went to live near her parents in Cherry Fork, Ohio, about 80 miles east of Cincinnati. Dale and Donna didn't have enough money for the move so Donna's parents, Ivan and Marie Barnett, sent it to them. The Barnetts knew of a trailer near their house that the Hendersons could live in. Donna's brother Joel offered Dale a job in his garage.

Even though he still had three months to go on his parole, Wyoming prison officials said it was all right for Henderson to leave the state. In late October of 1981, with a new family and a job, Dale Henderson's future was finally looking bright.

Once the Hendersons got to Ohio, however, things went downhill instead. Donna noticed a moodiness in her husband that had not been apparent in Wyoming. After a few weeks her brother had to lay Dale off at the garage because he was drinking on the job. Henderson collected unemployment checks and spent his days driving around southwestern Ohio. He told his wife that he was unsuccessfully looking for another job. On one occasion guns and watches appeared in the Henderson trailer and Dale had a dubious story about their origins. He later sold them out of the trunk of his car.

One day Donna's brother walked into a bar in Cherry Fork and saw Dale Henderson drinking with a woman. Unseen, Joel watched as the couple left. He did not tell his sister about it. Other members of the Barnett family were also expressing their concern over Henderson's behavior. There were arguments, and animosities grew.

On January 15, 1982 Dale Henderson returned from his daily driving foray and sat in front of the television set. He uncharacteristically paid rapt attention to the local newscasts, which were full of news about the Anderson Township housewife who had disappeared the day before from the Eastgate Mall. Some relatives kidded Dale about his interest, but he didn't seem amused.

From that point on his condition deteriorated rapidly. He was drinking heavily and acting as if he was wired on some drug. Marie Barnett commented on her son-in-law's increasingly eerie and even threatening demeanor. "Dale had the devil in his eyes," she said.

On January 21 Dale Henderson left his trailer, saying he was going to collect his unemployment check. A few hours later he appeared at Joel Barnett's garage. "It was the worst I'd ever seen him," Barnett later said. "His eyes were all bloodshot. He asked me twice what time Mom and Dad would eat dinner." Henderson had been asking a lot of strange questions about his in-laws recently, questions about how much money they had and whether they kept it in their house. Barnett went back to work as Henderson staggered to his car and drove away.

By now the devil was in Dale Henderson's soul.

The Cincinnati Crime Book

Later that afternoon Joel Barnett drove past his parents' home and noticed Henderson's car parked outside. He continued on to his own home. That evening he returned to his parents' house. Now Henderson's car was gone. Inside the house Joel Barnett found a nightmare.

Ivan and Marie Barnett were dead. They had each been shot in the head as they sat in their living room drinking coffee. The coffee cups were still in their hands. Joel's younger brother Cliff was also dead. The eleven-year-old had been shot as he walked into the room with an armload of firewood. The murder weapon, a .22 caliber rifle, was on a bed. Two pistols − a .22 and a .38 − were missing along with a small amount of money. (As Henderson had suspected, the Barnetts did keep a large amount of cash in their home. But the $38,000 was well hidden and he did not find it.)

Joel Barnett called the police, who immediately began searching for the number one suspect in the triple murder: Robert Dale Henderson, Jr.

It wasn't until Sunday January 24 that police got their first lead. Early that morning they found Henderson's car abandoned near 3rd and Main Streets in downtown Cincinnati. By that time, however, he was already over 600 miles away.

Henderson had arrived in Charleston, South Carolina the day before. Calling himself "Billy Henderson" he spent his time drinking and playing pool in bars. In one bar he met a man to whom he sold the .38 caliber revolver taken from the Barnett home for $25.

Unfortunately for eight other people, Henderson would hold on to the .22 until he was arrested.

That Superbowl Sunday in 1982 the San Francisco 49ers played (and defeated) the Cincinnati Bengals. Like millions of other sports enthusiasts, Dale Henderson watched the game in a bar. In the final minutes of the game the bartender noticed Henderson going out the back door with a woman he had been shooting pool with. She was a 21-year-old part time model named Lucinda Lee Russell.

The next day one of Henderson's new Charleston friends went to pick him up at his motel to take him to a job. Henderson was not there. Later that day a hunter found the body of Lucinda Lee Russell in a rural area about 30 miles away from where she was last seen. She had been raped and shot once in the head with a .22. Her car, a brown Dodge Aries, was missing. Police began a massive search for "Billy Henderson."

But he had already left the area.

The same day Lucinda Russell's body was found, Henderson drove her car to Palatka, Florida, just south of Jacksonville. At around 11:00 a.m. the car was noticed parked in front of a western clothing store. Fifteen minutes later the car was gone. At that time a saddle repairman entered the store and found the clerk, Dorothy Wilkinson, lying dead on the floor behind the counter. Blood flowed from a bullet wound in the side of her head. About $50 was missing from the cash register.

The Cincinnati Crime Book

Even as police were beginning to investigate this murder, an ambulance was arriving a few miles away at the home of a 79-year-old retired doctor. Murray Ferderber had been found dead in his home. An invalid, Ferderber was found sitting in a chair with a bullet wound in the back of his head. It was soon determined that $150 was missing from his home.

Police later theorized that the killer spent the night of January 24 in a car in a wooded area near Ferderber's home. Upon awakening, he robbed and murdered the physician, and then killed Mrs. Wilkinson at the clothing store on his way out of town.

An all-points-bulletin was issued for the Dodge Aries. But again, Henderson was already out of the area.

Still on January 25 Henderson arrived in Valdosta, Georgia, located on Interstate 75 in the southern part of the state. In a small grocery store he noticed a young mother and her 12-year-old daughter. When the ladies left the store Henderson followed them out to the parking lot and then to their apartment two miles away.

While the daughter was in the kitchen of her apartment putting away the groceries, she heard a strange noise at the front door. When she went to investigate the noise she found her mother and the man from the store in the living room. The man smelled of alcohol. And he had a gun.

The gunman led the women into the bedroom where he took $20 from them. He forced them to strip, tied them up with panty hose, and gagged them with socks. Then he viciously assaulted the girl while her mother looked on.

Suddenly the mother had her hands free and was able to get the Henderson's gun. She smashed him in the head with it. "Don't shoot, don't hurt anybody," he begged as he tried to get away. The woman fired three shots at the attacker, but because of her distraught condition she was not able to hit him.

The daughter recovered and broke a glass candy dish over the man's head. But he was able to regain possession of the gun and run out of the building. It was about 5:30 p.m.

In his hurry to get away Henderson left behind some important clues. One was a four inch knife that appeared to have bloodstains on the blade. Another clue was a wallet. In the wallet was a picture of Donna Barnett and a business card from a bar in Charleston, South Carolina.

Two days later Dale Henderson's wanted poster arrived in Valdosta. The 12-year-old girl easily identified him as her attacker. But already the alcoholic drifter was hundreds of miles away in another state committing another murder.

When Henderson left Valdosta he headed north. Perhaps fearing that the Dodge Aries was too hot, he abandoned it near the bus station in Macon, Georgia. Then he bought a bus ticket to Mobile, Alabama. In Mobile he got another bus which dropped him off in the gulf town of Pascagoula,

Mississippi late on the morning of January 26. Using the name "Paul Reed" he checked into a local motel and rested overnight.

One mile straight down the road from Henderson's motel was the Singing River Hospital.

At noon on January 27 Sheryl McDonald arrived at the hospital to visit her ailing 88-year-old grandmother. After a two hour visit she bade her elderly relative good-bye and started back towards her car, which was parked in the hospital's huge lot.

At 4:00 p.m. Sheryl's husband Robert arrived home from work. Neither his wife nor her yellow 1978 Mercury Marquis were at the house. Sheryl McDonald was very devoted to her family, and if she ever had to go somewhere unexpectedly she always left a note behind for her husband. This time there was no note. Robert McDonald notified the police.

The next day a Jackson County Deputy Sheriff was patrolling on a remote country road near an abandoned cemetery. There, alongside the road near a pile of empty beer bottles, he found the body of the missing housewife. Her wrists were tightly bound together. She had been raped and shot once in the head. Her purse and credit cards were found nearby. Money hidden in the purse was still intact, but a diamond ring and Sheryl's car were missing.

Deputies put out an alert for the car, but yet again Henderson had already left the area. The afternoon the body was discovered he was in Port Allen, Louisiana, a small town about 120 miles west of Pascagoula. He stayed there in a motel, again registering as "Paul Reed."

On January 29 Henderson entered a bar and ordered a rum and coke. Chatting with a barmaid, he mentioned finding a diamond ring in a parking lot. The woman agreed to buy the ring for $40. Henderson left that bar and later appeared in another one, The Casa Loma Lounge.

Samuel Corrent was the 61-year-old owner of the Casa Loma. He was at a happy time in his life. Not only was he anxiously looking forward to an upcoming vacation, but he was even thinking of getting out of the bar business altogether and retiring. "I feel better than I have all my life," he'd recently told a friend. "I'm thinking of taking it easy, selling the place, and relaxing. I've worked hard all my life."

At 8:30 p.m. on January 29 Dale Henderson walked into the Casa Loma Lounge and ordered a beer. He spent the evening drinking and socializing with some off-duty workers from a nearby chemical plant. By 11 o'clock he had switched his drink to rum and coke. By midnight the last of the plant workers left and Henderson was the bar's lone customer.

Sam Corrent didn't like late night problems with troublesome drunks, so he always closed up at midnight instead of the legally allowed 2:00 a.m. When Henderson ordered his last drink he got it in a plastic cup to go.

That cup was still sitting on the bar the next morning at 8:30 when two friends of Corrent's stopped at the Casa Loma to see why the bar's neon sign had not been turned off.

The Cincinnati Crime Book

Samuel Corrent was lying behind the bar. He had been shot four times. $300 from the cash register and Corrent's .38 caliber revolver were taken, but $1500 in a money belt had been missed. Outside, a yellow 1978 Mercury Marquis was parked up against the building. Sam Corrent's truck, a silver Ford, was gone.

With Corrent's money and a new vehicle, Henderson was able to take a momentary respite from his killing ways. For the next few days he drove around aimlessly in Louisiana and Texas before heading back to his old, familiar territory, Florida. He was back in the northern part of the state by February 3. That day he picked up three young hitchhikers.

Frances Dickey, 23, was a young woman running away from an abusive husband. 27-year-old Vernon Odem was running away from a robbery charge in Mississippi. Robert Dawson, 19, had just been discharged from the Navy and was on the road because of youthful restlessness.

For the next three days Henderson and his three new friends moved from motel to motel, mostly drinking and engaging in sex. They also spent time devising various illegal schemes for getting their hands on some money.

But by the time the group reached rural Hernando County in central Florida on February 5 Henderson had decided that his traveling companions were more of a liability that an asset. Indeed, he had also come to the conclusion that the trio was plotting to murder him. So, finding a secluded area away from the main highway he forced everybody out of the truck, tied them up, and shot each one in the head with his .22 caliber pistol.

The next day Henderson abandoned Samuel Corrent's Ford and began hitchhiking farther south into Florida. He got as far as tiny Punta Gorda when he apparently decided that he'd had enough of his murderous life on the road.

At a shopping center he called the Charlotte County Sheriffs Department and told them that the stereo had been stolen from his car. When a deputy arrived to check out the call, he found Dale Henderson standing in the shopping center parking lot. A purple nylon bag was on the ground at his feet.

"My gun is in the bag," Henderson told the stunned officer. "I want to give myself up. I've killed ten or eleven people. I'm not sure how many."

Actually, the number of victims was twelve.

Henderson was immediately taken into custody. When police voiced skepticism about his claims, he backed them up by taking officers to the bodies of the three hitchhikers. He was arrested for murder and held without bail.

While in jail he made a complete confession to the crimes he had committed on his spree. When he told of a woman he had picked up in a Cincinnati shopping mall and left dead in a barn, police for the first time connected him with the rape-slaying of Jerilyn Stanfield on January 14.

Why did Dale Henderson embark on his serial killing rampage? The motive for the murders seems to have been to eliminate witnesses to his assaults and robberies. He had a record for both offenses long before he took his first life.

It may be that when Henderson left Jerilyn Stanfield in that Clermont County barn he didn't know if she was really dead. But when the days went by with no news of her being found, he must have known that she couldn't have survived. He probably then felt that he had nothing more to lose. As he later said, "Once you've killed one, it's no big deal."

Henderson took a gamble in killing the Barnetts, but it didn't pay off. He failed to locate their hidden money. By then the futility of his actions (and maybe of his whole life) may have overwhelmed him, with the resultant lethal consequences for the unfortunate people he met on the road.

The legal proceedings against Dale Henderson were as varied and confusing as his crimes. In June 1982 he pleaded guilty in Florida to the Ferderber and Wilkinson shootings. In exchange for the guilty pleas the state agreed not to seek the death penalty. He got two life terms. In November 1982 a jury convicted him of the murders of the three hitchhikers in Hernando County. He received three death sentences and went to Florida's death row.

On August 5, 1985 Henderson pleaded guilty to three counts of aggravated murder and one count of aggravated robbery in the murders of his in-laws three and a half years earlier. He got thirty years to life on each count.

The following February he was indicted in Clermont County for the murder of Jerilyn Stanfield. In September he entered a plea of not guilty, then changed the plea to guilty in exchange for the prosecution dropping the death penalty specifications.

Henderson went to the Florida State Prison at Starke. The state was very ready to execute him for the three hitchhikers' murders, but numerous appeals delayed his appointment with the electric chair. The man who took the lives of others so callously used every avenue the legal system had to offer to save his own life, which, to him, *was* a big deal.

But he couldn't postpone his fate forever. On April 12, 1993, over ten years after his crimes, Dale Henderson's time finally ran out. He was 48 years old. The eyes where Marie Barnett saw the devil were now sightless from a congenital vision disorder.

At 7:00 a.m. Dale Henderson was strapped into Florida's electric chair. He did not make a final statement. The executioner threw the switch, and Henderson's body strained as 2000 volts of electricity coursed through it.

He was pronounced dead ten minutes later.

The Cincinnati Crime Book

Dale Henderson. (*The Cincinnati Enquirer*/Michael Snyder)

**Dale Henderson kidnaped his Cincinnati victim from
this shopping mall parking lot.**

Alton Coleman And Debra Brown

Just two years after Dale Henderson made his murderous mark on Cincinnati another series of brutal crimes rocked the area. But unlike Henderson's case, wherein the true extent of his crimes only became known after he was already in custody, this time the public was aware that the killer was at large and possibly still in the area. Because of that, Cincinnati felt the fear of being held hostage by a serial killer – a fear it had not experienced since the Cincinnati Strangler case almost twenty years earlier.

At about 3:15 p.m. on Friday July 13, 1984 a young woman bounded up the steps of a green, two-and-a-half story wood frame house at 4118 Floral Avenue, in Norwood, Ohio. Norwood is a centrally situated suburb completely surrounded by the City of Cincinnati. The house on Floral Avenue was in one of Norwood's better neighborhoods, a tree-lined street of homes comfortably located away from any major thoroughfares.

The woman's purpose for being at the house was to visit her parents. But the minute she opened the front door she knew this was not going to be a routine visit.

The usually neat home was a shambles. Furniture was out of place, papers and material were tossed around, and broken glass was everywhere.

Very concerned, the daughter called out for her parents and began to make her way through the house. When she got to the basement, her search was over.

The parents, Harry and Marlene Walters, were lying on the floor. Harry Walters was handcuffed and had a bucket placed over his head. Marlene Walters had been bound with an electrical cord. Her head was wrapped in a bloody sheet. Blood was splattered everywhere around them. Both had obviously been savagely beaten.

The daughter called Norwood Police, who almost immediately arrived from their station on nearby Elm Avenue. They determined right away that Marlene Walters was dead. Her husband, though, was still alive. Police called an ambulance, and Harry Walters was rushed to University Hospital, where he was listed in critical condition.

The Cincinnati Crime Book

Police cordoned off the property and began their investigation into the murderous assault. Inside, the house looked like it had been ransacked. Outside, everything appeared to be normal. A pop-up camper trailer, with a sign marked "For Sale," was parked in the driveway. The Walters' car, a burgundy colored 1983 Plymouth Reliant, was missing. Two 10-speed bicycles were in the driveway. The daughter told police that the bikes did not belong on her parents' property.

Neighbors of the Walters couldn't believe what had happened. They were shocked not just by the attack itself, but that it happened to the Walters. "They were extremely vigilant, careful people," one neighbor remembered. "(They were) the last people you'd expect to be victims of a crime. They were very aware of what was going on. In fact, they were more or less like vigilantes. Harry saw a guy stealing a woman's car battery once and almost caught him. He jumped in his truck and chased him." The neighbor added that the Walters had three German Shepherds.

"You always hear about something like this in other people's neighborhood, but not your own," said another resident of Floral Avenue. "I could see it if it was on Montgomery Road, but not in this area."

Other neighbors were simply terrified by the crime. "I told my husband his gun doesn't (even) make me feel safe anymore," said one woman. "Even when you have guns at home, like police officers do, it's (just) another thing you have to worry about when you go into your home. Is somebody already there? Does somebody have the guns?"

Police spread through the neighborhood and questioned everyone to see if they had any information about what had happened that Friday afternoon. One neighbor recalled a telephone conversation with Marlene Walters earlier that day in which Marlene told her that her husband had just left to go to a bank with two strangers. The strangers, a young black couple, had appeared at the Walters' house on bicycles and expressed an interest in buying the camper in the driveway. After the couple decided to buy the camper, Mrs. Walters said, Harry and the two strangers went to the couple's bank to get the money to pay for it. This story was backed up by at least seven other neighbors on Floral Avenue who had noticed the pair at the Walters residence. That was the last thing anyone knew about Harry and Marlene Walters until they were discovered by their daughter at 3:15.

This information dovetailed with finding the two strange bicycles at the Walters house. The information was also important because the description of the young black couple matched that of two persons who had been sought for almost three months for a murderous crime spree that had ranged over six states. Six persons were already believed to have fallen victim to the homicidal pair. The male member of the couple had just been added to the FBI's 10 Most Wanted list as a "Special Addition" two days before the deadly assault on Floral Avenue. His name was Alton Coleman.

The Cincinnati Crime Book

Alton Coleman grew up in Waukegan, Illinois. People who knew him in his old neighborhood described him as "a charmer" and "someone everyone likes to be with." But the neighbors' recollections were oddly tempered by a fear of the fugitive. None wanted to be identified in the press because, "We're afraid he'll come get us."

Coleman was raised on the south side of town, a mostly black and Hispanic area. His neighborhood had been the scene of intense race rioting during the 1960s and '70s and would later be described as a "rough" place. There was no father figure in young Alton's life and even his mother was not present much. Coleman, along with six siblings, was raised for the most part by his maternal grandmother. Ironically, the grandmother's sister, Alton Coleman's great aunt, was Addie Devost, a woman who was charged in one of the most sensational series of murders in Waukegan history. According to police, DeVost had murdered three of her husbands – one with an axe, one with a gun, and the third by stabbing and beating with a hammer, screwdriver, and tire iron.

By the time he was 28 years old Alton Coleman already had a substantial criminal history. In 1973 he was charged with kidnaping and rape in Waukegan. Convicted on a lesser charge of robbery, he spent two years in Joliet Prison. In 1976 he was again charged with rape in Waukegan. While awaiting trial he was charged by other prisoners in the county jail with "deviate sexual behavior." The prisoners wouldn't testify against him, however, so these charges were dropped. Coleman was later acquitted on the rape charge. In 1980 he was acquitted in the rape of a woman in Chicago.

Over the next several years Coleman was charged four times with various sex related crimes. In three instances the charges were dropped when victims refused to testify. In one case the presiding judge responded to the victim's allegation that her identification of Coleman was a lie that had been coerced by police. "I've heard what she has to say." the judge said, "(and) I find it completely implausible. I think the woman, as she stands here today, is terrified by this man (Coleman)."

On May 29, 1984 Coleman kidnaped 9-year-old Vernita Wheat after befriending the girl's mother. Two days later he learned that he was suspected in the disappearance of the young girl. He fled the area.

By now Coleman had a companion, a 21-year-old woman named Debra Denise Brown.

Debra Brown was also from Waukegan. One of eleven children, she was engaged to another man when she met Alton Coleman at a nightclub in 1981. Brown's mother later recalled, "Debra's a good girl. She liked music and she liked dancing." Although Debra's mother had met Coleman and "he was nice" around her, she noticed how her daughter had changed for the worse since she met him. "Debra used to be real close to her sister. Since she's met Coleman, she's different. If I could just talk to her, away from (him)...." The mother had been upset when Debra said she was moving in with Coleman. "I asked her not to. Coleman had a bad reputation, but she said she was a grown girl and could do what she wanted."

Police knew that Coleman rented an apartment in Gary with Debra Brown and they questioned her there on June 1 regarding the disappearance of Vernita Wheat. She said she didn't know anything about the missing girl. After police left, she apparently joined Coleman on the run. One FBI personality analysis of Brown said she was "dominated, manipulated, and controlled" by Alton Coleman.

On June 18 Tamika Turks, 7, and her 10-year-old cousin Annie Hillard vanished on their way to a store in Gary, Indiana. The next day Annie was found in a wooded area near Gary. She had been beaten and raped. Her young cousin was also found, dead.

That same day the body of Vernita Wheat was found in an abandoned building in Waukegan.

In Gary, a woman reported to police that her daughter, Donna Williams, had disappeared on June 19. Five days later a woman was kidnaped by a young couple matching the description of Coleman and Brown. This woman later managed to get away from her captors.

On July 7 Toledo, Ohio authorities discovered the bodies of a woman and her young daughter stuffed into the crawlspace under their house. Elsewhere in Toledo an elderly couple reported that their car had been stolen by suspects who matched the descriptions of Coleman and Brown.

Four days later, on July 11, Donna Williams' body was discovered in an abandoned building in Detroit, Michigan.

By then, Alton Coleman and Debra Brown were in Cincinnati.

Because of the belief that he was responsible for the attack in Norwood, police charged Alton Coleman with aggravated murder, attempted aggravated murder, aggravated robbery, aggravated burglary, and auto theft in connection with the incidents at the Walters' residence. Police said that Brown was not a suspect in the Walters case; they only wanted her for questioning.

Norwood police said that Coleman and Brown had no known friends in the Cincinnati area, but added that the couple must have stayed somewhere during their time in the Queen City. They appealed for those persons to come forward with information.

One person who came forward was the Reverend Sterling Price, an interim pastor at the Wyoming (Ohio) Baptist Church. Wyoming is another suburb of Cincinnati, located several miles northwest of Norwood.

Pastor Price recalled that on the day before the attack in Norwood a man matching Coleman's description had appeared at the church asking for assistance. "There's an infinitesimal chance that it wasn't him," Price said, "but I'm convinced that it was."

Price said that the stranger had been alone and had asked for money for rent and for a heart bypass operation for his mother. "He wanted to know if he could wash the windows of the church for money. I was sympathetic to the fellow, but there was nothing I could do for him." The preacher offered the man cookies and water, which he accepted and ate.

Price said he did not see anyone else with the man or any kind of vehicle. "He was in a hurry to get some money, I can tell you that. His behavior was very exemplary. He didn't scream and shout, he didn't threaten. He didn't overtly insist on the money. (But) I can tell you that he smelled to high heaven. The thing that stood out most about him was that the perspiration was just dripping off him." Price's visitor left after fifteen minutes.

"When it happened, I just thought of him as another poor soul who needed help and I felt bad that I couldn't help," the minister concluded. "Now, I just have an eerie feeling...."

Price's experience fit the known modus operandi of Alton Coleman. Coleman was regarded as a smooth talker who easily made friends, especially with people predisposed to reach out to other people, like ministers and social workers. Coleman frequently approached black churches for help. Police began to interview other clergymen the suspect might have tried to contact.

When the identity of the suspects became known, Harry and Marlene Walters' neighborhood reacted true to the reputation of the white, working class suburb that Norwood is. One woman, who had taught Sunday school with Marlene Walters, said, "I don't think they're still around here. If it's who they think it is, they'd be fools to stay here. They'd be lynched."

Another neighbor added, "There are a lot of strong feelings about blacks around here anyway. They're seen with suspicion. And now it will look like those suspicions are justified."

But authorities were quick to put an end to speculation that the crime had been racially motivated. "This man is wanted nationwide," said Norwood Police Sergeant John Murphy. "He's killed more black people than white people and he is just a killer, not a person venting one race against the other. He doesn't seem to care what race a victim is, so why should anyone here try to make it out as a racial slaying?"

On Sunday July 15 Harry Walters' condition was upgraded from critical to serious. His room at University Hospital was still under 24 hour guard by police.

Late that same night police got their first break in the case. The Walters' missing car was recovered from a cornfield in a semi-residential area in northwest Lexington, Kentucky, about five miles from the city's downtown and a half mile from Interstate 75. The location in the field was so secluded that even some nearby residents were not aware of it until police questioned them about the car found there.

Lexington Police and FBI agents went door to door in the surrounding neighborhoods, which were predominantly black and middle-class, and tried to determine if anyone had seen Coleman and Brown. Because the car had been found in such a secluded spot, police thought that the suspects might be familiar with the area or even know people there. But they didn't find any link

– just terrified neighbors. "I didn't sleep a wink last night," said one resident. "I wish to God they would find him. It sure would ease my mind."

As news of the Norwood tragedy and the missing suspects spread, Cincinnati police began to receive many reports of sightings of the wanted pair. Although the officers checked all of the sightings out, none of the people seen were Coleman and Brown. The panic over the killers continued.

The next lead in the case was the kind that law enforcement officers anticipate with dread: the perpetrator struck again.

On Tuesday July 17 police in Dayton, Ohio were called to McCabe Park in the west central area of the city to check out a suspicious vehicle. When they checked the vehicle they discovered that a man was locked in the trunk.

The man was Oline Carmical Jr, age 39. Luckily, he was still alive. Carmical told police that he lived in Williamsburg, Kentucky and that he taught political science and history at the Cumberland College there. He was in Lexington for the summer while he attended the University of Kentucky on a fellowship program.

The professor was unharmed, at least physically. "I was threatened, but nobody laid a hand on me," he said. "(But) they threatened to blow my brains out."

The description Carmical gave of his kidnappers fit Alton Coleman and Debra Brown.

The discovery of Oline Carmical was quickly linked to another incident that occurred in Dayton that day. A few hours before the discovery of the abducted history professor an elderly couple had been beaten in their home in West Dayton. And, true to Alton Coleman's MO, the man in the couple was a minister, the Reverend Millard Gay.

Reverend Gay and his wife were not beaten seriously. Gay readily identified his attackers as Alton Coleman and Debra Brown. He said that a week or so earlier, from July 7 to the 9th, Coleman and Brown had stayed as guests in the Gay home. He said the couple called themselves "Paul and Diana Fisher." After the visit, Gay said, he and his wife gave the two strangers a ride to Cincinnati. In Cincinnati everybody attended a service at a church on West Wyoming Avenue on the evening of July 9. When they came out of the service they discovered that the tires on the car had been slashed, so Rev. and Mrs. Gay and "the Fishers" all spent the night in the vehicle. The next day the tires were repaired and Gay dropped the couple off at the corner of Central Avenue and 7th Street, downtown. Gay and his wife then went home and did not see the couple again until they reappeared at their home in Dayton on July 17 and beat them. The suspects took the Gays' car, a 1975 Buick station wagon.

With Coleman and Brown apparently moving around very freely, fear continued to build in the Midwest. Nobody knew where the murderous couple would strike next. Police noted that the pair would often befriend someone and then return later to attack them. Because police theorized that Coleman and Brown must have stayed with someone in Cincinnati between the time the Gays dropped them off downtown and the time the Walters were attacked, they were especially concerned about those individuals. "We believe very strongly there are other people in Dayton and Cincinnati who befriended Coleman and his associates," said Dayton Police Chief Tyree Broomfield. "Anyone who has aided Coleman is obligated to come forward and share that information. They have the responsibility to share whatever they know."

FBI Special Agent Richard Dorton said, "It's a very real concern of ours that he could be in another place because the individual or individuals he stayed with have not come forward, and we are afraid he is covering his tracks. It's been his pattern in Ohio to stay with someone."

Also on July 17 a funeral service was held for Marlene Walters in Norwood. Relatives, friends, and neighbors packed the Grace United Methodist Church on Slane Avenue, just a half block away from the Walters home, to mourn the slain woman. Mrs. Walters had worked in the church library and taught Sunday School there. Reverend Bud Allison called Marlene Walters "a mother to everyone who knew her," and asked mourners to remember the victim for the person she was – a loving wife and mother – and not for the way she died.

Another mourner said, "You can't find any nicer people anywhere than Marlene and Harry. The man who did this, I wish there was a way for him to feel the pain of (the Walters) family."

Harry Walters did not attend the memorial service. He was still in serious condition and under police guard at University Hospital.

The fear spread. With recent crimes perpetrated by the fugitive couple occurring in Norwood, Lexington, and Dayton, it appeared that Coleman and Brown were moving around and striking at will, without being affected by the massive manhunt that was looking for them. Residents throughout the Midwest wondered where the pair would strike next. Wisconsin, Illinois, Indiana, Michigan, Ohio, Kentucky – Coleman and Brown could have been anywhere.

But after three more days of tension the suspense finally ended. On July 20 Alton Coleman and Debra Brown were finally apprehended as they sat in a park in Evanston, Illinois. Evanston, a suburb north of Chicago, was about 250 miles from the suspects' last known whereabouts in Dayton, Ohio.

The arrest came after another patron of the park noticed that Coleman and Brown had a handgun. That person called police. When police arrived on the scene, they found the fugitives seated at a picnic table. They arrested them without incident. The gun, a revolver, was found in Debra Brown's purse. In addition to the firearm, police also confiscated a steak knife from Alton Coleman's sock.

Coleman and Brown were initially held on a concealed weapons charge, but after their identities became known more charges were added. They were eventually held on a variety of federal charges with a combined bond of $45 million. They were detained at Chicago's Metropolitan Correctional Center.

In justifying the extraordinarily high bond, the U.S. Magistrate who imposed it declared, "This nation has been under a siege. This nation has been under a reign of terror not knowing when the next victim was to be taken. (By imposing this high bond) I am going to make sure that no other victim will be subject to this man."

But while the arrest of Alton Coleman and Debra Brown meant the residents of six states could breath a sigh of relief, it didn't mean that the horror was over.

A day before the arrests, on July 19, a Cincinnati realtor was showing a property to a prospective buyer. The property was an unused and somewhat dilapidated building at 2826 May Street in Walnut Hills. The potential buyer was considering remodeling the former multi-family dwelling into doctors offices. As the two men inspected the first floor of the red-brick Victorian style building they found the bound and badly decomposing body of a young black girl. Above the body, on a wall, was written "I hate niggers. Death." The men, both badly shaken, quickly left the building and called police.

The next day the dead girl was identified as Tonnie Storey of Mohawk Place in Over-the-Rhine, downtown. Storey had been reported missing on July 12 after vanishing the previous day.

Tonnie Storey was a 15-year-old eighth grader at the Bloom Junior High School in Cincinnati's West End. She was described as a good student, earning mostly Bs in English, French, science, and advanced math. "The intelligence was there and the ability to become a success was there," her principal remembered. "She had a pleasant personality and she got along with her teachers and along with the students."

Tonnie was also active in school sports, playing on Bloom's volleyball, softball, and track teams. A teacher remembered her as "always smiling, all the time, and she was a person who was always pleasant, even when she was being reprimanded."

One woman who knew the girl said that her friendly manner may have been a factor in her death. "She was a nice girl. Maybe that's what happened. She was too nice. She got to talking with (Alton Coleman).... I think her friendliness ended her life, that's what I think."

In the summer of 1984 Tonnie Storey had been taking a summer school course in computer science. The last day of that class was July 11. After completing that last day of classes she was seen by witnesses at about 1:00 p.m. at the corner of Elder and Republic Streets in Over-the-Rhine. That was the last time anyone saw her until she was discovered in the house on May Street.

Cincinnati Police began investigating Tonnie Storey's death as a homicide because, as Homicide Lieutenant Hugh Burger said, "It's highly unusual to find a dead person with hardly any clothes on in a vacant building." He added,

"I can't say for sure this is Coleman's, but I can't say for sure that it isn't, either. We do know that Coleman was in Cincinnati from July 9 to July 13 and as far as we know, (the dead girl) could have died in that time period." Burger said that the Hamilton County Coroner was performing tests to determine how Storey died and whether she had been sexually assaulted.

Cincinnati Police quickly located witnesses who claimed to have seen Alton Coleman in the neighborhood around the May Street house.

One man recalled, "He was smooth talking. The way he used words really got your attention. He just slid over to talk to us and he fit right in. It was maybe 9:30 at night. I saw him across the street, with a girl, and he came over and asked to buy a bag of weed and some (rolling papers). And he was talking about the girl. He said she lived around the corner, in an apartment. He said he was from out of town. She was nice looking, and he was saying they were going to go lay up and smoke some weed."

The description of the girl seen with the suspect did not match Tonnie Storey.

Another witness said, "His face looked familiar, but I didn't recognize him. After he got caught, I saw his picture over the TV and I knew it was him."

A woman in the neighborhood said she was approached at her home on May Street by a man and girl who wanted to rent a room. The woman was sure the male visitor had been Alton Coleman.

On July 26 Cincinnati law enforcement officers announced that Alton Coleman and Debra Brown would begin their series of trials on the multiple and multi-state charges against them in Cincinnati.

One reason Cincinnati was selected to go first was because the evidence in the crimes committed there was strongest. "We do have evidence of a substantial nature to present to a jury, if the case goes to a jury," Hamilton County Prosecutor Arthur Ney said. "And we are prepared to go to trial."

Another factor in picking Cincinnati was the consensus that a conviction in conservative Hamilton County would lead to "the swiftest imposition of the death penalty," said Ney. "We've tried seven aggravated murder cases with the death penalty in Hamilton County since (Ohio's new death penalty) law went into effect (October, 1981), and we've had seven convictions."

In Chicago, United States Attorney Dan K. Webb echoed this hard line. "We will not be satisfied with one conviction. After the first convictions, then we'll proceed in all other jurisdictions to get murder convictions and death penalties in as many states as possible.... We want to make certain that (Coleman's execution) occurs. We believe the likelihood of obtaining the death penalty is substantial."

Alton Coleman and Debra Brown were transferred from Chicago to await their trials for the murders of Marlene Walters and Tonnie Storey. It was decided that the defendants would be tried separately, but simultaneously, on both charges.

The Cincinnati Crime Book

The trials of Alton Coleman and Debra Brown for the murder of Marlene Walters and assault on her husband both began in April, 1985.

The jury in the trial of Alton Coleman, consisting of four men and eight women, was selected by Friday, April 19. But things didn't go smoothly. Coleman accused his attorneys of being involved in a "plot" with the prosecution which allegedly allowed him to have conjugal visits with Debra Brown in exchange for a guilty plea. "Right now we don't even have a defense," Coleman told Hamilton County Common Pleas Judge Richard Niehaus. "We might as well flip a coin. I might as well not have any defense lawyers. (Do) you think I trust my life with these guys (his court-appointed attorneys)? I'm not satisfied. (Do) you think we're playing marbles here? I have no more faith in (them)."

Prosecutor Ney denied there was any plot and said that Coleman's attorneys had "gone overboard" in defending him.

Coleman asked Judge Niehaus to dismiss his lawyers and allow him to defend himself.

Down the hall, Debra Brown was being tried before Judge Fred J. Cartolano. In opening the case for his client, defense attorney Daniel Burke said, "The defense will admit that a crime has been committed, but we believe evidence will not show that Debra Brown committed any crime of aggravated murder (against) Marlene Walters."

On Monday April 22 Judge Niehaus granted Alton Coleman's request to be allowed to defend himself as a co-counsel of his court-appointed attorneys. As part his opening statement, Coleman thanked the jury for their service and said, "I have a lot to say, but I don't want to go into it now. I realize I'm on trial for my life."

In the state's opening argument Prosecutor Ney said that the evidence would show that Alton Coleman was responsible for the murder and assault that occurred on Floral Avenue. Coleman's co-defense attorney Peter Rosenwald countered, "it was not Alton Coleman who acted with prior calculation and with design" to commit the crime.

Meanwhile, in Fred Cartolano's courtroom, testimony began in the aggravated murder trial of Debra Brown.

Among the first witnesses called in her trial were neighbors of Harry and Marlene Walters who testified that at about 10:30 on the morning of the murder they had seen Alton Coleman and Debra Brown at the Walters' house talking with the Walters.

Then Harry and Marlene Walters' daughter testified about July 13, 1984, when she visited her parents' Norwood home early in the afternoon. Debra Brown sat expressionless while the young woman remembered the events of that day. The witness and defendant never made eye contact with each other.

"A man and woman had come to look at our camper," the daughter recalled. "I didn't see him and I just saw the back of her head." The daughter said that her mother said "the people were going to buy the camper. (But) she didn't think they would come through with the money. She didn't trust them."

The witness remembered her later return to the house and the horrifying scene she found there. "I went in and hollered, 'I'm home', which is usual. I saw my dogs tied up, which is unusual." She noticed that the house had been ransacked. Then she heard her father's voice crying "Help" from the basement. She went downstairs and found her parents bound and bloodied. "I tried to untie them," she said. She pulled back the sheet which was over her mother's head. "I lifted it up, and the back of her head was caved in."

Brown's attorneys did not cross-examine the Walters' daughter.

The state called the paramedics who had responded to the call for help after Ms. Walters discovered her parents. Harry Walters, one paramedic said, "tried to move away. He seemed to be afraid of us. He didn't know who we were. All he would say is 'Marlene.' (Mrs. Walters was) in a state where we would say she was obviously dead. The body was blue. Her arms, behind her, were stiff."

The next day a fingerprint expert testified that he found 23 fingerprints at the Walters' residence that belonged either to Alton Coleman or Debra Brown. The specialist said that Debra Brown's prints were on a serrated knife, a coffee table, a coffee cup, an envelope, and on a red ten-speed bicycle. Coleman's prints were found on a piece of a broken soft drink bottle, on a table, inside the camper, and on a yellow ten-speed bicycle. "I have never made a mistake on fingerprints in court," the specialist emphasized.

On April 25 three couples from Dayton and Toledo Ohio testified about being beaten and robbed by Coleman and Brown in July of 1984. This testimony was part of a prosecution strategy of showing a pattern of beatings and robberies consistent with what happened at the Walters residence.

The first couple described how Coleman and Brown had initially approached them at a garage sale and then led them at gunpoint to a bedroom where they were tied up and gagged before being robbed. They lost a television set, $150, and their car.

The second couple was the minister and wife who had befriended the two defendants and knew them as "Paul and Diane Fisher." Reverend Gay described how Coleman and Brown had returned to Dayton about ten days after he and his wife dropped them off in downtown Cincinnati. By then the minister had read newspaper accounts about the wanted fugitives. "I said, 'The police have been looking for you.... If I were you I'd get out of town.'" Instead, Coleman produced a handgun, tied the minister and his wife up, and threatened to beat them. "He started to hit us with a crowbar, but he changed his mind," the minister recalled. "He said, 'I'm not going to kill you. We don't generally leave them alive.'" The robbers stole the Gays' car.

The third couple recalled being restrained with a telephone chord, handcuffs, and gags, and being forced to lie on the floor while Coleman and Brown robbed them of about $100. This couple was not injured.

The Cincinnati Crime Book

On April 26, Harry Walters was called to the stand. He described how Coleman and Brown had showed up at Floral Avenue at about 11:00 a.m. on July 13, just as he and his wife were preparing to go on a weekend camping trip near Wilmington, Ohio. Walters said that he talked with Coleman about selling the camper to him. Then he drove Coleman and Brown to an apartment house in Evanston so Coleman could get the money to pay for it. "(Coleman) told me he was a recent military release and wasn't flushed with money. He wanted me to come down on the price (of the camper). I said I wouldn't come down." Walters said they returned to his house and were talking in the living room. "Shortly thereafter, I don't remember what happened. I vaguely remember some pain at that point.... I just know I was in pain." Harry Walters also remembered being on his knees and asking that Marlene not be hurt. The next thing he remembered was waking up at Good Samaritan hospital, two months later.

The director of University Hospital's neuro-trauma division testified that Harry Walters had received a "severe, life-threatening injury to the head."

Hamilton County Deputy Coroner Ross Zumwalt testified that Marlene Walters had been beaten about the head over twenty times, probably with a four-foot-long wooden candlestick holder that had been in the basement. "Many of (the blows) in and of themselves could have caused her death," Zumwalt said. The coroner accompanied his testimony with 22 graphic color slides of the dead woman.

After that testimony, the prosecution rested its case.

Defense attorneys were ready with their side of the story, but conceded that the main problem with preparing a defense had been the defendant herself. "She has been unwilling to basically follow any suggestions I have offered as a matter of defense," her attorney, Joseph Dixon, told the press. "The main character in this thing has been Alton Coleman (and not my client)." Dixon said it was unlikely that Brown would take the stand in her own defense. "She doesn't do that well on the stand," he said. "It wouldn't be of any benefit to her."

The lawyer who had represented Coleman and Brown earlier on the charge of kidnaping the professor in Lexington (they had already pleaded guilty to the charge) concurred. "I can accurately say that representing them was one of the worst experiences of my legal career. I don't envy the attorneys in Cincinnati at all." Defending the pair was like "a dentist trying to pull teeth.... (Brown) has (apparently) decided to tie her future in with (Coleman) for whatever result. That's something that's always troubled me from the very beginning. (It's) as if she's under some sort of mystical, hypnotic trance. There is no doubt in my mind that Alton Coleman has a certain effect on Debra Brown."

On Monday April 29 Alton Coleman called Debra Brown as a witness in his murder trial. Acting as his own attorney, he questioned his former companion about the events of July 13, 1984.

Brown recalled that she had done drugs that day. "I was smoking (marijuana) a lot and sniffing (cocaine) a lot. I can't recall where I was at."

After arriving at the Walters' house, "Did you get into a fight with Marlene Walters?" Coleman asked.

"Yes I did," Brown said.

"Did you cut her?"

"Yes I did."

"Did you hit her on the head?"

"I hit her, but I can't recall hitting her on the head."

"Did you hit her on the head a whole lot of times?"

"No."

"Where was I when you were in the basement?"

"Upstairs."

"You didn't even tell me what happened until later?"

"I can't remember."

When prosecutors cross-examined Brown, she then recanted most of what she had just testified to, saying she didn't remember tying or beating Harry and Marlene Walters in the basement of their house. Despite the testimony elicited by Alton Coleman only minutes earlier, she now told Assistant Prosecutor Carl Voolman that all she remembered was sitting on the Walters' porch discussing the camper.

Debra Brown's trial ended on April 29. In closing arguments her defense attorney tried to put most of the blame for the crime on Alton Coleman. Still, the lawyer admitted, "I don't intend to be up here and paint this woman a saint."

Jurors were given the case and deliberated for five hours before returning with a verdict: guilty of aggravated murder and attempted aggravated murder. The jury did not convict Brown on the specifications of acting with prior calculation, trying to kill two or more persons, or killing during the commission of another felony. Thus, she was spared the death penalty.

Brown's jurors later said that they had been "confused" by Judge Cartolano's instructions, not realizing that if they acquitted her of the specifications she would not be eligible for the death penalty. "We actually thought she would be given the death penalty (just) from the aggravated murder charge," said one juror. Two others said they wished the judge had given them written instructions.

In a news conference later, Judge Cartolano defended the verdict. "(Jurors) were never confused by the law. They were deliberately never told by the court what the result of what a guilty or not guilty verdict would be.... Jurors should only be concerned with the facts of the case (not with the possible outcome of their verdict)."

When Alton Coleman was told of the outcome of Debra Brown's trial he commented, "Best news in the world."

The Cincinnati Crime Book

Jurors in Coleman's own trial had been given that case the same afternoon. Testimony and evidence presented at his trial was virtually identical to that presented at Debra Brown's. His attorney, Peter Rosenwald, argued that Coleman had never intended to kill Harry Walters, that he hit the Norwood man in the head with the candlestick holder "(just) to control him, to put him in a position to place handcuffs on him." Rosenwald said that Debra Brown was the actual killer of Marlene Walters. Prosecutors disputed this, claiming that Brown was too small and frail to render such savage beatings as had occurred on Floral Avenue.

Coleman's jurors deliberated five hours before being sequestered overnight. The next day they returned to work and soon arrived at a decision, finding the defendant guilty of aggravated murder and attempted aggravated murder. They also found him guilty of aggravated robbery and burglary. The jury further decided that Coleman was guilty of the death penalty specifications in that he was the principal offender, that he acted with prior calculation and design, and that he committed the acts while trying to kill two or more persons. Hearing the decision, Coleman rolled his eyes at the ceiling.

The next day a sentencing hearing was held to determine if there were any mitigating factors that would result in Alton Coleman's death penalty verdict being altered. Coleman made an unsworn statement (meaning he could not be cross-examined) in which he recalled his version of a deprived childhood and admitted that he had no respect for the law. He admitted being a robber and said, "I would take the fall for Mrs. Walters, but I didn't kill her." Recalling his frame of mind during the incident he said, "Get the money, get the car, let's go. I didn't have no intention of killing anybody. I feel sorry for the woman." Coleman said that Debra Brown committed the murder, saying she could "get aggressive when she's all doped up. All I did was tie the people up. Where I was going, I didn't know. I was too far gone to stop." Referring to the possibility of the death penalty, he asked the panel not to condemn him just to impress the public or to make up for the fact that Debra Brown had not received the death penalty. "(The verdict) will be the talk for the rest of the week. 'We got somebody. We didn't get Brown but we got Coleman.' That's all you got to do, is paint a pretty picture.... (But) to kill me, that's not the truth."

Jurors were unimpressed by the statement and quickly recommended that Alton Coleman be put to death in the electric chair. As he was led from the proceedings Coleman said, "It wasn't a fair trial, period. I wasn't responsible."

On May 6 Judge Richard Niehaus formally sentenced Alton Coleman to death for the murder of Marlene Walters. Niehaus also sentenced him to 7 to 25 years for the attempted murder of Harry Walters, 10 to 25 years for burglarizing the Walters' home, and 10 to 25 years for robbery. The sentences were ordered to be served consecutively. In his sentencing statement Niehaus characterized Coleman as "the epitome of an Exhibit A to be attached to an argument in favor of the death penalty." Coleman became the 11th person to be sentenced to death row from Hamilton County since the reimposition of the death penalty in Ohio in 1981. His case would automatically be appealed.

Debra Brown was formally sentenced on May 14. Judge Cartolano sentenced the 22-year-old woman to life in prison at the Ohio Reformatory for Women. He also sentenced her to additional consecutive terms of 10 to 25 years each for the charges of attempted aggravated murder, aggravated burglary, and aggravated robbery.

But Cincinnati was not yet finished with Alton Coleman and Debra Brown. The pair still faced trial for the murder of Tonnie Storey.

As in the case of the crimes committed at the Walters house, Coleman and Brown were scheduled for separate and simultaneous trials for Storey's murder. Defense attempts to have the trials moved because of publicity about the first trials and verdicts were denied. Judge Simon L Leis, who would preside over the second trial of Coleman said, "There's no question that there has been extensive coverage, but I am thoroughly convinced (he) can get a fair trial."

The jury in Alton Coleman's trial was selected by Friday May 24. Two men and ten women would hear the case.

Assistant Prosecutor Mark Piepmeier opened the state's case on May 29. He began, "Sometime between June 28 and July 5 (Alton) Coleman entered what was to be his deadliest state, Ohio, a state that yielded four victims" to him. He said that the defendant's MO was "to find an unsuspecting young black female who (Coleman and Brown) would assault or kill, then find an escape out of town." To further establish this pattern of behavior, Piepmeier recounted the other similar crimes Coleman was accused of in Illinois, Wisconsin, Michigan, and Toledo and Dayton Ohio, and said that the surviving victims of those crimes would testify against the defendant.

The defense countered that while "Evidence will show that Coleman and Brown passed through that (May Street) house that summer....The prosecutors didn't know who killed Storey and still don't. They cannot show even where she was killed. They don't know, can't even show you beyond a reasonable doubt the how, why, or who killed Tonnie Storey."

The first order of business was a trip by the jury to view the crime scene. Alton Coleman exercised his right to accompany them, although he remained handcuffed and manacled and was kept in the back of a Sheriff's patrol car. Jurors viewed both the house where Tonnie Storey's body was found and a corner market where a witness would testify he saw Coleman on the day of the fifteen-year-old girl's murder.

Back in court, early testimony in the prosecution's case came from Tonnie Storey's parents and teacher, all of whom recalled the last time they saw the girl on July 11, 1984. A classmate remembered seeing Storey with Coleman and a "light-skinned, skinny" black woman the same day. (Debra Brown was light-skinned and thin.) The real estate agent testified to finding the body on July 19.

The Cincinnati Crime Book

Then prosecutors began presenting the testimony of the similar crimes.

The first witness in this phase was Jaunita Wheat of Kenosha, Wisconsin. Ms. Wheat recalled meeting Coleman, who then called himself "Robert Knight," in May of 1984. After the two struck up a friendship, "Knight" talked Wheat into letting him take her nine-year-old daughter Vernita with him while he supposedly went to get some stereo speakers for the Wheats. Instead, Coleman took the girl to Waukegan, Illinois. On July 19 Vernita's decomposing body was found in an abandoned house located just two blocks from Alton Coleman's home. Weeping, Ms. Wheat looked at the defendant and said, "I trusted him. I didn't think he'd kill her. You don't have a heart, I swear."

Next to testify was the surviving member of the pair of young girls who were attacked in Gary Indiana on June 18, 1984. The girl said that she and her 7-year-old cousin met Coleman and Brown at a hot dog stand. Coleman asked the girls if they wanted some new clothes. When they said no, he forced them into a car and drove them outside of town. There, the witness said, "They took off their belts, tied them around my neck, and choked me." The girl saw Coleman rape and strangle Tamika Turks. Then he turned on her and attacked her. "I passed out." When she regained consciousness she was alone. She wandered around the semi-rural area until she found a stranger, who called her mother. Defense attorneys did not cross examine this witness.

On June 4 a Cincinnati Police Division criminalist testified that Debra Brown's fingerprint was found on a button of pop star Michael Jackson that had been found about ten feet from Tonnie Storey's body in the May Street house. Tonnie had been a big fan of the entertainer.

A Hamilton County Coroner testified that Storey's bound body had been so badly decomposed when it was discovered that it was impossible to determine how she died. But in his opinion she had been asphyxiated.

While Coleman's trial was progressing, an almost identical trial was held for Debra Brown down the hall. Her jury was finally given the case on Thursday, June 6. They deliberated for eleven hours over two days before finding her guilty of the aggravated murder of Tonnie Storey. She was also convicted of the specifications which made her eligible for the death penalty. Prosecutors were satisfied with the verdict, since the death penalty specification made up for the life sentence meted out after the trial in the Walters homicide. "We were crushed after the first trial," admitted Co-Prosecutor Claude Crowe. "We couldn't leave on that note."

Alton Coleman's jury also got its case on June 6. It deliberated two days before returning with its verdict finding him guilty of murder with the specification that the crime was committed during a course of conduct (his entire crime spree) in which he killed or attempted to kill two or more persons. The jury found him innocent of aggravated robbery and dismissed the other death penalty specifications. "It's a well-thought-out verdict," commented

207

Prosecutor Piepmeier. "It shows that (Coleman) killed just for the sake of killing. It all fits."

Asked by a reporter for his reaction to the verdict, Coleman smiled and said simply, "What can I say?" The reporter remarked that Coleman didn't seem upset. "Why should I be?" he responded.

The jury returned to court Sunday for the mitigation hearing to determine whether the death penalty recommendation should be altered.

Prosecutor Piepmeier urged the jury to stick with death because Coleman had committed an "unprovoked, premeditated attack on a child.... Alton Coleman is probably the most serious criminal to ever step foot in Hamilton County."

Coleman's attorneys countered with an anti-death penalty argument that included a graphic description of death in the electric chair.

As in his trial for the murder of Marlene Walters, Coleman took the stand and made an unsworn statement on his own behalf. But the jurors were not moved by Alton Coleman's famous silver tongue and reaffirmed the decision that he die in the electric chair for Tonnie Storey's murder.

In a statement directed at the jury after its decision Coleman said, "I'm not upset. I'm disappointed. I had intentions of begging for my life, but the media has made it a joke. I guess the picture is drawn up that I am the nastiest person in the world. I lost my life (got the death penalty) in the first trial.... (So) with your decision or somebody else's.... I'll die in the death chair. I haven't even been in some of the places they want me for."

And then, as if to show that he had no hard feelings against the jurors, Coleman told them, "Have a nice day, you hear?"

Alton Coleman was transferred to Ohio's death row at the Southern Ohio Correctional Facility at Lucasville.

On June 10 Debra Brown had her own mitigation hearing. She also took the stand and made an unsworn statement recalling her association with Alton Coleman, remembering how they first got together and how she first made the decision to choose him over everything else. "Me and my mother got into an argument because she didn't like his background. I told her if she didn't like Alton she didn't like me. So I moved in with Alton." As for the crime she had just been convicted of, Brown said, "I didn't have nothing to do with Tonnie Storey's death and I didn't take any of her property."

After this statement she heard her fate. The jury recommended that she be put to death for her role in the slaying of Tonnie Storey. For the first time in the proceedings Debra Brown's stony composure left her, and she broke down and cried.

"We missed her the first time (the Walters trial) in regards to the death penalty," said Co-prosecutor Melba Marsh, "(so) I am satisfied with the recommendation. I'm glad it's over."

After her trial Debra Brown was taken to the Ohio Reformatory for Women in Marysville where she joined three other women on Ohio's death row.

The Cincinnati Crime Book

Alton Coleman and Debra Brown still had numerous charges filed against them in the other states where they committed crimes, but they would only return to court with regard to one. In 1986 both were convicted in Indiana for the murder of seven-year-old Tamika Turks. They were both sentenced to death.

In 1991 Debra Brown made the news again when outgoing Ohio Governor Richard Celeste, in one of his last acts as governor, commuted the death sentences of eight female Ohio death row inmates to life in prison. One of the reprieved prisoners was Debra Brown. "The decision to grant or withhold executive clemency is probably the most awesome responsibility that comes with being governor," the Governor explained. "It was such a responsibility I accept, and one which I could not in good conscience leave unexercised as I reach the end of my term in office." Celeste was a long-time opponent of the death penalty. He said he commuted Brown's sentence because of her low I.Q. and because the "violence she suffered as a young person" had created in her an "extraordinary vulnerability" which made her susceptible to falling into a "master-slave" relationship with Alton Coleman. Commenting on the victims of the reprieved inmates, Celeste said, "I feel enormous pain for them. (But) I can't heal that for them."

In response to the commutations, a prosecutor who worked on the Storey case said, "You have to say, 'Is the system being cheated?'"

Harry Walters, who had nearly been beaten to death in his Norwood basement, said, "There's no way the woman deserves the right to live. It (the commutation) is just a disgrace to the whole legal system."

Officials in Indiana, where Brown was still under a sentence of death for her part in the murder of Tamika Turks, said that they would seek custody of her for execution in that state.

Although Alton Coleman was prosecuted in Hamilton County in hopes of a swift imposition of the death penalty, he immediately began appealing his death sentences and delaying their application. In February 1998, after losing all appeals of his Ohio death sentences on the state level, he was denied at the first level of federal appeals. He is expected to appeal that loss to the U.S. Court of Appeals.

Alton Coleman. (*The Cincinnati Enquirer*/Michael Snyder)

Debra Brown. (*The Cincinnati Enquirer*/Michael Snyder)

Alton Coleman and Debra Brown killed a woman in
this Norwood residence.

**15-year-old Tonnie Storey was found dead
in this building in Walnut Hills.**

Cincinnati's Angel of Death

Hospitals scare many people. Of course, a lot of people die in them, and that's scary. But people also fear hospitals because they feel so helpless in them. In no other circumstance do people turn their welfare over to other people who are, for the most part, total strangers. And yet these strangers have complete control over hospital patients. If a health care worker comes into your room at two in the morning and tells you to take a pill, you probably will.

Occasionally one might hear a nightmare story about a doctor who forgets a sponge in a patient or an anesthesiologist who miscalculates a dose and leaves a patient permanently comatose. But in the majority of cases medical procedures are carried out to the best of the staff's abilities and the results fall within the perimeters of recovery that a patient can expect. In the vast majority of instances, health care workers are dedicated professionals with nothing but the well-being of their patients in mind. And for the most part, a person who is convalescing in a hospital doesn't have to fear a person clad in medical attire who comes into the room and makes an adjustment to an intravenous feeding unit or tells them to swallow a certain pill.

But what if the person in medical attire is a murderer?

John Powell was a forty-four year old resident of Delhi Township. When he wasn't working at the General Electric plant in Evendale, he enjoyed outdoor activities, including motorcycle riding. Unfortunately, when he rode his bike he frequently chose not to wear a helmet, and in July 1986, while riding, he collided with a car and sustained major injuries to his head. He was rushed to a hospital where the staff worked feverishly and saved his life.

But Powell had suffered massive damage to his brain, and he soon slipped into a coma. He was then transferred to Drake Memorial Hospital, a long-term health care facility. Drake Hospital was located on Galbraith Road a few blocks west of Vine Street, just inside the Cincinnati Corporation line near the suburbs Wyoming and Lockland.

213

The Cincinnati Crime Book

John Powell remained at Drake until March 7, 1987 when a nurse's aide found him dead in his bed.

Even though Powell had been in bad shape for some time, his family was naturally saddened by his passing. They scheduled a funeral mass for March 10 at the St. Dominic Church in Delhi Township and requested that contributions in his memory be made to Drake Hospital.

Because Powell had apparently died as a result of his motorcycle accident with another vehicle, an autopsy was performed in order to determine the exact cause of death to establish legal liability in the event that any court action resulted from the accident. The autopsy was performed by Dr. Lee Lehman, a Deputy Coroner for Hamilton County.

As Dr. Lehman began examining Powell's body, he noticed nothing that would lead him to believe that the death was the result of anything other than the motorcycle crash. The dead man's lungs showed evidence of pneumonia, but that is a common enough natural cause of death for many people who are hospitalized for long periods of time.

But when Lehman examined the stomach everything changed. As soon as the doctor cut into that organ he recognized the distinct "bitter almond" odor of cyanide.

Cyanide is a poison that affects the body by preventing it from utilizing oxygen. Lacking oxygen, the body's cells begin to die. When the part of the brain that controls breathing shuts down the person ceases breathing and suffocates to death. It only takes a small amount of the poison to kill an adult human being.

Surprised by his find, Dr. Lehman sent tissue samples from the body to an independent laboratory for another analysis to confirm the presence of the poison. When those tests came back positive, Lehman knew there was a problem: there is no innocent reason for cyanide to be present in a human body.

The Cincinnati Police Department was notified.

Police began their investigation into the death with interviews of all of the people who worked at Drake Hospital, as well as John Powell's doctors, family members, friends – anyone who could have poisoned the dead man. One of these persons was a thirty-five-year-old nursing assistant named Donald Harvey. Donald Harvey was the nurse's aide who discovered that Powell was dead.

Donald Harvey was born to Ray and Goldie Jane Harvey on April 15, 1952 at the Mercy Hospital in Hamilton, Ohio. Goldie was 17 years old when Donald was born; Ray was 32. Shortly after Donald's birth, his parents left Hamilton and returned to the place they had grown up, Island Creek, Kentucky. Island Creek is a very small settlement – just a few houses – in Owsley County, in the southeastern part of the state. Soon Donald was joined by younger siblings – a sister in 1958 and a brother in 1960.

The Cincinnati Crime Book

Although the beauty of south-central Kentucky might seem an idyllic place for a child to grow up, the reality is that the area is a tough place to make a good living. There is little land suitable for farming and no major employers or industries. People in Owsley County barely get by. In 1980 the county had the fourth lowest per capita income in the United States.

Ray Harvey worked odd jobs, but an eye injury prevented him from doing many things, so he was frequently unemployed. Often the Harvey family had little money and less food. It was a hard life.

Life was especially hard for Donald. Although he was generally well-liked by his neighbors, Donald was also regarded as a Mama's boy and "sissy" who would rather play with girls than boys.

There was a dark reason for Donald Harvey's apparent effeminacy: since he was about five years old he was abused sexually by both a male relative and a neighbor man. Harvey later explained that these encounters left him wary of contact with males, and thus he never became manly.

At the time, Donald told no one about the abuse. In many respects his life appeared fairly normal. He did well in school, but dropped out in the ninth grade. He and his family regularly attended the Walnut Grove Baptist Church.

In 1969, when he was 17, Donald Harvey left Island Creek to visit his grandfather, who was a convalescing at the Marymount Hospital in London, Kentucky. There, he befriended a man who worked as an orderly in the hospital. The orderly said that it would be no problem for Donald to get a similar job. Harvey was more than anxious to get out of Island Creek, so, a year later, he returned to Marymount and got a job at the hospital.

Everything went well at for a while. But two years later Harvey was in trouble. Inexplicably, he burglarized a neighbor's apartment and set a fire in another apartment. He was caught the same night. He pleaded guilty to reduced charges (petty theft), paid a small fine, was ordered to undergo treatment as an outpatient at a Frankfort mental health clinic. Then he was released to the custody of his parents.

Ray Harvey, in an attempt to make his son more masculine, urged him to join the armed forces. In June 1971 Donald joined the Air Force and was stationed at Travis Air Force Base in California, near San Francisco. He visited the city and its large homosexual community often. He also overdosed on drugs twice. As a result of these overdoses, he was dismissed from the Air Force on March 9, 1972 with an honorable discharge. The discharge noted that Donald had a "character/behavior disorder."

Disgraced, Harvey returned home to Kentucky. He quickly took another drug overdose and had to spend four months recovering in the Lexington Veterans Administration Hospital. Then he underwent another eighteen months of outpatient treatment.

He also resumed his career in the health care field, working variously at Lexington's Cardinal Hill Hospital, the St. Luke Hospital in Fort Thomas, Kentucky, and at Cincinnati's Christ Hospital. Finally, in 1975, he began working at the Cincinnati Veterans Administration Medical Center. Harvey worked at the VA Hospital for the next eight years, in the morgue.

At this same time Harvey began a long term homosexual relationship with Carl Hoeweler, a cosmetologist from Cincinnati. Everything went well for Donald for the next several years.

But in 1983 Harvey was transferred out of the morgue. Simultaneously, his relationship with Hoeweler began to go bad. Both men accused the other of being unfaithful. Harvey never denied his infidelities. "He talked about all the people he picked up," a friend later said. "He was constantly on the prowl. He liked Carl for Carl's generosity, but I don't think he really had any kind of personal feelings toward anybody." As the relationship worsened, Carl Hoeweler frequently became sick with some illness that doctors could not quite diagnose.

Harvey worked two more years at the VA hospital after leaving the morgue. He didn't end his association with the facility under the best of circumstances. In July 1985, as he was leaving the hospital, a security guard asked to inspect the contents of his gym bag. The guard found a coke spoon, occult books, needles and syringes, human tissue samples mounted on slides, and a .38 caliber revolver.

Donald Harvey's career at the Cincinnati VA hospital was over. In addition to being terminated, he was given a fifty dollar fine for possession of a weapon on federal property. (Harvey pleaded guilty to this offense. He was not prosecuted for any more offenses because the search of his gym bag may not have been legal.)

After losing his job, Harvey began drinking heavily and picking up one-night stands in gay bars. He finally broke up with Carl Hoeweler in early 1986. By then Donald Harvey had found another job. In February he began working at Cincinnati's Drake Memorial Hospital, as a nurse's aide.

He was still working there when John Powell died on March 7, 1987.

Since Donald Harvey had worked on John Powell's ward, he was asked to take a polygraph examination to determine whether he had anything to do with the man's apparent murder. Everyone else who worked on the ward had taken a similar test and passed.

Harvey missed the first appointment for his test, so it was rescheduled. When he showed up for the second test he refused to be strapped to the polygraph machine. Instead, he admitted that he had killed Powell by introducing cyanide into the his intravenous feeding tube. He said he did it because Powell had no hope of recovery. The death, Harvey said, was "an act of mercy."

Donald Harvey was arrested and charged with aggravated murder. A few days later he pleaded innocent by reason of insanity. His trial date was set for July 27.

If authorities thought the arrest of Donald Harvey was the end of this case, they were sorely mistaken. Although hospital spokesmen assured everyone that the Powell poisoning was a singular incident, other people who worked in the facility thought otherwise. Many other nurse's aides had noticed what seemed to be an unusually high death rate among Drake patients since Donald Harvey had begun working there. The employees even remembered how Harvey used to joke about the deaths. More than once, as he left the room of one of his patients, he had cracked, "Well, I just took care of another one."

And, sure enough, these patients were soon found dead.

When the employees took their suspicions to hospital higher-ups, the administrators refused to hear their complaints or to investigate any of the other deaths which had occurred on Donald Harvey's shifts. Since the employees were not getting anywhere with the hospital, they took their suspicions to a local television news anchorman.

In 1987 the local news anchor for Cincinnati's WCPO-TV Channel 9 was Pat Minarcin. After the hospital employees contacted him, Minarcin quickly became convinced that this was a big story and he decided to begin an in-depth investigation of the situation. For two months he and his news team dug into the case, interviewing hospital staff members, relatives of possible victims, and experts on poisons and serial killing. After two months of work, Minarcin and his team were ready to present their findings on the air.

On June 23, 1987 viewers of the *Channel 9 Local News at Six O'clock* witnessed a first in local news coverage. The entire half hour program was devoted to the results of Minarcin's investigation. There were not even any commercials. Stunned viewers watched as the news anchor presented his very convincing case that Donald Harvey had killed many more people at Drake Hospital than just John Powell. Minarcin said that as many as 23 deaths at Drake may have been caused by the gentle, soft-spoken nurse's aide. The report also included interviews with anonymous hospital workers who said that their suspicions about questionable deaths at the facility were ignored by hospital administrators. The workers presented statistics indicating that the number of deaths increased in Harvey's ward after he started working there.

Channels 9's program rocked the Tri-State area. But ordinary citizens weren't the only ones who took notice of the news broadcast. It also caught the attention of Hamilton County officials. Since Drake Hospital was owned by Hamilton County, any malfeasance there fell under the purview of the Hamilton County Commissioners. Within days of the news program the commissioners announced that there would be a special investigation to look into the allegations raised by Channel 9's report.

Still, Hamilton county officials were reluctant to assume that the charges were true. Expressing dismay that they had not been made aware of Channel 9's investigation until it was broadcast, one commissioner said, "I believe we should have been informed immediately, and to this date, I don't know why we weren't. (But) I do not intend to overreact to one report. You do not approach this with the presumption that someone is guilty until proven innocent."

The Cincinnati Crime Book

A spokesman from the Hamilton County Coroner's Office also downplayed the information in the broadcast. "We had all those (high death rate) figures and we determined that they were not significant," the spokesman said. "There is nothing pointing to this being a string of mercy killings."

Hamilton County's investigation into the deaths soon included law enforcement officials. On June 25 County Commissioners met with Hamilton County Prosecutor Art Ney. Ney later conferred with Cincinnati Police Chief Lawrence Whalen and County Coroner Frank Cleveland.

Drake Hospital promised complete cooperation in the probe. On June 27 a hospital official declared that they were allowing all of their employees to contribute to the investigation and that "no retribution will be taken against anybody for any statement they have made, and that is a categorical promise. We have encouraged total cooperation between our employees and any authorities investigating this case."

Channel 9 also promised complete cooperation with Hamilton County's investigation into the deaths.

On June 30 county officials announced that a special grand jury would be impaneled to investigate the deaths at Drake. Officials at the hospital said they welcomed the inquiry.

The grand jury was sworn in on July 6. Two days later, Donald Harvey's attorney, William Whalen, Jr. approached Hamilton County Prosecutor Art Ney and offered a deal: Harvey would plead guilty to all the Drake murders in exchange for a sentence of life in prison instead of the death penalty. He would also provide detailed information about any other killings he may have committed. Ney, who at that point lacked enough physical evidence to corroborate Harvey's earlier statements and win convictions for multiple murder, agreed to the deal, saying he wanted "to settle once and for all the questions surrounding the crimes this man committed."

On August 18, 1987, in a packed Hamilton County courtroom, Donald Harvey pleaded guilty to 24 murders in Hamilton County, including 21 at Drake Hospital. No one in the Cincinnati area had ever been convicted of that many murders. The historic proceedings were broadcast live by local television stations.

Art Ney stood by a large placard which listed the names of the victims, the dates of their deaths, and the means by which they were killed. Relatives of the deceased shook their heads and wept.

Characterizing Donald Harvey as a man with "a compulsion to kill like someone else might have a compulsion for malted milk or cold beer," Ney disputed claims Harvey had made that the killings were done out of mercy for the sick. "He killed because he liked to kill. This man is sane, competent, but is a compulsive killer. He builds up a tension in his body, so he kills people."

Ney described some of the methods Harvey used to dispatch his victims. Some ingested fatal amounts of arsenic or rat poison that had been put in their food. One was smothered with a plastic bag. Mixtures of water and cyanide were given to patients, either through intravenous feeding tubes or by direct injections. Another patient got a lethal dose of cyanide in a cup of coffee. Others got the poison in orange juice. Yet another died after Harvey gave him an injection of a petroleum-based cleaning fluid.

After each of the 28 counts was read, Harvey and his attorney were asked if they accepted the prosecution's version as the truth. William Whalen and Donald Harvey both stood up each time. "Yes," answered Whalen.

Harvey made no statement during the hearing. He seemed comfortable and often smiled as he spoke with his attorney. "He seems to have detached himself (from) the proceedings," said a relative of one of the victims. "He's just sitting there, so calm and cool. It's beyond belief."

"He acted like it was a joke," said another.

With the guilty plea entered, Hamilton County Common Pleas Judge William S. Mathews passed sentence: 20 years to life on each of the 24 murder charges. Three of the sentences were to be served consecutively, the rest concurrently. Harvey was also sentenced to 7 to 25 years for attempted murder. He would not be eligible for parole for 60 years.

Prosecutor Ney defended the plea bargain, saying, "If I could have found one more body (with evidence of poisoning) I would have put (Harvey) in the chair. (But) we have effectively removed a terrible and horrible cancer from our community."

An editorial in the *Cincinnati Enquirer* called the plea "a shortcut to justice" and pointed out that while many people thought Harvey deserved the death penalty, there was actually little, if any, evidence that would have resulted in proof of guilt beyond a reasonable doubt if the state had been forced to go to trial.

With the guilty plea it was at least certain that Donald Harvey would never walk the streets again. Now all that remained was for him to make his detailed statements to police about all the murders he committed. When he did the extent of his murderous career, as well as the detachment with which he recalled it, horrified his listeners. It was a story almost too incredible to be believed.

According to Harvey, his career in crime began almost sixteen years earlier when he had begun working at the Marymount Hospital in London, Kentucky. He claimed the first death had been a mercy killing, a woman with cancer who wanted to die. In June 1970, Harvey said, he obliged her by turning off her oxygen tank.

One month later he discovered a better way to kill. He had attached an oxygen tank to a patient, not realizing that the gauge indicating the amount of oxygen in the tank was broken. The gauge showed the tank being full when it was really empty. The patient hooked up to the tank soon died from lack of oxygen, but the death appeared to be from natural causes and no investigation was made. When Harvey realized what had happened, he wasn't shocked. Rather, he was surprised at how easy it was for him to kill without being detected. He kept the broken valve and used it on the oxygen tanks of at least eight more people he felt were ready to die.

Death in this manner is not easy. A person deprived of oxygen can put up quite an agonizing struggle for life before they finally die.

Not everyone at Marymount met their death from lack of oxygen. Harvey developed an antagonism against an older patient. At one point the two men actually came to blows. Still, despite the known bad blood between the pair, Harvey was allowed to attend to the man. He eventually killed the elderly man by inserting a coat hanger up into his catheter and puncturing his bladder.

Harvey killed another patient at Marymount by holding a pillow over his face until he suffocated. He injected oxygen into the bloodstream of another. He used an empty oxygen tank to kill the only black patient at the hospital because he resented having to take care of him.

Harvey eventually pleaded guilty to the murders of nine patients at Marymount, although he claimed to have killed thirteen people there. He was sentenced to life in prison for each murder, the sentences to run concurrently with those he was already serving in Ohio.

As a partial justification for these killings, Harvey claimed that he had been traumatized because he was raped shortly after his arrival at London. "I thought I had put all that (being a victim of homosexual abuse) behind me when I left Island Creek, but then it happened the first night I got to London. I really think that may have triggered something."

Even so, Harvey showed little remorse for any of his acts. "Some of (the victims) might have lasted a few more hours or a few more days, but they were all going to die," he told a newspaper interviewer. "I know you think I played God, and I did.... I believe God has forgiven me." He mocked the grief of the survivors. "If they get two, three million out of this (from lawsuits) they are not going to be too grief stricken. I'm going to make rich men and women out of a lot of these people." And he added a warning. "I think there are several other Donald Harveys out there. I think my case is going to make them more cautious about what they do."

(Actually, there *are* several other Donald Harveys out there. In fact, health care workers killing patients under their care is a common enough phenomenon that books have been written about this type of killer. They are known in criminological circles as "Angels of Death." A recent example of this is the case of Orville Lynn Majors. Majors, a licensed practical nurse, was arrested in Clinton, Indiana in December 1997. Charged with killing six people, he is suspected of killing as many as 165 persons over a 22 month period.)

Harvey also claimed to have killed as many as 17 people during his ten years at the Cincinnati Veterans Administration Medical Center between 1975 and 1985. But when the FBI investigated these claims they concluded that "many of the things he said he did, he couldn't have done." Harvey was never

The Cincinnati Crime Book

charged with any of the murders he claimed to have committed at the VA Hospital.

The victims of Donald Harvey were not always confined in hospitals. His tumultuous affair with Carl Hoeweler resulted in several more murders. Harvey admitted that he killed Hoeweler's mother because she was too demanding on her son. He killed Hoeweler's father as well, but said it was a "mercy killing." He poisoned a friend by giving her a cup of coffee laced with hepatitis because he felt she was causing problems between Hoeweler and himself. That woman survived.

Once convicted, Donald Harvey began to tell his story to many people other than those in law enforcement. The revelations of his crimes came at a point in media history when television programmers began to appreciate that a large segment of the public has an interest in true crime and that that interest could translate into profitable ratings points for television programs. The era of the celebrity criminal was under way.

Donald Harvey was much sought after by members of the news media who wanted to interview him. And he readily agreed to talk. He was interviewed by newspapers and by local television stations for their news broadcasts. Pat Minarcin must have felt some satisfaction as he questioned Harvey through the glass in the visiting room at the Hamilton County Justice Center. Harvey told the anchor that "I felt what I was doing, except for the exception of two or three, I had done right. I did not feel that I had done wrong. There are a lot of people that believes in mercy killing, but they never have the nerve to carry it out."

Cincinnati television station WXIX broadcast a one hour special on Harvey and his crimes called *Angel of Death*. This show also included an interview with the convicted killer.

Harvey's story appeared on the tabloid news show *A Current Affair* as well as in updated news segments on Cincinnati area television channels. He was featured in a CBS News *Eye on America* segment dealing with serial killers. The case was also made into an episode of the Lifetime Channel's *Confessions of Crime*. Harvey was re-interviewed for most of these programs.

At one point there was also talk about Harvey doing a book on his life story. Harvey told an interviewer, "If I ever do get a book done, I will not describe the details of how the people died, whether they were in pain or went peacefully. I would like to protect the families from all that. After all, I'm not totally heartless."

Pat Minarcin won a George Foster Peabody Award (television's answer to the Pulitzer Prize) for his work in uncovering the Donald Harvey story. In October 1988 he announced that he had sold the movie rights to his story of the case to a Los Angeles-based production company. The company hoped to have the film on the air by 1989. It would portray Minarcin as a heroic TV news anchor who single-handedly exposed one of the country's worst serial killers. "I have wrestled with this decision for a long time," Minarcin said of the deal. "The families (of the victims) had always indicated to me that they want to see (a film) done. The cutting issue to them was that if something like this case was done (on film), maybe it could prevent something like this from happening again."

Plans for the TV movie were eventually dropped.

Donald Harvey has survived. In spite of the fact that his guilty pleas to 37 murders made him perhaps the most prolific serial killer in American history, he will never face the death penalty. Instead, he will likely spend the rest of his life in the care of the State of Ohio at the Warren Correctional Institution near Lebanon in Warren County, just northeast of Cincinnati.

Harvey was interviewed on Cincinnati television as recently as March, 1998. In a session with Clyde Gray, one of Pat Minarcin's successors as anchorperson at WCPO Channel 9, the Angel of Death said, "I never considered myself a killer," and added that he was merely "Dr. Kevorkian without the license."

Drake Hospital has survived as well. After the Donald Harvey incident many patients refused to go there, and the facility lost some accreditations. Relatives of two dozen of the persons who were killed by Harvey filed a multimillion dollar lawsuit against the facility. (Drake settled out of court for $2.3 million in 1990.) The hospital almost went broke.

But most Hamilton County residents knew that the facility was a good one, and in 1989 60% of county taxpayers voted in favor of a special tax levy to support Drake Hospital. The hospital also became affiliated with the University of Cincinnati Medical Center.

By 1992 the hospital, now called simply "The Drake Center," was the most profitable hospital in the Cincinnati area. Drake's chief executive officer Earl Gilreath explained the miraculous comeback by saying, "We rehabilitate people – now we have rehabilitated ourselves."

Donald Harvey killed over twenty people when he worked at Drake Hospital on Galbraith Road.

Donald Harvey. (Courtesy Hamilton County Sheriff's Department)

Della Dante Sutorius

The last several cases recounted in this book were remarkable mostly because they involved multiple victims. And while the individual murders of Dale Henderson, Alton Coleman and Debra Brown, and Donald Harvey were certainly tragic enough, it is really only the high number of victims that makes their criminal careers more memorable than those of most single-victim killers.

But in 1996 a single murder occurred that was, in itself, enough of a story to command the public's attention. The case of Della Dante Sutorius had just enough of the right stuff to make it a major news story not just in Cincinnati, but in the rest of the country as well.

It was a first-rate media event from the very beginning. "Gunshot kills surgeon; wife held" read the banner across the top of the front page of the *Cincinnati Post* on Tuesday, February 20, 1996.

The previous day the Hamilton County Sheriff's Department received a phone call expressing concern for the welfare of one Dr. Darryl J. Sutorius. The call was made by coworkers of Sutorius who were concerned because the conscientious doctor had not shown up for work and he was not responding to pages to his beeper.

Darryl Sutorius was 55 years old. He lived with his wife in a rambling one-story house at 9014 Symmesridge Lane in Symmes Township, a suburb located about 15 miles northwest of downtown Cincinnati.

At a little after 10:00 a.m. deputies arrived at the Sutorius residence. Their knock on the door was answered by Darryl Sutorius' 45-year-old wife, Della. She let the deputies into the house and told them that her husband was not there.

The deputies asked to have a look around the house. Della consented. When they got to the basement of the house, they found Darryl Sutorius lying on a couch.

Nobody bothered to ask the doctor if he was all right; he was obviously dead. There was a large gunshot wound in his head just behind the right ear. A .38 caliber revolver lay on the floor nearby.

The Cincinnati Crime Book

The deputies went back upstairs and told Mrs. Sutorius what they had found. She acted completely surprised by the news.

Because a person killed by gunshot had been found on the premises, the deputies then conducted a thorough search of the entire house. In Mrs. Sutorius' bedroom they found a tin box which contained a small amount of cocaine. In a jacket pocket they found the business card of a shooting range in Sharonville.

Della Sutorius was taken into custody and arraigned on a charge of drug abuse. She was held on a $25,000 bond.

With the Sutorius house now vacant, Sheriff's investigators began a thorough examination of the premises in order to determine a reason for the shooting. "We're not really sure if we've got a crime," said Sheriff's Department Captain Don Coyle. "We don't know if it's suicide or foul play.... We have no reason to arrest anyone at this point. We're trying to figure out which direction to go – homicide or suicide."

There were a couple of things that concerned the investigating officers. For one thing, the death gun had been fired twice. One round entered the head of Dr. Sutorius; the other was recovered from the couch he was lying on. "We don't know the significance of the two bullets," Coyle said. "There are a lot of different possibilities. The gun could have been fired (first) to check out if it was working. It's happened before in suicides."

Another concern was the discovery of cocaine in Della Sutorius' bedroom. This discovery indicated that something was going on beyond the seemingly respectable appearance of the well-appointed house in the upscale neighborhood. Authorities knew that this was not a routine case. They began digging into the pasts of the individuals involved to try and make some sense out of the situation.

Darryl Sutorius was a cardiovascular surgeon with a longtime reputation as a dedicated perfectionist. He was born in Columbus Ohio on March 2, 1940. He got his BA degree from Capital University in Columbus, where he also played defensive tackle on the school's football team. He received his medical degree from the University of Cincinnati (U.C.) College of Medicine in 1965. After graduating, Sutorius went into private practice, eventually opening an office at 10496 Montgomery Road in Montgomery, Ohio. He also practiced at Bethesda and Christ Hospitals and had practicing privileges at Deaconess, Good Samaritan, Jewish, and Mercy Anderson Hospitals. In addition to all this work he taught classes at the University of Cincinnati.

By 1980 Darryl Sutorius was earning $380,000 a year from his practices and his position on the U.C. Faculty. Among his other achievements he was also chief of surgeons at the Cincinnati Veterans Affairs Hospital, chief of thoratic surgery at Bethesda Hospital, and a fellow in the American College of Surgeons.

A colleague later recalled Sutorius' dedication to his career. "You had to be all work around him. He didn't tolerate any errors. He was always very,

very dedicated." The colleague also provided an insight into the late doctor's personality. "People around him would be a little bit scared of him, but that was just Darryl."

A physician who worked with Dr. Sutorius said, "He was a big man – over six feet tall – with a gruff appearance. But he had a heart as big as gold. He was one of the nicest persons you would ever know. When I heard yesterday (about the shooting) I was very upset and very shocked. He was a good man."

Another doctor who worked with Sutorius, though, said that the dead man had changed in recent years. "He had been somewhat depressed, unhappy, and grumpy the last three or four years," the doctor said. "But I don't know if that could have led to suicide. I had never thought of him as unstable like that. His death was a shock to me. It just floored me." The doctor added that there didn't seem to be any problems between Dr. Sutorius and his wife. "They seemed very happy together," he said. "They talked with people (at a party they attended recently) and mixed very nicely. I thought she was a very nice person, sweet and engaging."

A former landlord of Della Sutorius agreed with this positive assessment of the dead doctor's wife. "The person I knew for two years was a nice person. She was very pleasant, very polite. She was a decent tenant. I never saw her do much drinking and absolutely no drugs. I thought she was a pretty straight arrow."

Daryll Sutorius married Della in March 1995. Prior to that he had another marriage of 30 years duration which ended in divorce in November 1994. That first marriage produced four children, all of whom were grown and had moved out of their father's house.

Naturally, the Sheriff's investigators were very interested in Dr. Sutorius' new widow. "She has been cooperative with us," said Captain Coyle. "She has been married and divorced several times, and we're checking into her background."

It would turn out to be quite a background. Della Sutorius was born as Della Faye Hall on August 8, 1950 at Mercy Hospital in the Cincinnati suburb Mariemont. Della's father, Jim Hall, was from Kentucky. Her mother, Olga, was from Liverpool, England. After Della was born the Halls had another daughter, Donna. Mr. Hall died of cancer when Della was three. Her mother remarried quickly and had several more children.

Della grew up in Western Hills and Norwood. She attended the Our Lady of Lourdes Elementary School in Westwood, the Bridgetown Junior High School, and the Oak Hills and Mother of Mercy High Schools. She did not graduate from high school.

Della first married in 1969 in Kenton County, Kentucky. That union lasted four years and produced one child, who continued to live with the father after the divorce. In 1974 Della married again, to an employee of the sewer department. That marriage ended in divorce almost five years later with both parties charging the other with cruelty and neglect of duty. Della's third marriage lasted just eight months. It ended in another divorce in August, 1990. On the divorce papers for this marriage Della listed her middle name as "Dante," and from then on she preferred to be addressed as that. A source later claimed that Della made up the new middle name because "it sounded rich." Della married for the fourth time on Valentine's Day, 1992. This marriage, to a man twelve years her junior, lasted three years.

Three of Della's divorces had been handled by the same attorney. Referring to her and the problems she had with her husbands, he said, "She was real nice, but she wanted a hell of a lot more than any of the guys could give her. She wanted the big home and the big time."

According to one husband, Della loved to lounge around the house in her bathrobe watching daytime TV talk shows and tabloid new shows. She probably never imagined that her own life would one day be the subject of those same programs.

Della never fell into a career, but on her 1992 marriage license she claimed she was a "governess." She also claimed that she had never been married before.

On March 2, 1995 Della married her fifth and final husband, Darryl Sutorius. Dr. Sutorius had just been divorced from his wife of thirty years. "He just didn't want to be alone," a friend later said, explaining the marriage.

Della met Sutorius through an exclusive dating service they both signed up with in late 1994. On her application at the service, Della described herself as "a very sensitive and gentle person; sometimes passive, sometimes aggressive. I'm very unpredictable."

After dating for a few months, Della and Daryll decided to get married. On the marriage license Della said she was unemployed. She again did not list any of her previous marriages.

Besides this matrimonial history, authorities also discovered that Della had a record in the Hamilton County court system. In 1979 her then current husband had obtained a restraining order against her, claiming that she was a threat to his property and person. In 1990 she had been convicted on a charge of menacing. The complainant in that case claimed that "I was speaking to (Della) on the phone – she accused me of causing her a great amount of stress. She's pregnant (I do not know if I am the father) and threatened my life if she miscarried. Prior to that, she stated her intention to purchase a derringer.... On September 20 (1990) at approximately 11:30 she attempted to kill me with a .22 pistol."

On February 20, 1996, two days after the shooting death of her fifth husband, Della posted her bond on the drug charge and was released.

Meanwhile, authorities continued their investigation.

They learned that Dr. Sutorius' divorce from his first wife had not been without rancor. "The parties are incompatible and defendant (Dr. Sutorius) is guilty of gross neglect of duty," the wife charged in one court filing. "Our standard of living was lavish," the document continued. "(Now) he has left me and my children and.... threatens to cut his income, work hours, and child support." According to the divorce records Sutorius was a wealthy man. He earned almost $400,000 a year. He owned a Porsche, a Jaguar and had two vacation condominiums, one in Cancun, Mexico. He was also a frequent traveler to major foreign cities.

The Sheriffs knew that a wife of thirty years suddenly being cut off from a luxurious lifestyle and left alone to fend for herself could probably work up a lot of anger. Enough to shoot her ex-husband?

Investigators went to the shooting range whose business card was found in Della Sutorius' jacket pocket. They found out that the range also sold guns. A trace on the gun found next to Darryl Sutorius' body revealed that it had been purchased for $235 at the range just two days before he was shot. Federal firearms records showed that the gun had been purchased by Della Dante Sutorius.

A clerk from a discount store came forward and said he remembered a transaction in the store's gun department, also just two days before the shooting. The clerk said that the customer in that transaction was Della Sutorius.

"She was kind of nice but she didn't know anything about guns," he later said. "she seemed hesitant at first.... and just asked for hollow-point bullets."

Hollow-point bullets generally cause much more damage when they hit a target than standard round-point ammunition does. But they are also more expensive than regular bullets.

The clerk recalled that Della decided to go with the cheaper standard ammo.

The clerk also remembered Della saying that her husband had confiscated her previous firearm. "It kind of freaked me out when she told me her husband took away her last gun," he said. "But who am I to know that she might shoot someone?"

Hamilton County Sheriffs continued to call the death "suspicious." As a routine part of the investigation they did a test to see if gunpowder residue was present on the hands of the dead man. If the residue was present, it would indicate that he had recently fired a gun and would strengthen the theory that he committed suicide by shooting himself. Deputies also made a test for gunpowder residue on the only other person who had been living at the Symmesridge Lane house, Della Sutorius.

Police also considered the possibility that Dr. Sutorius was killed by a stranger. Random slayings, unfortunately, are no longer uncommon anywhere, even in well-to-do neighborhoods such as the one where Daryll Sutorius lived. On February 23, 1996 an 82-year-old woman was killed in a home on nearby Symmes Creek Drive. Iran K. Alavi, who was visiting her family, was found stabbed to death in the basement of the house. Robbery was the suspected motive in that case. (No arrest has been made in that murder.)

The Cincinnati Crime Book

On the evening of February 27 a memorial service for Daryll Sutorius was held at the Lutheran Church of the Good Shepherd in Kenwood. Dr. Sutorius had intended to walk one of his daughters down the aisle of the same church to get married in October. Instead, over 300 people were now there to listen to eulogies from family members and friends, and to mourn the loss of the popular physician.

But the news of this church service was greatly overshadowed by an event earlier in the day.

Ever since the shooting, the Sutorius home had been staked out by both Sheriff's deputies and members of the news media. At 4:45 on the afternoon of February 27, the deputies finally moved in and arrested Della Sutorius for the murder of her husband.

As the news cameras caught the scene, she was led from the house in handcuffs. She wore only a white bathrobe. She was then placed into the back of a squad car and driven to the Hamilton County Jail.

Della Sutorius had hired an attorney, R. Scott Croswell III, the moment she realized she was under suspicion in the death of her husband. After her arrest for murder Croswell denied his client's guilt, telling the press, "The state has made an allegation and they will have to prove it. I don't think there is a key piece of evidence." As for the arrest itself he said, "I feel (it) was a staged media event. She had made arrangements to surrender, if necessary. (Instead), they dragged her out barefoot."

Authorities were quick to release the "key piece of evidence" they believed they had against Della Sutorius. Results of the tests for gunshot residue did indeed reveal traces of gunpowder on the hand of Dr. Sutorius. But the tests also revealed much more of the residue on the hands of Della.

Della Sutorius was housed at the Hamilton County Justice Center in downtown Cincinnati. The next day she appeared in a courtroom packed with spectators, reporters, and cameramen from the news media. As she trembled and covered her face with her hands, she was charged with aggravated murder. The presiding Judge, Timothy Black, set her bond at $225,000.

In addition to the gunpowder residue tests there were other reasons why authorities had zeroed in on Della Sutorius as the main suspect in her husband's death. Interviews with some of the doctor's relatives revealed that the marriage between the two had been less than idyllic.

One relative said that Sutorius had not known about his wife's previous marriages when he married her, nor about her criminal conviction on the misdemeanor menacing charge. The relative said that Dr. Sutorius feared his second wife and planned to divorce her.

The relative went on to say that Sutorius feared his wife so much that he spent as much time away from his house as possible, often going to his father's home in Columbus, or staying with friends, or even going to hotels. "He said (Della) told him she was going to kill him," the relative claimed. "She had told him so many times. He was after a divorce. She didn't want a divorce. She had a rich man."

Another source said, "(Sutorius) was in love with her, until he found out who she was. (Then) he just wanted his life. But no, she couldn't do that."

After her arrest one of Della's former husbands also recalled this alleged dangerous side to her character. The man described how a few months after his marriage to Della he had discovered two sharp carving knives concealed in the furniture of their apartment. When he questioned his wife about the knives, she responded, "I could kill you and the world would be a better place for it."

"I'll never forget it," the ex-husband recalled. "She scared me to death."

Another ex-husband remembered his brief marriage to the accused woman in 1990. "I endured months of brow-beating, mocking, and mental abuse. She'd work your head and work your head until your emotions were wide open. And then she would just filet them. I'm (still) frightened of her. This lady is very, very scary."

A third ex revealed that he had been so scared of his wife that he hid the ammunition for the .44 caliber handgun he owned. "If I hadn't hid the bullets, it would be me on the couch with the bullet to my ear," the man said. "It still feels like she haunts me."

On March 6 Della Dante Sutorius was indicted by the Hamilton County Grand Jury on one count of aggravated murder and one count of drug abuse. Hamilton County Prosecutor Joseph Deters said the accused woman had "a serious problem with rejection" and a history of being a threat to the men in her life.

"It's obvious there is a clear pattern here," Deters said. "We believe there was planning. This (the shooting) was not an accident. She knew what she was doing." Deters said that the prosecutor would ask for the maximum sentence allowable by law under the circumstances, life in prison with a first chance for parole after 24 years. He said that the death penalty was not an option because the state could not prove aggravating circumstances, as required by the law. Commenting on the limited possible punishment, Deters said, "I guess they (the Sutorius family) were disappointed, but they understood."

Della's attorney, Scott Croswell said that the evidence against the defendant was "completely circumstantial" and that she would be acquitted at the trial.

After the hearing Della was returned to her cell. She had not been able to secure her $225,000 bond.

On March 13 Della Sutorius formally entered her plea of not guilty to the charges against her and asked for a reduction in her bond, claiming that she had no money.

The prosecution said that the bail should be increased to $1 million because "her ex-husbands and members of the Sutorius family all expressed concern about her getting out." Prosecutors also expressed the fear that if released Della would flea the area, either to California or Texas.

Attorney Croswell countered that because Della had no money she could not afford to go anywhere. He denied that his client was a threat to anyone, and added, "I just fear by the time this case is finished, my client will be tried by rumor, innuendo, and speculation."

After listening to the arguments Hamilton County Common Pleas Judge Richard Niehaus increased the bond to $400,000 and set Della's trial date for May 20, 1996.

Sitting in the Hamilton County jail, Della Sutorius now found herself to be the subject of interest of the same daytime TV and tabloid news programs that she herself used to enjoy so much. At least three daytime talk shows and two tabloid programs expressed interest in her story. Several made-for-TV movie producers were also said to be interested in the case. "America does have a sick fascination with sick things," said one anonymous TV source.

A spokesperson for another show called the details of the case "highly dramatic."

"Everyone in the United States has called," said Scott Croswell. "(But these programs) are in no fashion newsworthy. They serve no purpose other than to sensationalize this (case). There is a clear distinction between TV news and print news and these so-called news shows and talk shows. The proper place to try this case is in the courtroom and not in the press."

On May 1 a pretrial hearing was held in Hamilton County Common Pleas Court to lay the ground rules for what kind of evidence would be allowed at the trial.

The state wanted to introduce statements from Della's former husbands that she had threatened them. The defense said that the statements were not relevant to the case and would only prejudice the jury against the defendant. Judge Niehaus said he would allow the statements to be admitted.

The defense wanted to exclude certain statements made by Della Sutorius to Hamilton County Sheriff's deputies on the grounds that they had questioned her for over seven hours before arresting her on the cocaine charge and finally advising her of her rights. "If someone's liberties are restrained and they are the subject of a criminal investigation, they should be advised of their constitutional rights," said Scott Croswell. "I've never seen anyone interrogated for seven hours without (the police) giving them their rights."

A sergeant with the Sheriff's Department testified that Della had not been informed of her rights because she was only considered a witness, not a suspect, when she had been questioned.

Then the defense announced its intention to introduce evidence that Darryl Sutorius had been suicidal. That theme would become the heart of the defense case. They would claim that Sutorius was a depressed man who killed himself in the basement of the Symmesridge Lane house. "The defense believes that the decedent in this case had dealt with issues of suicide and had contemplated taking his own life," said Scott Croswell. He read from a Symmesridge Lane neighbor's statement characterizing Daryll Sutorius as "always very gloomy, very solemn, very depressed, very unfriendly, never smiled, never would speak to you – just Gloomy Gus."

On the second day of the hearing a Hamilton County Sheriff's sergeant testified that police had zeroed in on Della Sutorius as a suspect only hours after Dr. Sutorius' body was found. The deputy also said that after news of the discovery of the body had been made public, the Sheriff's Office received many calls from friends, co-workers, and relatives of the dead man. They all pointed their fingers at Della. "(One caller) called to tell me that he was a very close friend of Dr. Sutorius, and that the last time (he) had talked to him, Dr. Sutorius said, 'If you find me dead, Della did it. Make sure you tell police.'"

Another caller was Della Sutorius' own mother. "She felt that if Dr. Sutorius was dead, Della was responsible for that," the sergeant recalled.

Prosecutors disputed the idea that Daryll Sutorius was suicidally depressed. Pointing at Della, Assistant Prosecutor Steve Tolbert said, "The only thing bad about Dr. Sutorius' life in early 1996 and late 1995 is sitting over there at that table in a black dress."

Judge Niehaus considered the evidentiary issues raised by both sides and decided to allow everything but portions of the statements police obtained from Della during the six hour questioning session after the discovery of the body.

The trial of Della Dante Sutorius began as scheduled, on Monday, May 20, 1996. The courtroom was jammed with spectators and reporters.

That first day, in an early ruling favorable to the defense, Judge Niehaus ruled that Della Sutorius could have access to whatever clothing and makeup she would need to "present a reasonable appearance at trial." This ruling on appearance was important to the defense because Court TV, the cable television channel dedicated to trials and other legal news, had secured permission to record the trial for extended presentation to its national audience.

By Wednesday a jury of nine women and three men had been selected. Each side then presented its opening statement.

Speaking for the state, Assistant Hamilton County prosecutor Thomas Longano presented the case against the defendant.

Longano said that Daryll Sutorius was afraid of his wife. In January 1996 he had taken a gun from Della's bedroom and turned it in to police. "The doctor's concern was that Della was taking control, and he feared for his safety," Longano said.

The prosecutor revealed the Daryll Sutorius had prepared divorce proceedings against his second wife which were scheduled to be filed on February 19, 1996, the day after he was killed. He suggested that the pending divorce was the motive for the murder. "Della stood to gain over $900,000 in assets if (Sutorius) died of natural causes or suicide. Through divorce she gets zero....(Dr. Sutorius) underestimated his wife.... he exercised plain bad judgment."

Longano said that Sutorius told friends that he feared his wife would kill him if he filed the divorce papers. "These statements took place immediately preceding the doctor's death. He is concerned that if he proceeds with a divorce, she will kill him and she will get away with it. He is in fear for his life." The prosecutor added that the physical evidence found at the death scene in the Sutorius basement was inconsistent with a suicide. "From the very beginning, everything is wrong with Della's plan." He said that Dr. Sutorius' body had been found in a sleeping position, which was not consistent with a suicide. He pointed out that the gun had been fired too far away from Sutorius' head for the wound to be self-inflicted. "It was not a contact wound. That's totally inconsistent with suicide."

Longano said that Darryl Sutorius probably lived for fifteen minutes after he was shot. Conceding that Sutorius' fingerprints were found on the gun, he said that Della Sutorius held the gun in her dead or dying husband's hand and fired it a second time in order to get his fingerprints on the gun and gunpowder residue on the hand

Robert Croswell countered with the defense theory that Daryll Sutorius had committed suicide. "He is concerned that Della Sutorius would tell his colleagues that he was an alcoholic," Croswell said. "That she would call the IRS and tell them he was a tax cheat. But what he really was afraid of was that she would tell people that he was impotent.... and that he was very dirty physically. He was very unhappy about that prospect.... He was depressed."

Croswell admitted that his client was not exactly a saint. "You may not like Della Sutorius when this case is over. You might not want to invite her over for dinner. But I'm telling you, don't punish her because you don't like her."

On Thursday the jury was taken to Symmesridge Lane for a tour of the house where the shooting had occurred. Much of what they saw inside contrasted sharply with the image of a peaceful suburban lifestyle presented by the exterior appearance.

They saw that Dr. and Della Sutorius slept in separate bedrooms on separate floors.

Her room had been fitted with locks to keep her husband out. The jury saw knives that Sheriff's deputies found under her mattress. There was a box of .38 caliber bullets on her dresser.

Daryll Sutorius secured his own door with a small stepladder under the doorknob. Neither husband nor wife had photos of each other in their bedrooms.

In the basement, jurors viewed the death scene. Bloodstains were still visible on the carpet.

Back in court that day, the state called several witnesses to bolster their contention that Della Sutorius had an active interest in and influence on her late husband's financial affairs.

An assistant manager from a Montgomery bank testified how Della had set up a joint checking account for Dr. Sutorius and herself with instructions not to send the statements to Dr. Sutorius.

Dr. Sutorius' own attorney testified, "A few months after they were married, (Della) demanded that (Dr. Sutorius) meet with her certified public accountant, so she would have an understanding of their financial affairs." The lawyer added that Daryll Sutorius had not been a man who seemed to be contemplating suicide. He was looking forward to his life after his divorce. He had scheduled a meeting with the attorney to discuss the divorce on February 19. "He never made that appointment," the lawyer recalled. "He wasn't alive at the time."

In cross-examining the lawyer the defense brought out that in 1992, when Darryl Sutorius was divorcing his first wife, he had expressed his despair over the situation with a remark about suicide. "He said, 'Maybe my children would be better served by my insurance (money).'" Sutorius' lawyer remembered. "I found that (remark) disturbing and referred him to a psychiatrist. We had no more discussion about it."

"If it's true in 1992 that he could meet his obligations to his children by committing suicide, then isn't it also true in 1996?" Scott Croswell asked.

Next, one of Dr. Sutorius' daughters was called to the stand. The 26-year-old woman recalled the first time she met her future step-mother. "My father had his arm around her. She was not very affectionate. She seemed kind of cold to me."

The young woman recalled discussing her own wedding, which had been scheduled for October, 1996, with Della. "I said, 'I don't want an elaborate wedding. I was really thinking about a simple wedding.' (Della) said, 'I hope so. Because you're only a waitress and you can't afford to have a nice wedding.' I looked at my dad, and he just looked away."

The daughter said that her father's marriage to Della had deteriorated from the start. She described how Della had eavesdropped on a telephone conversation between her and her father. She confronted Della. "I told her I didn't appreciate that (eavesdropping) and I wanted my private time with my dad back. I said she was one of the most insecure, selfish people I had ever met in my life. I told her she needed to see a shrink. She called me back the next day and said, 'I hope you know you're not getting a penny for your wedding.'"

Dr. and Della Sutorius had a tremendous argument over this situation. The daughter played a tape recorded phone message for the court where Sutorius begged her not to call him at his home anymore.

"It's your father," Daryll Sutorius cried on the tape. "I asked you not to say that we had talked; you didn't. I don't know if I'll ever be able to talk to you again. Now this – why can't you just do what I ask? Please. You don't know the situation. Don't call Dante. Don't talk to Dante. If you and I talk, just keep it between the two of us, please. Don't, don't do this to me. I mean, I may not live through this. I'm serious. Please don't do it."

Sutorius then called his daughter back. "This is Dad again. Please don't call my office and leave any kind of message on my message machine that you don't want Dante to hear because she also listens to all those. Be careful what you say."

The daughter said that the day after his argument with Della her father had scratches on his face. "I decided to leave him alone," she said. "I didn't want to agitate the situation. I was afraid also at this point."

To support the claim that Della Sutorius killed her husband for his $900,000 estate, the state called her half-sister, who said that a couple of months before the shooting she had a phone conversation with Della. "She told me how she'd be worth a million dollars if he wasn't there," the sister testified. "I asked her if she loved the man and she said, 'I tried that once and look where it got me.'"

The Sutorius' marriage counselor testified that Dr. Sutorius was constantly showering his wife with expensive gifts, but that he feared she would never be satisfied. "(Sutorius) told me he made a big mistake," said the counselor. "The doctor said, 'I'm afraid she will kill me in my sleep.'" When asked whether Daryll Sutorius was depressed, the counselor responded, "He looked forward to being free after the divorce. I would say that he was not suicidal."

Other relatives of the dead doctor also said that Sutorius had been enthusiastic about his future without Della. They recalled him looking forward to planting a rose garden that summer and attending his daughter's October wedding.

A sister recalled that Sutorius had been afraid of Della. "He was very frightened, (and) I was very frightened for him."

When court resumed on Monday May 27 the audience to the proceedings became national as Court TV began its in-depth coverage, beaming the Sutorius affair into over 25 million households.

"It's a good choice by Court TV," said a University of Cincinnati communications expert. "(It's) the flip side of the O.J. (Simpson) trial, with a woman accused of being the dangerous partner. (Here) we have an accused woman who is very attractive and allegedly very dangerous. The history of her marriages reveal a pattern that will be absolutely fascinating to people. The doctor is also interesting to many people because of what he did – get a divorce after 30 years of marriage and marry a woman who had been divorced four times. Many men go through a mid-life crisis where they make some pretty foolish decisions and this looks like a classic case."

A spokesperson for Court TV said the trial was chosen for broadcast "because we thought it was a really gripping local trial which would have a great national interest. It seems to touch on a lot of intriguing human interest issues. We have a prominent surgeon. We have a woman with five [sic] ex-husbands. It offers a lot beyond a simple murder trial. Our grand goal is to teach people about the legal system, and we hope by choosing interesting trials we will encourage people to watch, learn, and keep on watching. You have to balance important legal issues with interesting elements."

Viewers were not disappointed.

Clerks from the gun store where Della purchased the death weapon testified that she had been a "motivated customer."

A Montgomery businessman testified that Della had told him, "I'm just gonna get rid of (Daryll). I think I'll poison him."

A range instructor from the gun store where the weapon had been purchased testified that Della had practiced with the weapon at the store's firing range on February 17, the day before the shooting. Asked about her shooting skill, the instructor said, "In my opinion, she was doing outstanding."

A psychiatrist who had been treating Daryll Sutorius for depression was called by the state to testify as to his non-suicidal state of mind. "I think he felt that he was going to be able to get the divorce," the doctor said. "He wasn't trapped anymore.... He was looking forward to the future. I do not think he was suicidal."

Under further questioning by the prosecutor the psychiatrist added, "One time he (Sutorius) told me, 'If anything happens to me, you'll know who did it.'"

"Who was the doctor talking about?" asked the prosecutor.

"His wife," the psychiatrist said.

But the defense got the psychiatrist to admit that many symptoms found in suicidal persons, such as depression, low self-esteem, and financial worries, were present in Daryll Sutorius.

The defense then went on to suggest that Daryll Sutorius planned to commit suicide and make it look like he had been murdered by Della. Remarking on the fears for his safety that Dr. Sutorius allegedly made to so many people, Scott Croswell said, "It almost sounds as though he wanted to make sure she got blamed for it, whatever happened. It seems to me whether Della shot him or he shot himself, he was going to make sure she got blamed for it."

Croswell suggested that Sutorius killed himself because Della had threatened to tell his friends he was an impotent alcoholic who was about to lose his medical practice and go under financially. To support its contention that Sutorius was depressed and in financial trouble, the defense introduced witnesses who testified about his mood and character. One of them, a neighbor, recalled, "(Dr. Sutorius was a) very unpleasant person.... He was a Gloomy Gus."

On May 30 the prosecution presented a woman who had befriended Della Sutorius after her arrest for murder. The woman said she had known Della slightly before the murder through Dr. Sutorius' hospital work. "I felt sorry for her," the woman said, explaining how she had approached the defendant after seeing her on TV. "She appeared very frightened and seemed to need a friend." A few weeks after they first got together, the woman claimed, Della confessed the killing to her. "She told me she shot him. She told me that the first shot, she shot around him and — this is an exact quote — she said that he didn't even move. And the next shot she shot behind one of his ears."

Defense attorneys brought out that Della's supposed "friend" was actually an inmate at the Butler County jail awaiting sentencing on two felony charges of illegally obtaining prescription drugs. Croswell also suggested that the woman was a habitual liar. He pointed out that the woman's claim that Della fired the shot into the couch first did not fit the prosecution's scenario that the couch shot was fired after the shot that killed Darryl Sutorius in order to get gunpowder residue on his hand. Croswell was skeptical of the witness's altruism, noting that she didn't report the alleged murder confession until it was to her advantage. "You were carrying around the confession, the keys to the vault, but you don't call police until you're sitting in a jail cell," he said.

On May 31 the prosecution called one of its main witnesses, Hamilton County Coroner Carl Lee Parrott, Jr. Parrott testified both to the scene of the shooting in the Sutorius basement and to the condition of the body of Dr. Sutorius. Neither of these, he said, were consistent in any way with a suicide.

Parrott said that the evidence at the scene indicated that Dr. Sutorius had gone down to the basement with a glass of red wine. Sutorius drank the wine, emptied his pockets, placed his glasses on a coffee table, and set his shoes neatly by the couch. These actions, the doctor said, were not consistent with someone contemplating suicide. "It's consistent with someone getting themself ready to go to sleep."

The Coroner said that the death weapon had been held about an inch from Sutorius' head when it was fired. The trajectory of the bullet, from behind the right ear to above the left eye, was inconsistent with a self-inflicted wound.

Dr. Sutorius lived for perhaps 15 minutes after he was shot, the Coroner said. During that time he cupped his right hand under his chin. Blood had sprayed out of his mouth and onto the hand. When Sheriff's deputies first arrived on the scene, however, both of Dr. Sutorius' hands were hanging off the couch. This suggested to the Coroner that the body had been moved. Also, Dr. Parrott said, there were blood smears on the couch out of reach of the dead doctor. This too suggested that someone had manipulated the scene.

Parrott said that blood on the death weapon indicated that it "was handled by someone with a bloody hand." It would have been impossible, he said, for Darryl Sutorius to shoot himself in the head, get blood on his hand, and then handle the .38 again.

Prosecutor Tolbert asked Parrott, "Can you tell us who fired the shot into the back of Dr. Sutorius' head?"

"No sir," Parrott replied.

"Can you tell us, forensically, scientifically, or medically, who did not fire that shot into Dr. Sutorius' head?"

"Yes."

"Who didn't?" Tolbert prompted.

"Dr. Sutorius," Parrott said.

That, said Tolbert, made it clear who did. "There was only one other person in the house," he said, "And that's Della Sutorius."

Scott Croswell attempted to undo the damage done by the Coroner's testimony by suggesting that since Parrott had not typed the blood on the revolver he could not even say with certainty that it was Darryl Sutorius'. He also said that the out-of-reach blood smear on the couch could have been made by the Sutorius' dog.

On June 3 prosecutors played audio tapes of telephone conversations between Della Sutorius and her half-sister. The tapes had been made on February 20 and 24, the week after Darryl Sutorius' death. The half-sister said she recorded the calls because she thought Della had killed Dr. Sutorius. "I wanted to see if Della would admit to what she had done, and I didn't want her to use me as an alibi," she said.

On one tape Della painted an unflattering picture of her dead husband. "He didn't have one friend in the world," she said. She blamed her mother for contacting police and telling them that she had something to do with Sutorius' death. "She starts bad mouthing me. She's trying to hang me. Wouldn't you know that the people who are against me are my family? How would you feel if Mother called and tried to get you into serious trouble? Hurt your feelings?"

The sister replied, "You know what? That wouldn't be on my mind. My husband being dead would be my utmost concern."

At two points in the conversations, Della made what prosecutors claimed were self-incriminating statements. At one point she tearfully recalled, "All day.... I have been in a daze all day thinking, 'God, I came so close to killing me too.'" Later, discussing her chances for bail, Della said, "I'm not going to go around killing someone. I'm not a danger to society.... The fact that you killed your husband doesn't mean you're going to go start robbing banks and killing people."

"I'm not a bad person," Della concluded, "(but) I have a lot of problems, and I know where a lot of them come from."

The last day of the prosecution's case came on Tuesday, June 4. Most of the day was spent discussing the .38 revolver recovered from the scene of the shooting.

A firearms examiner from the Hamilton County Coroner's Office testified that ballistics test confirmed that the gun was the death weapon. An employee of the gun store where Della purchased the gun testified that it had been "in reasonably clean condition.... (with) no stains" when it was sold. The defense had earlier claimed that blood found on the used weapon, blood which had never been conclusively determined to be either Daryll or Della Sutorius', may have been left over from the previous owner. But that previous owner, a police officer in Springdale, Ohio, now testified that the gun was clean when he sold it to the gun store.

The next day the defense began to present its version of the case.

The first witness was the director of the Center for the Study of Suicide in South Carolina. The witness, who had not known Daryll Sutorius, said that the dead doctor had been a good candidate for suicide. A divorce from Della, he said, would not have ended the Sutorius' problems. "The real problem is not Della, it's himself. Even if he gets a divorce, he still has to live with himself."

He said that Sutorius had been upbeat in the days before his death not because he anticipated life after divorcing Della but because he had decided to kill himself. "If I'm feeling at the end of my rope and I formulate a plan to kill myself, I'd clearly be more upbeat. The feeling is that now I'm going to solve my problems."

The second witness was another suicide specialist, who also had never met Daryll Sutorius. This witness, too, testified that Sutorius exhibited signs of being suicidal.

After just these two witnesses, the defense rested its case. Della Sutorius did not take the stand on her own behalf. "She wanted to testify," Scott Crosswell said, "and she was willing to testify. But I made the decision myself that it wasn't necessary based on the state of the evidence. I think she wanted to tell her story, but I think it's also been told."

Closing arguments were given on June 6.

Referring to Della as a "black widow," Assistant Prosecutor Jerry Kunkel said, "She knew that if Dr. Sutorius died while they were married she would get close to a million dollars. And she knew that if he divorced her, she'd get almost nothing. (So) she had a million reasons to want (her husband) dead. She didn't marry him because she loved him.... All she wanted was his money."

Kunkel said that the physical evidence of the blood on the couch made it "impossible" for the death to have been a suicide.

Pointing at Della, the prosecutor continued, "That woman is the most dangerous person you'll ever see in your whole life. That's because she doesn't look like it. She'll sneak up on you, find out your weaknesses, and she'll use them against you. She'll blackmail you, and if you don't go for the blackmail, she'll kill you."

Defense attorney Croswell countered that the state had the legal burden "to exclude any and all possibility that (the death) was a suicide." It had not done that, he said. He said the prosecution case was not about facts, but "about creating an atmosphere of hate and dislike for Della Sutorius, because it will be easier to convict an innocent person if you don't like her."

The jury began deliberating on the afternoon of June 6. They did not reach a verdict that day.

The Cincinnati Crime Book

The next day they resumed deliberating and soon announced a verdict: guilty of aggravated murder.

Della Sutorius began to cry. She needed assistance as she was led from the courtroom.

Some of the jurors later explained the reasoning that led to the verdict. "We entertained the thought of suicide," said one, "but with the Coroner's report, you would almost have to disbelieve all the information he gave us."

Another juror said that Della's guilt was obvious. "The bottom line is, nobody could explain (the blood smear on the couch out of the reach of Daryll Sutorius). It all came down to the physical evidence.... She waited for that opportunity (to shoot her husband).... We felt that she calculated the plan and she carried it out. I think she's the kind of person who, if you look at her, you can feel sorry for her.... She can be very loving one minute, and a killer the next. I think she's a very scary person. She didn't have a lot of love in her life and it shows. I think it's unfortunate that Dr. Sutorius had to pay for it with his life."

A daughter of Dr. Sutorius said she was relieved with the verdict but, "I don't want to say anything to Della because she is getting out in 20 years, and I'll still be as afraid (of her) that day as I am today."

Della's mother, though, had no such hesitation. "We can't cover it up and say, 'Oh, she's innocent,' when you know in your heart she's not. This is the worst thing in the world anyone could do. But when your God is money, I guess you'll do anything."

Scott Croswell said, "The jury has spoken. They're competent, fair people and I'm not going to second guess (them). It is a tough case and a tough situation. There are two sides to every story, and they chose to believe the prosecution's side."

Della Sutorius was sentenced on June 24. Judge Niehaus did not mince words as he gave her the maximum allowable sentence, 20 years to life on the murder charge, plus an additional three years for the use of a handgun in a crime and eighteen months for possession of cocaine. "You have the attitude that the world owes you something," Niehaus told the convicted woman. "You have now earned something (the sentence) for probably the first time in your life. You will receive your just due: life imprisonment for the coldly calculated murder of your spouse."

Judge Niehaus disputed the prosecution's characterization of Della as a "black widow." "A black widow does not disguise itself. It is what it appears to be. I believe you are more suitably compared to a creature I have observed while scuba diving. That creature is a lion fish. The outward appearance of this creature completely belies its deadly, poisonous, aggressive nature. The lion fish attracts prey through its appearance and then consumes all who come close to it. That creature is you.

"This sentence is inherently fair because you, with your lifelong history of aberrant behavior, are probably, at least in my opinion, beyond any hope of rehabilitation."

After the judge's remarks, Della Sutorius was led from the courtroom for the last time.

Prosecutor Longano said, "She's led a very violent life. We think the system has finally caught up to her."

Defense Attorney Croswell said he would appeal.

With the sentencing, the case against Della Sutorius was over as far as the state was concerned. But to the family of Dr. Darryl Sutorius, it was not over.

"Now we can try to get on with our lives," said one of the doctor's daughters. "(But) Della's taken our father from us, and we can't get him back. It's not over for us. It's not ever going to be over for us until she's dead. They'll never be able to repay me for what she's done to me and my family, to my dad. There's nothing too bad for her."

Nor did the public's interest in all things Della end with her conviction and sentencing. She was in the public eye again in March 1997 when Hamilton County prosecutors announced that they would auction off eleven pieces of her jewelry in order to pay some of the $26,000 cost of her murder trial. One of the pieces was Della's wedding ring, which was appraised at $5,800. But the auction was not a great financial success. An Oakley realtor bought the whole lot for just $5,100.

In February 1998 Pocket Books published the paperback book *Della's Web*, by true-crime writer Aphrodite Jones. The book immediately rose to the top of local bestsellers lists and stayed there.

A month later Court TV broadcast a one hour special program on the case based on its earlier extended coverage. The story of Della Sutorius was still a good ratings-getter.

It is likely to continue to be one for some time.

Della Sutorius is currently serving her sentence at the Ohio Reformatory for Women at Marysville. She will not be eligible for parole until the year 2021. She will be 70 years old.

•

Della Dante Sutorius. (*The Cincinnati Enquirer*/Michael Snyder)

The Symmes Township house where Dante Sutorius killed her husband.

Afterward - Cincinnati Crime Scenes Today

The stories in this book occurred in practically every part of the Cincinnati and the surrounding Tri-State area. While I originally planned to include maps with this work, I dropped the idea because there were so many locations spread over such a large area that too many maps would have been involved. But any interested reader can find many of the places described in this book with any good, detailed Cincinnati map and maps of Ohio, Kentucky, and Indiana.

The Murder Of Pearl Bryan - In 1953 the 9th Street rooming house occupied by Scott Jackson was demolished to make room for a parking lot. But the other side of the street is still the same as it was in 1896. The Cincinnati Dental College, formerly on Central Avenue, is long gone, as is Dave Wallingford's saloon at Plum and George Streets. John Legner's saloon, at 9th and Plum Streets, may be gone; there is only one building left on that intersection that dates from the 19th Century, and none of the accounts I read gave the exact street address of the saloon. The former Lock farm in Fort Thomas, Kentucky, where the body of Pearl Bryan was found, was sold in 1962 and subdivided into residential lots. For years the Locks kept registry books for the visitors that came to the crime scene. Thousands of people came, even into the 1950s. The old Newport jail, where Scott Jackson and Alonzo Walling were hanged, was torn down in 1995. The valise which may have concealed Pearl Bryan's severed head has been on display since 1996 at the Campbell County Historical and Genealogical Society on Main Street in Alexandria, Kentucky. Pearl Bryan is buried in the Forest Hill Cemetery in Greencastle, Indiana.

The King Of The Bootleggers - You can still drive the route that George Remus took when he followed his wife to their ill-fated rendezvous in Eden

243

Park. Start in front of what's left of the old Hotel Alms (now the Alms Hill Apartments) at Victory Parkway and William Howard Taft Road. Drive south on Victory until it turns into Eden Park Drive at the bottom of Park Avenue. Cross the bridge and enter the park. Continue past the Krohn Conservatory and around the curve by the reservoir. Not much has changed at the spot where the King of the Bootleggers killed his wife. It happened on the right side of the northbound road, near the gazebo. Remus' Price Hill mansion and the Death Valley Ranch are both long gone.

The Head And Hands Murder - Captain Harry Miller's former summer residence still perches on a hillside about a half mile outside of New Trenton, Indiana. It is located on Barbour Road. The General Butler State Resort Park in Carrollton, Kentucky, with its lake, is still a popular spot for recreation seekers. The residence of Flora Miller, on Crown Street, was torn down to make way for the Interstate 71 right-of-way. The house where she kept her massive collection of art and bric-a-brac, on Lennox Avenue in Avondale, is still standing.

Anna Marie Hahn - The years have claimed several of the locales associated with the case of the poisoning blond. The Hahn residence, which was located at 2970 Colerain Avenue, is gone. A gas station is now there. The nearby home of George Heis is also gone. A modern building occupies the spot on Central Parkway where Albert Palmer's house once stood. The neighborhood where George Gsellman lived on Elm Street is in such bad shape that it took me three trips before I could tell if his house is still there. It is, standing alone between two newer buildings. 1717 is the doorway on the right. The main entryway to the building where Jacob Wagner lived on Race Street has been bricked up, but the building, at Findlay Market, is still in use. The Clifton Avenue home of George Obendorfer has been remodeled with exterior siding but is otherwise intact. At the sidewalk level you can still see where he had his shoe repair business.

The Pugh Murder Mystery - Although a few new homes have been built on Hill and Hollow Lane since 1956, the former Pugh residence is still a secluded house. Surrounded by trees and bushes at the end of the private street, it is barely visible.

The Stories Of Edythe Klumpp - The home Edythe Klummp shared with William Bergen is still on Bloomingdale Avenue in Mount Washington. Stratton Road, where Louise Bergen was shot to death, has been developed, but it is still an isolated place. Cowan Lake, where Louise Bergen's charred body was found, remains one of Ohio's most popular state parks.

The Cincinnati Strangler - Enough of the locales associated with this case are unchanged today that someone could do a "Strangler Tour." The Verona and Clermont apartment buildings are the same as they were when the Strangler prowled their basements. The Price Hill apartment building where Frank and Lois Dant lived is unchanged. Electric lighting has been added to the Chipmunk Hollow Nature Trail in Burnet Woods, but it is still a secluded walkway through thick woods. The building which housed the Lark Café was converted to industrial use before finally being torn down. The intersection where Barbara Bowman was murdered is just as it was on that rainy night in 1966. Her apartment building still stands at 2902 Warsaw. When I first visited it in 1989 it was abandoned and vandalized – a real ghost. Now it has been rebuilt and people inhabit it again. The Clifton garage where Alice Hochhausler was slain is the same today. The Vine Street house where Lula Kendrick lived was torn down shortly after her murder there. The Brittany Apartments on 9th Street downtown are virtually unchanged. The Soul Lounge, in Madisonville, eventually went out of business. The building which housed it is now for sale.

The Bricca Family Murders - Except for some remodeling of the front porch area, the house where Jerry, Linda, and Debbie Bricca were stabbed to death in 1966 is unchanged today.

The Easter Sunday Massacre - The former home of Charity Ruppert on Minor Avenue in Hamilton, Ohio is exactly as it was the day James Ruppert killed eleven members of his family there. The Ruppert family is buried at Arlington Memorial Cemetery on Compton Road in Mount Healthy. The grouping of ten graves (Leonard and Alma are buried together) is inside the front entrance and to the right, near an evergreen hedge in the section just beyond the Garden of the Sermon of the Mount with its statue of a seated Jesus. Alma Ruppert's father, Frank Allgeier, who committed suicide three years to the day after the shootings, is also buried in the plot. He is the twelfth victim of the Easter Sunday Massacre.

The Devil In His Eyes - Only the models and years of the cars have changed at the Eastgate Mall parking lot where Dale Henderson abducted his Cincinnati victim. I was unable to find the barn where he left her body, and I did not go to Cherry Fork.

The Cincinnati Crime Book

Alton Coleman And Debra Brown - The former Norwood residence of Harry and Marlene Walters on Floral Avenue is now a different color, but is essentially unchanged. The May Street building in Walnut Hills where Tonnie Storey's body was found stood vacant for years before being renovated into business offices.

Cincinnati's Angel Of Death - Drake Hospital, where Donald Harvey committed the majority of his local "mercy killings," is still on Galbraith Road, just west of Vine Street. It is now called the Drake Center.

Della Dante Sutorius - The former Sutorius residence, on Symmesridge Lane in Symmes Township, is unchanged from the day Della Sutorius shot her husband there.

Further Reading

Many of the cases described in this book have been treated as chapters or entries in various true-crime anthologies and encyclopedias. It would be impossible to list all of those works. But below is a list of books that are of special interest.

DiSalle, Michael V.; *The Power of Life or Death*; New York; Random House; 1965. Former Ohio Governor Michael DiSalle's treatise on the death penalty contains an account of his involvement with the case of Edythe Klumpp.

Fortin, Roger A.; *One Man's Justice*; Cincinnati; Ohio Book Store Inc.; 1990. A novelization of the George Remus murder case.

Hopkins, William Foster; *Murder Is My Business*; New York; World Publishing Company; 1970. Foss Hopkins' lively memoirs of his career as one of Cincinnati's foremost defense attorneys includes long chapters recounting the trials of Robert Lyons and Edythe Klumpp.

Jones, Aphrodite; *Della's Web*; New York; Pocket Books; 1998; ISBN 0-671-01379-3. A book-length account of the Della Sutorius case.

Kuhnheim, Anthony W.; *The Pearl Bryan Murder Story*; Alexandria, Kentucky; The Campbell County Historical and Genealogical Society; 1996. A 26-page book on the Pearl Bryan murder.

Reston, James; *The Knock at Midnight*; New York; Norton; 1975; ISBN 0-393-08710-7. Published as a novel, this book is a much-fictionalized account of the Cincinnati Strangler case.

Rosenberg, Albert and Armstrong, Cindy; *The American Gladiators*; Aimwell Press; 1995; ISBN 0-9648784-0-2. A non-fiction account of the life of George Remus, with emphasis on his murder trial and the conflict between Remus and Hamilton County Prosecutor Charles P. Taft.

(Photo by M. J. Moonighs)

About the Author

George Stimson was born in Cincinnati, Ohio in 1954. Raised in East Hyde Park, he attended the Kilgour Public Elementary School and graduated from Walnut Hills High School in 1972. He also received a bachelor degree in German from Hobart College in Geneva, New York.

As a long-time interested observer of the criminal side of man, he has investigated and studied murder cases for over twenty years. He has had many true-crime articles published in magazines and books.

This is his first book.